PRAISE FOR *HUMAN EX*

MW00776919

This topic has never been more challenging or important. Ben Whitter offers pragmatic tips and tools as well as compelling employee experience (EX) research. The result is required reading.
Stuart Crainer, Co-founder, Thinkers50

People will go above and beyond if you appreciate, trust and empower them. This book provides an excellent insight into the importance of a positive human experience at work. Recommended reading for any business leader.
Joanna Swash, Group CEO, Moneypenny

A strong, human-centred company culture is what separates market leaders from every other employer. *Human Experience at Work* navigates through best practices in hiring, leading and growing employees who develop a healthy organization in return.
Wiktor Schmidt, Co-founder and Executive Chairman, Netguru

Having the right people culture is integral to the success of any company. *Human Experience at Work* provides crucial advice to help you motivate your colleagues, get them on board and keep them there.
James Collier, Co-founder, Huel

Today's world is undergoing major changes unseen in a century. It has become a business mandate to promote a human-centred management philosophy and practices. This is more urgent than ever before and relates to all business activities. This new book from Ben Whitter features groundbreaking research and exploration. It is a masterpiece worth reading.
Mao Zhongqun, Chairman and President, FOTILE Group

Organizations have shifted their focus way beyond profit. Every leader has a responsibility to our planet, our people and our purpose as a human race. Having a systemic way to think through a different workplace experience and beyond, will help many more to immerse themselves in their own way of creating something special. The future of work is already here and the more we co-create it, the more 'skin in the game' we have – this book will help you to co-lead it!

Raj Verma, Chief Diversity and Experience Officer, Sanofi

People make organizations successful. Successful organizations are progressing humanity, society and the planet. In this new book, Ben Whitter not only presents a compelling case for why creating a meaningful human experience at work for all stakeholders is the key to organizational success, but he also provides a holistic development approach that is both profound and pragmatic. His work is leading-edge and revolutionary!

Dr Xuan Feng, Assistant Professor of HRM and Organizational Behaviour, Nottingham University Business School China

Very powerful. This excellent book brings front and centre the importance of people to the social fabric of the business. Ben Whitter brilliantly captures the essence of what purpose-led organizations must do to create an environment where their people can thrive. A must-read book for anyone interested in building an organization fit for the 21st century.

Joseph Healy, Co-founder and Co-CEO, Judo Bank

Everyone who is concerned about creating a positive culture within your organization, who wants to create a great place to work and cares about employees and their experiences, should read *Human Experience at Work*. This book will give you a great framework and ideas to move forward in building an experience that will keep your employees happy and wanting a long career within your organization.

Lisa Dillon Zwerdling MSN, RN-BC, HEX, Chief Employee Experience Officer/VP of Internal Care Coordination, Visiting Nurse Association Health Group

Employee experience (EX) and wellbeing is the cornerstone of every company now. Based on years of research from all over the world, Ben Whitter shares his findings and ways of bringing EX to life in a human-centred and holistic manner. If you want a deeper understanding of what HR will look like in the future and how to successfully enable your business through your people, this book is absolutely essential reading!

Monir Azzouzi, Vice President, People Experience, GoJek

Human Experience at Work

Drive performance with a people-focused approach to employees

Ben Whitter

KoganPage

Publisher's note

Every possible effort has been made to ensure that the information contained in this book is accurate at the time of going to press, and the publisher and author cannot accept responsibility for any errors or omissions, however caused. No responsibility for loss or damage occasioned to any person acting, or refraining from action, as a result of the material in this publication can be accepted by the editor, the publisher or the author.

First published in Great Britain and the United States in 2021 by Kogan Page Limited

2nd Floor, 45 Gee Street	122 W 27th St, 10th Floor	4737/23 Ansari Road
London	New York, NY 10001	Daryaganj
EC1V 3RS	USA	New Delhi 110002
United Kingdom		India
www.koganpage.com		

Kogan Page books are printed on paper from sustainable forests.

ISBNs

Hardback	978 1 78966 765 3
Paperback	978 1 78966 763 9
eBook	978 1 78966 764 6

British Library Cataloguing-in-Publication Data

A CIP record for this book is available from the British Library.

Library of Congress Cataloging-in-Publication Data

Names: Whitter, Ben, author.
Title: Human experience at work : drive performance with a people-focused
    approach to employees / Ben Whitter.
Description: London ; New York : Kogan Page, 2021. | Includes
    bibliographical references and index. |
Identifiers: LCCN 2021010254 (print) | LCCN 2021010255 (ebook) | ISBN
    9781789667639 (paperback) | ISBN 9781789667653 (hardback) | ISBN
    9781789667646 (ebook)
Subjects: LCSH: Human capital. | Work environment. | Personnel management.
Classification: LCC HD4904.7 .W54 2021 (print) | LCC HD4904.7 (ebook) |
    DDC 658.3/14–dc23

Typeset by Integra Software Services, Pondicherry
Print production managed by Jellyfish
Printed and bound by CPI Group (UK) Ltd, Croydon CR0 4YY

CONTENTS

ABOUT THE AUTHOR

Ben Whitter is the CEO of HEX Organization and the Founder of the World Employee Experience Institute (WEEI). His previous book, *Employee Experience* (2019), was also published by Kogan Page.

Ben was recognized by Thinkers50 as one of the top management thinkers in the world for 2021 for his 'compelling' EX research. Ben is best known for pioneering and popularizing the concept of employee experience worldwide. He shares his work and research through popular keynotes, advisory services, executive coaching and the global HEX Practitioner Programme.

His work has reached 18 million people, inspired the first EX conferences, and has been featured in publications and by organizations including *The Times, The Telegraph, Forbes*, the *Financial Times, The Economist*, MIT Sloan, Thomson Reuters, *People Management*, and HR publications worldwide. His acclaimed 2015 article, 'Bye, Bye HR', introduced employee experience to a global audience of one million. His content online and across publications is respected and recognized throughout the business world.

Ben is a prolific global keynote speaker on human and employee experience topics and has introduced his ideas to audiences in more than 30 countries. His background as a multi-award-winning practitioner has created a strong foundation on which to build his research and ideas. Ben has lived and worked in six countries including the UK, Australia and Japan, and for three years was the Director of Organizational Development at China's leading international university. As a result, Ben brings a deep global and local perspective to his work, which informs his approach as a frequent adviser, speaker and strategic coach to the world's top global companies. Ben supports organizations in the development of their holistic, human-centred and experience-driven business strategies.

In normal times, Ben spends most of his time between England, Wales and China, but the world is his workplace. You can work directly with him through HEX Organization, whose clients include companies such as JP Morgan Chase, Ogilvy, Suntory, GSK, Sanofi, Chubb, Deutsche Telekom, FedEx and many more. Explore partnership services and join the HEX Nation at www.hexorganization.com

FOREWORD

This foreword is written by the HEX Nation, which is a global collective of colleagues working to deliver exceptional experiences in work. No matter what our role, we are working every day to enhance and make a positive impact on the human experience. We represent a workforce of millions around the world. The HEX is the lens we use to target our work and capture the essence of our impact across the human and employee experience. The driving force behind our approach and work is that we lead in a *holistic, human-centred* and *experience-driven* way.

Work and life converge

A full merger of work and life has become reality on an unprecedented scale and this will extend well beyond a hybrid world of work. Improving experiences at work – to set the frame for people to do their best work – is now setting up an immediate chain reaction from work to families, to societies, to the life on this planet – as leaders, we have more impact than ever before!

The concept of work is integrated into the lives we have and we, as practitioners, need to continue to learn to care for the holistic employee experience. Connecting employees to a larger purpose, beyond the business. Grounding experiences in a way that not only touches people's work but also their lives. In order to drive successful business transformation, our foundation is cultivating belonging that contributes personal and professional growth. *Human Experience at Work* will help you to be successful in all those areas.

Yet, this is a profound moment of real transformation. The moment you work on something – however small or big you think the act might be – you connect directly or indirectly with others through your creation and shape a tiny piece of our world. Millions of tiny pieces connected make up what we call life – the human life. Developing yourself on the unlimited potential of positive, holistic and sustainable experiences should be on the curricula of any business and school.

Why work on the human experience at work?

The only question to ask yourself is: can you afford not to? Everyone, irrespective of the organizational role they play should take time out to understand humanity in the workplace. We owe it to one another. The world has been pivoting for some time and to create the curve of change you have to start with those who will experience it most – people. The research is too hard to ignore now and those that do prioritize the human and employee experience are seeing results.

It's been a gradual awakening across the economy, but an awakening nonetheless – one which was accelerated in the most dramatic of ways during the global pandemic. Life brings people the lessons they need to learn by whispering first. Then the message starts getting louder and louder until it makes sure that people hear. Given COVID-19 and its impact on work, the messages and themes that are covered by *Human Experience at Work* are getting very loud indeed. What does it say then? To us, it says that up until this point, as a global society, we have prioritized everything else but the human experience so far, and failed at almost every attempt to create companies that are good for planet, people and society.

For some, it's an effortless, instinctive and natural transition; others are dragged kicking and screaming, and are simply following a trend. Traditional approaches to company building endure, but that doesn't necessarily mean they are the right ways to create thriving businesses. We are very different people today. We view the world differently. This means organizations must adapt with us.

Taking a stand through the human experience

Despite the rise of digitization, AI and automation, people will continue to be one of the most important aspects of any business. As HEX Practitioners, we couldn't be more excited to have been able to adopt HEX principles to contribute meaningfully to the experience of employees as well as the business. The HEX is an easy-to-understand lens and framework that addresses individual, team, organizations and the general population. It helps to demonstrate how important it is to ensure that everyone has a voice, that everyone matters within an organization, and helps create a trusting relationship that brings so much more back to everyone by building a positive culture and experience. It brings value to every level employee/person.

Most companies have been working on or are at least starting to prioritize the need to address the human and employee experience. From our companies, we have found that there are definitely benefits to ensuring that employees are happy and having a positive experience at work. Happy employees are more productive, safer, take less time off work, are excited to come to work and eager to speak up with ideas. Business performance is positively impacted in a variety of ways including uplifts in profitability, innovation and customer satisfaction. Employees also report higher levels of happiness in their overall lives as they bring that excitement and energy home at the end of the day. Leaders that follow the HEX path will be more open to including all employees in decisions being made and empowering employees, which creates stronger overall trust and collegiality amongst their teams, and across the organization. Another primary outcome of adopting a business approach that places the human experience as a high priority is that, in a nutshell, it makes us better, more considerate and kinder people and companies. Do we really need to create yet another PowerPoint presentation to help companies understand why that is important anymore?

Creating value and building trust with all stakeholders

Working with the HEX is easy, inclusive and targets organizational goals for a positive employee experience. Within our organizations, there have been many changes over the past few years. With the use of the HEX lens, we see noticeable changes and there are proven metrics to demonstrate positive change. We have gone through many changes and even with COVID-19 and all the obstacles that this has brought on, our teams have been stable and actually up for the challenges that this has created. We work as a team and everyone pitches in when needed. Hearing so many positive remarks from employees regarding the confidence and trust they now feel and how happy they are to work in companies that really care about them is incredibly rewarding for all stakeholders. These outcomes are common across companies putting people at the heart of their business model.

HEX work brings and creates value for humanity, business and the planet in the following ways:

- Humanity – co-creation brings employees and their perspectives into experiences early. We have an approach that helps us to design the organization *with* employees, not *for* them. This enriches and enhances their overall work and life experience.

- Business – creates a better business approach that promotes cross-functional collaboration. HR does not own the human experience at work. The collective view and experiences require organizations to work in new ways across disciplines to deliver an improved end-to-end experience for employees. There is a shared ownership within a broader ecosystem that makes it feel more like a movement than a management project.

- Planet – cultivating deeper levels of meaning for employees by connecting them to how they are impacting the world, not just their work. Similarly, integrating business and people with the communities that they want to impact most is good for the planet and the brand.

Getting under the skin of the human experience at work

If you are interested in getting deep and under the skin of your employees at work, you must understand the role that their experience plays and how to harness that for a competitive advantage. COVID-19 has brought to the surface what is really important to people in the company they chose to work for. Those companies that thrived in the global pandemic were prepared to listen, be open and create new ways of working with their employees. The HEX lens has proved invaluable by shining a light for companies to invest and align with the emotional needs of their employees. This allows employees to be and bring their true self to work, which is a win for all.

Motivated HR practitioners and business leaders strive and work towards supporting their companies to deliver high engagement, productivity and performance levels. If you dig into engagement, it's all about experience. To meet our goals, we must focus on the experience of the employee and all the people associated with our companies – only then will we truly understand our people and see them flourish. Having a systemic way to think through a different workplace experience and beyond, will help many more to immerse themselves in their own way of creating something special. Everyone deserves to work in a great environment doing something they're interested in. Sometimes people don't know what they want that environment to be or what they want to do; in HEX terms, they don't know their Truth – purpose, mission and values. This is where our work can make a major difference and establish a bridge for people to achieve their higher potential.

Organizations were already starting to shift to being more empathic, promoting connection and community, and deepening a sense of purpose. As a result of COVID-19 and social justice experiences around the world, the human experience at work has come into even sharper focus. The question became more centred on how we care for our employees and how we evolve the ways they work, receive support and feel connected in this new abnormal. As HEX Practitioners, we must build empathy for our people and invite their voice/be their voice when they do not have a seat at the table. This means that we must balance the tension between what our business wants and what our employees need. When we do this well, we co-create meaningful impact through the experiences we design holistically.

An enduring human obsession

Do you want to be known as a leader who can advocate, influence and directly deliver positive change for the workforce and the business at the same time? If so, focusing on the human experience at work will enable you to do that. We're not afraid to challenge the status quo and are ruthlessly consistent in our mission to serve people and the business. There isn't anything we would rather do or anything that could possibly take precedence over this. HEX has become totally intertwined into everything we undertake.

Right now, it's inconceivable to think of anything that could be of greater priority. The start of this decade will be talked about forever. Our world and humankind are at critical junctures. How we respond to adversity defines us as humans. Creating better human experiences is the very least we can do for one another and arguably one of the easiest things to achieve in practice. Change has its challenges, but the upsides are limitless when we work together.

Our advice to you in applying the ideas and insights from this book

There is no right or wrong – it's about creating different experiences for different people at different times in different ways in different organizations. Don't be deterred by any obstacles you encounter. Creating human-centric work experiences is a duty we all share, and is no longer optional. Keeping your passion alive, your patience high, and seeing barriers as a learning journey are all key to success. It may take time, but the impact will come. The most important insight for others to understand is that this is all possible; it's not just frilly consultant-speak. The end result may take longer in some organizations, look different than 'expected', or require a lot more effort in some contexts, but establishing a workplace that supports a positive human experience is possible. And it is so worth the effort to make it happen.

Our journey together

The HEX journey brings together like-minded and like-spirited companions to travel the road ahead. With every bold stride another opportunity presents itself to touch the lives of many and make a difference that matters. What else do we need to be motivated for this kind of work? To be open, willing to learn and acknowledge that we can all always do better is a good place to start. To hold ourselves, and others, to account for treating people like humans – not resources or 'bums on seats' is also a wise position to take within this journey.

Why? Because what we do and what we deliver within and beyond our companies always has the potential to have a profound effect, not only on the people who live the experience we help to co-create, but on the families and friends waiting for those people to come back home and enjoy their company after a long day at work. Our job, when it is done well, is to keep on creating human-centred experiences that will linger fondly in the memory after the workday has gone, and long after the employment relationship has ceased.

As people in business, regardless of our role, every single day we all get the absolute privilege of influencing the experiences that people around us have at work, and the choice to be able to put people first – what a special gift to have. Every day we make too many decisions to count, from the ones so small they seem insignificant (they're not) to the big hairy ones. This means that every single decision you make will have an impact on people's experiences at work, and you get to choose if that is positive... or not.

Reading a book is no different than listening to the person who wrote it, and Ben is someone we definitely deem worthy of listening to; and behind Ben are many, many people who share his career-long mission to humanize workplaces all over the world – and you are very welcome to join us.

HEX Nation
www.hexorganization.com/hex-nation

ACKNOWLEDGEMENTS

A big part of the human experience – seeing friends, family and loved ones – has been missing for all of us in the past year or so. I'm looking forward to the day when we can all meet again in person. That will be a good day indeed! I wish you and your family all the best at this challenging period of human history. It will get better.

My readers are my primary co-creators and allies in this journey – without your overwhelming support for my first book, there would not have been the chance for another. I am eternally grateful to you, but also incredibly inspired with your amazing work to bring our ideas to life in your organizations. It's been excellent to work so closely with you through the programmes and services my organization delivers too. We've built a really supportive global community and it amazes me every day. As one colleague put it, 'the HEX is now much bigger than Ben', and I am very proud of that. Thank you.

Writing a book often starts as a solo adventure, but then quickly transforms into a collective endeavour. I am grateful for the support, encouragement and wisdom of all the people who have contributed to my work from around the world.

I reserve special thanks to those who have contributed their time, energy and insights with me throughout a long period of research, dialogue and discussion: Christina Chateauvert, Colleen Schuller, Kiersten Robinson, Mao Zhongqun, Joanna Swash, Wiktor Schmidt, Joseph Healy, Helen Matthews, Sarah Langley, Nabeela Ixtabalan, James Collier, Lisa Dillon Zwerdling, Raj Verma, Elizabeth Shaw, Nick Ellsmore, Nicole Bannell, Sarah Oquist, Alan Barratt, Oscar Fuchs, Ms Sheng, Kevin Graulus, Robert Pender, Emily S. Cox, Orcun Irfan, Julie Wix, Sabine Weishaupt, Charlene Lee, Peter Cheese, Gary Hamel, Eleni Aslani, Mert Bay and Francesca Gino.

Thank you to my publisher, Kogan Page, for all of the support provided throughout the production of this book. It's been another enjoyable experience working with you throughout the writing and production process. A special mention too for Dr Xuan Feng for her great support throughout the project – our thoughtful discussions were always a real pleasure and very helpful.

I would like to place on record my sincere thanks and appreciation to our fantastic and global HEX Practitioner community, our clients and the HEX Nation generally. For several years, I travelled the world introducing employee experience to various audiences. I was often the only one speaking specifically about employee experience. It was a lonely place back then! So, I can't tell you how pleased I am that this idea about focusing businesses on humans and their experiences is now mainstream management thinking. Even more pleasing is the joy I get from being a member of one of the best and most human-centred teams in the world. I've found my tribe, finally! On a related note, thank you to *The Times*, *Forbes*, *The Economist* and Thinkers50 for recognizing and sharing my work with your audiences, and I am very grateful to all colleagues who proactively share, promote and support my books and ideas around the world.

Finally, thank you to my family and friends for their constant support and belief. It's been quite the year for everyone. I can't wait to see you all again. We'll definitely enjoy the experience!

This book is dedicated to the Whitwahs, Harry and Emmie.
The most important part of my human experience.

Introduction

If you received an instruction manual at birth, please do share it with the rest of us because this is the very thing we haven't been able to create through science and any kind of technology that is currently presented to us on Earth. Our psychological, physiological, financial, spiritual and emotional challenges are never far away. If there are fees for participating in life, you will find many of them across these elements that are associated with human life and human suffering. Yet, all that we are as human beings is truly inspiring. People can demonstrate stunning levels of compassion, creativity, ingenuity, and there are no limits on what can be achieved in life. Yet, people still struggle to realize their full potential in and out of work. Indeed, I can confidently say that many of us barely scrape the surface of our true power and strength in life. Sometimes people get in the way of themselves, and other times, organizations can play a role in limiting the potential of their people. On the other side of this are people and organizations that thrive. They get the best out of each other and make progress, together. The human experience is understood, respected and leveraged to deliver outcomes, as you'll see from several case studies I present within these pages.

The longest relationship human beings experience in this world is the one we have with oxygen. It is the relationship that we cannot do without. It is the relationship that is vital to our survival and a long-term necessity within our life. This is a deeper and more profound relationship than we ever seek to explore. It is taken for granted in most cases, yet our existence entirely depends on it. There is no thinking required on this point. It is an automatic and rapid understanding of our world for all humans. We don't acknowledge it yet our relationship with oxygen serves as the ultimate reminder of how we are connected to the wider world. The producer of the air we breathe must be protected at all costs for the human species to remain intact. This understanding brings companies, people and communities much closer together in our minds. When we allow companies to flourish that are, in some cases, literally taking away or seriously impacting our ability to breathe, we need to do something about it. The ignorance of this has led to all manner of social and environmental movements, and relates, in no small part, to our individual freedoms as human beings. Our basic human rights may well be understood and enshrined in law offering basic protections against unjust treatment, yet there is never ever any promise of a positive experience for human beings, and there is often very little help when it comes to the experience of our own minds and our own journeys through life and work.

As we'll see throughout this book, in the context of human experience, the organization takes on a whole different role to rise to meet the social, environmental, technological, political and even spiritual challenges that are being experienced by people across the world. It was just a matter of time before the human experience became a key consideration within the strategy of successful businesses and enterprises. The evolution from organization and management-centricity to a deeper commitment to human-centricity in the grand scheme of things has been relatively quick. Just a few decades ago, the economy was well and truly in service to industrialists and those concerned only with profit as an indicator of progress. Fast-forward to the present day, and we have witnessed the emergence of the employee experience field, which continues to enjoy impressive growth and increasing recognition, not just within HR circles, but in business more generally. The research for my previous book, *Employee Experience*, which covered some of the world's leading companies, indicated that businesses that put people first and consider the organization holistically, not only deliver exceptional business outcomes, but also human ones too. The idea that organizations and humans can flourish at the same time is one that grows in stature every year – it is an idea whose time has come.

Broaching this topic is not easy by any means, and in writing this book, once again my own thinking has been profoundly challenged. Certainly, my thoughts on what the human experience is, and what role an organization and work plays in it, have been questions that warranted some deeper introspection and dialogue with colleagues in different parts of the economy and at different stages in their lives and careers. The examples in this book offer two things: inspiration and impact. Without the former, we cannot expect the latter. Leading business in a human way naturally challenges the status quo, established thought and will provoke reactions. The whole point is to create organizations where people can reach as high as they wish to go – to co-create astonishing things.

It's important to remember that what is right for one context may not be right for another. Every company and person is unique, but I hope your experience with this book will support you in growing and enhancing your human-centred and experience-driven impact. It's rather exciting to discover and work with companies and colleagues that are doing bold things to advance the human experience at work, and my research here aims to contribute some new thinking about how we can do just that. As a result, I suppose this book presents an opportunity to challenge and radically reshape our organizations and the world of HR as a priority. This is not based on hacking, disrupting or refining the current model. It's about a next big step in minimizing the gap between people and companies, making work more human and our experiences more valuable.

Human experiences, not human resources

The exploration I have been on, which took place before and during a global pandemic, has resulted in a radical idea that is centred on where organizations have seen, felt and experienced the best results. Across smaller companies or global enterprises, what is being called for and actively encouraged is an overhaul of organizations, and their internal support functions, to become more trusted, valued and respected within and outside of their business and industry. These are key measures of success. Trusted organizations are created through trusted leaders and professionals who are consistently amplifying what matters most to a business and the people within it. They help their companies share and live their truth. To that end, rather than silos, functions and departments being set up in competition with each other – fighting for resources and influence with the top team – the organization that is best geared up to deliver on the human experience is the one set up purely with humans in mind. Humans care about their planet, their performance and all the roles they play in life – companies that can be considered as a progressive force for good will, increasingly, be defined by their impact across all of those areas as opposed to a narrow focus on simply delivering a return to shareholders. A profitable business does not always translate into a positive and progressive brand – one that has a celebrated impact in the world.

One hypothesis that is gaining traction is the idea that human experience as an approach and business philosophy essentially replaces human resources as we know it today. Though the profession is so much more than those two words 'human' and 'resources', to achieve its full potential it has to transform itself up to the next level of collective consciousness rather than seeing people as simply resources. The incremental and very positive steps into organization development, talent management and employee experience are commendable, but it is not enough to truly align with an experience-driven economy. To deliver sustainable and tangible progress, I believe HR will need to reposition its identity, brand and role within business. Thinking of brand HR and impression, perception and trust management, the conclusion to be drawn is that 'human resources' may be ready to be retired as a term and as a way of thinking about the role, and impact, that HR professionals have within business. In my opinion, no progressive 21st-century people-centric CEO would tolerate their people being referred to as resources. It's just not on and it needs to stop. In saying this, it must be noted that I didn't fall into or end up in HR by chance; I made a conscious decision to move into the field over 15 years ago as I felt that, of all business functions, HR was the best positioned to play a significant business leadership role. There is no doubt that HR has a big influence over the quality of the experience within an organization, but challenges remain in the way the function is set up, positioned and perceived within business. As we'll see from this book, companies are responding in a positive way by accelerating new paradigms for their support services that are more closely associated with the two things that are most important to any brand: humans and their experiences.

The great human movement within organizations

I'm fortunate in my role to work with many progressive companies and individuals that are absolutely committed to their people, witnessing and experiencing the shift to human experience at work. What is of note across many of these organizations is the depth and breadth of their commitment. It is not one thing. It is all things. There are no shortages of places to look for evidence that an employer supports and stands with its people. There is evidence in abundance being freely shared across all facets of media and all measures within an organization. It runs through the business in a way that resonates with many within and beyond the marketplace.

In acknowledging a great employer, we are acknowledging great leadership – at least, what I define as world-class leadership anyway. Whatever reputation has been created, you only need to look at the people at the top of the company to find out exactly why an organization's culture is the way that it is. What is tolerated, permitted and celebrated gives us real clues as to what's really going on inside businesses. Often, an exceptional employer is taken for granted. In the drive for profits, and in pursuit of what is perceived to be progress, people and companies can often lose their way. Those that stay the course and continue to elevate the outcomes of their people as well as the organization should be studied and held up as the inspirational entities they are. Done well, brands in this human mode rightly command respect and attention.

People just know when they're working for a great company because, from whatever angle you look at it, they are being supported. Across the entire human experience, you will see well-defined and well-designed programmes, policies and processes that are there to help people be as good as they possibly can be. Think about an employer from your career where you had a very positive experience. What was so special? What were the aspects that stood out? I ask this a lot of people and in almost all cases the response starts with an emotional response. We *felt* something. This tells us all we need to know about the impact of our experiences in work. Conversely, think about the worst experience you've ever had in work. What was happening there? What went wrong? It could be a lack of care, a lack of compassion or a lack of respect. Any one of these is enough to bring a healthy relationship to a close. So why do some employers allow it to occur at all?

By human experience, I am very much centred on people within the workforce for this book, yet when I talk about the human experience I naturally refer to and include any human that is associated, in any way, to a company and brand. All those experiences matter. They could be the fuel behind major success or they could be destroying any chance at a successful future in business. In practice, the human experience should be an organization's top and most enduring priority. Nothing else should come close.

The journey through this book will be guided by in-depth examples, case studies and insights from my work and research. We will question the very foundations of business and the HR function, and how we can develop our organizations to better serve humanity and the planet. Truly, our moment has arrived. This is our opportunity to build organizations to be proud of, that stand the test of time, and leave a positive legacy in the world. If you're reading this, I consider you an ally in this human-centred movement and I wish you well in advancing the human experience at work wherever you are. It is an honour to share this journey with you. Welcome, and enjoy the experience.

01

The human experience

The welcome experience into life is well defined and well established. We are born. We are introduced to our key network (our family) and we learn the basics that enable us to function effectively within our family and society. We are schooled through education, learning things that vary greatly in terms of their usefulness in life, and our education, hopefully, clarifies a path forward into a vocation or further education, where we secure specific knowledge, skills and behaviours that are helpful in securing our independence from our families through 9–5 employment. This then sets us up to make our own lifestyle choices and to meet our responsibilities as citizens until retirement. Rinse and repeat for billions of people with related cultural, economic and contextual nuances, and that is that. Society, in the main, remains locked in this pattern and cycle of life, which continues to dramatically shape and influence our human experience from day one. Is this it? Is this the best we can hope and plan for?

In this chapter, we'll explore how work connects to the human being and the experiences we have in life. This may sound like an easy opening, but it's not. Treating people like human beings, in an organizational context, has only just begun to surface its potential as a management idea, yet it is fundamentally important to building 'successful' companies. What is success anyway? From my experience, the very nature of organizational (and human) success has been irreversibly altered in recent years. It used to be completely wrapped around money – financial standing and financial outcomes. Whether from the personal and organizational view, forgetting all other considerations, this has been the measure applied to humanity and companies: bigger houses, bigger offices and bigger bank balances. We know this and we've all lived with the pressures and stresses related to this fixation on an endless chase for profit, gain and wealth.

Life is difficult enough without suffering additional and avoidable stress of our employer's making. Our workplaces are designed for a different age – an age where people would happily sleepwalk into servitude followed by retirement at the appropriate government-sanctioned time. What kind of life is that to live? Controlled by a system that treats people as numbers and liabilities. If you ever had the inclination to step back – I mean really step back – and consider the world of work holistically, I'm not sure how inspiring your conclusions would be unless you're working for companies that build and develop things that genuinely progress humanity and the world forward.

Understandably ruthless, competitive and driven in large part by ego, humanity has not come up with anything better than the market economy. As a model it has unlocked many benefits and many excesses. It is created by humans and is a reflection of them. The good and the bad all locked into one enduring system of trade, commerce and value-creation. Yet, even this well-established vision of capitalistic business success is under increasing scrutiny by more enlightened workers and more enlightened leaders who feel the inequalities it creates. Should business now consider the needs and values of all stakeholders, and place a firm emphasis on doing the right thing by people?

What is the 'right thing'? What do people really want from life and work? It is extremely difficult to consider the experience of being human without very quickly going down a path that leads to more philosophical, and often spiritual, conversations and thoughts. In fact, it is almost impossible to avoid the bigger questions when it comes to dealing with our own humanity and existence in the world. People can devote their entire lives to discovering who they are and what they are here for. Yet, at the end, they may still be none the wiser. This challenge is perplexing and grows bigger the more thought you throw at it. A conclusion can be drawn quite readily: we don't know why we are on this planet and those espousing that they have the answers are only working based on their best guess. No one knows what the grand plan is and no one really knows what life is really all about.

A best guess that resonates with me comes from author Bill Bryson, who sums life up in terms many of us can relate to:

> To attain any kind of life in this universe of ours appears to be quite an achievement. As humans we are doubly lucky, of course: We enjoy not only the privilege of existence but also the singular ability to appreciate it and even, in a multitude of ways, to make it better. It is a talent we have only barely begun to grasp. (Bryson, 2004)

It's a fitting quote to stimulate reflections, because what is our ultimate purpose in life? Perhaps it's to create and accelerate human progress. At the very least, there is some kind of unwritten human duty to leave this world in a better state than that in which we found it. It's no different in business. What are we doing as leaders and business professionals if our work does not advance the human experience? A large group of colleagues are constantly finding ways to innovate in this regard and set the pace for the rest of us. An equally large group of people resent this work and what it symbolizes because, in all cases, it means change. It means doing things differently in order to create better things and experiences. I can see how this would be threatening for those who depend on, and subsequently defend, the status quo. It's not in their direct interest to change. They may be living life quite comfortably. This could be a person or an entity, but significantly they represent established thoughts rather than evolving ones. We see this in society. We also see this within our businesses. Traditional versus progressive. It's a duel that has played out since time began. It must be acknowledged. If we are to stand a chance in building more human-centred companies, we will urgently need to revisit the role of organizations in the world of people. In this book, we will start to explore this to bring about a deeper connection between life and work.

A changed world; a changing workplace

Something has dramatically changed. The set prescription and structure of life is under intense pressure and scrutiny from a wide range of angles. People have an incredible number of choices available to them to forge a new career and life path that allows them to experience life on their own terms. Historically, work has presented limited choices. People go to a designated building or place for eight hours a day for five days a week and in exchange they get money, and over the years, an increasing number of benefits. Let's be clear: it's still like that in many companies – a very transactional relationship. And if companies in the 20th century like Ford in the US and Boots in the UK didn't realize the value of giving people some time for themselves at 'weekends', we wouldn't really have moved very far beyond these cold employment relationships. In every generation, pioneering companies often step up to mobilize social change – to push humanity further forward. In this economy, what we're seeing before our very eyes is a radical transformation of the way we experience work and how organizations play a greater role in the total human experience.

The chances of us even being here are so minuscule there are no statistics or odds that can adequately capture the unlikely event of our birth. One figure places the chance of you being born at 400 trillion to 1, and this is viewed to be a conservative figure. Whatever the reason for existence, we have a very human duty to make the most of the experience in work or life, or what we can simply term these days as 'life'. The convergence of our worlds accelerated quite profoundly in 2020 with a wide variety of challenges to grapple with, of which COVID-19 has no doubt sharpened our focus on the human experience. Work and life have converged in the most dramatic of ways.

This realization is dawning on people worldwide. We are seeing tensions between work and life that have given rise to significant issues around mental health, wellness and wellbeing outcomes. We are seeing pronounced fractures between people within our communities and companies. Pronounced in the sense that everything, being fuelled by technology, has become significantly more visible. Social media is showing us the best and worst of ourselves, sometimes in unequal measure. It's an alarming period in our history on this planet. That's certainly the pessimistic perspective. To balance this out for the more positively inclined among us, there has never been a greater opportunity to uplift human existence and increase the quality of our collective and individual outcomes.

A divided human experience

Data from the Health and Safety Executive suggests that 51 per cent of all work-related ill health in 2020 was attributed to stress, anxiety and depression (HSE, 2020). That is a remarkable figure, but who is responsible for it? The answer to this seems obvious. We all are. We have allowed this state of affairs to come to pass by what we permit, accept and promote. Through our choices, actions and decisions, we have made a contribution. With a society more inclined to reach for the remote control rather than reach out to people, we have lost something immensely valuable: connection. There is a disconnect at all levels of society – a disconnect with the people, places and the planet around us. People are more quick to judge, condemn and complain than they have ever been, and social media has fuelled this societal breakdown. Logging onto any social media platform these days is like standing in the audience at the Colosseum as people are ripped apart to the delight of the baying crowds. Reinforced and led by media, there has been a concerted effort to build walls between people, communities and countries in the last few years. This cannot be ignored nor can it be left unspoken within a narrative that focuses on the human experience.

We are, in many respects, simply beings of our time. To consider the human experience without thinking holistically and historically is flawed. The timing of our experience on Earth determines our outcomes greatly. The technology of our time, the societal movements that go on around, with and through us, the cultural developments over the generations, the health of the world, and the political changes within and beyond our countries all affect the quality of the experience we have in life. We are subject to conditions, rules and regulations that evolved over centuries, and systems that may well be ripe for further innovation. From education to employment, much of what is, has been before. It is merely reshaped for the mediums of our age and time.

The overriding and inescapable fact about humans is that we are conscious beings. We are consciously shaping ourselves through life and through experiences. In start-up terms, we are growing and defining our own brand. Every experience and interaction leaves an imprint. It shapes us in ways that we can't understand. For organizations, it is much the same. How intentional and conscious can companies be in building a robust connection between people, work and life? How far can a company go in helping people fulfil their true life potential? Answering questions like these elevates brands to a world-class level. They are thinking and acting with the whole human experience in mind. There is a conscious and systematic intent to better serve people. It differentiates them strongly in this economy.

A transactional, consumer-driven world

The driving force behind much of what people do and experience is grounded in consumerism. This is a very limited and transactional way of viewing the world, but it is a game that is largely played by all – the notion that we are all selling or working to sell something to as many people as possible. The 'American Dream' and the 'Chinese Dream' have had a profound effect on the way life is experienced. These, and dreams like them, have been responsible for generating tremendous economic growth and power, but the side effects have taken their toll across economies with historic and enduring inequalities in our economic and employment conditions.

Yet, wise people exist now and they have existed before. Confucius was on to something when he said: 'If your conduct is determined solely by considerations of profit, you will arouse great resentment.'

Resentment grows and for good reason. A 2019 report by the Credit Suisse Research Institute reported that 1 per cent of the world's population currently holds over 44 per cent of household wealth.

This is an incredible statistic that presents a major problem for societal harmony. Compounding this is executive pay. From 1978, CEO pay has risen 1,000 per cent. This contrast is sharp when compared with workers, whose average pay rose just 11.9 per cent over the same period (Economic Policy Institute, 2019). These are all human-created challenges based on a strong faith in market forces, but as Joseph Healy, co-CEO of Australia's Judo Bank, points out, capitalism is getting a bad rap, and people like Adam Smith or, indeed, Milton Friedman would not be best pleased with where their ideas have ended up. We'll take a closer look at this later in the book.

A unique human experience, every time

What is it to be a human being anyway? For some, this is a spiritual or religious journey. For others, a journey of survival, suffering and sacrifice. For others still, it is an opportunity to achieve something, leave a legacy or create some notion of success. Whatever 'it' is becomes very personal and unique to everyone. It stands to reason, then, that we all have profoundly different experiences and are here for very different reasons. It may or may not be a universal truth, that at our core, people want to do better and improve their lot in life. Generally, people want to make progress. Outside of starting your own enterprise or business, the primary route to achieve something is within the vehicle of an organization.

Co-creation of the human experience is taking place at a global scale through various platforms and technological innovations. Progress can often come at great expense to the environment and the world around us. This has been the trade-off. We have co-created the conditions to deliver a greater positive and negative impact on the world. We can travel more, eat better, buy more things that we don't need and have exceptional experiences with brands, yet some of these experiences are entirely dependent on a supply chain propped up by a 'cost-effective' workforce in places people care little to think about. The 'say and do' gap here is startling – a society that has been willing to tolerate the obscenest inequalities simply because they are out of sight and out of mind. If an exceptional customer experience or quality product is delivered, there has been an unspoken tolerance of the means to achieve that goal. Every time we put on our clothes and look at the label, we get a reminder of this. Whether through highly stressed people working in manufacturing plants in Asia, a fragile workforce of contractors fighting to survive or a population of people working three jobs to make a decent wage, the notion that this is just capitalism at work has prevailed, but does that mean it's right?

The declaration by 181 CEOs of the top companies in the world in 2019 to radically overhaul the reasons why companies exist was potentially a landmark moment (Gartenberg and Serafeim, 2019). The newly defined role of companies is to lead with purpose and build companies that have a positive impact on all stakeholders in society. This is a huge statement of intent and the reverberations will be felt in the years to come. In the old economy, high performance was all about the financials. In this emerging economy, backed by corporate power brokers, high performance is no longer related solely to financial outcomes. Doing good business now is simply not about profit, revenue and turnover. It is much more about placing purpose above profit and how companies interact with and serve their communities, societies and the environment in a sustainable way. At least that's what the marketing says. The truth much more closely resembles damage limitation. Scandal after scandal has left consumers questioning the integrity of businesses and trust has eroded significantly. In reality, there was no choice but to respond to try to strengthen trust and relationships. The cynics among us, and their grounded rhetoric, matters. Too often we have bought into something that didn't exist and a heavy price is paid by society to pick up the pieces.

For those of us who have been championing this position, the time has come to ensure companies effectively install this powerful rhetoric into the experiences of all stakeholders within and outside of a business. So, that's it. Carte blanche to create more purposeful companies that have a positive impact in the world. Well, not quite. The motives here are not entirely altruistic and it does make very good business sense. Indeed, based on 1.5 million employee-level observations across thousands of companies, those with high levels of purpose outperform the market by 5–7 per cent per year, on par with companies with best-in-class governance and innovative capabilities. They also grow faster and have higher profitability. If the company has a strong corporate purpose, employees will also feel greater meaning and impact in their jobs (Gartenberg and Serafeim, 2019).

The purpose and experience gap

For creative agencies, this is boom time as companies seek to bring their corporate purpose to life and ensure they are, at least, perceived to be working within the framework of this new economy, or in other terms, this commitment to a conscious and positive capitalism. There are going to be some major false steps in this work, with companies doing some exceptional work on their brand and marketing yet, as is often the case, the real substantive work on the employee and customer experience may well be lagging if they're not careful.

The say and do gap is very real and is open to strategic and tactical manipulation by employers. The world of work is awash with broken promises built on glossy marketing campaigns yet devoid of any real substance. This is now the wild west, as more companies fly the flag of 'purpose over profit', virtue signal and try to over-engineer something that simply does not exist. It's not the truth and they will get found out eventually. Interestingly, their very own marketing could be the fuel for viral exposure and not of the good kind – the kind that creates negative headlines and is written by their own employees. Genuinely purposeful companies create something special that people can believe in. It is very real, sincere and it satisfies one of our most fundamental desires to belong to something bigger than ourselves. This is a constant life pursuit. From observations of thousands of employees over the years, I can confirm that the search for meaning is very real. If people don't find it in work, they will try to create it elsewhere. This is partly why companies are starting to consider the entire experience of being human within and without their organizations.

In my research over the last few years on employee experience, the most significant finding was that the delivery of an exceptional employee experience is not about employees at all. It's about human beings – all of them, on the inside and outside of our companies. We can't vaguely throw together any model that focuses on experience without humans being the major part of it. This, as we find through our work as practitioners and leaders, leads us down a rabbit hole that demands answers to life's most challenging questions. As humans, why are we here? What impact can we have? How do we fulfil our potential? What is the right work for us to do? How do we make our difference?

Inevitably, this line of questioning is transformational as we no longer view work and life as separate entities. We need to consider everything around us holistically to start to realize and create the meaning we so desire. In this sense, for companies and people, everything about the human experience is now in question.

Not *what*, but *where* is the human experience?

This is a profound question, but it is necessary if we are to understand the art and science behind building human-centred organizations. Where does the human experience actually take place? In our offices, in coffee shops, at our kitchen tables, at our clubs or holiday locations, in our towns, villages and cities. Our environments can play an influential role over our lives, but there is one basic truth that none of us can ever escape: the human experience in its purest sense takes place within us. Our internal world matters more than anything. How we think and how we feel. Our mental and physical health. Where does joy come from? Who creates our happiness? Who controls and regulates our moods? Who is responsible for the way we experience the world around us? We are.

'Know thyself' is one of the most powerful expressions, and philosophies, in life. Originating in ancient Greece and carved into the Oracle stone at Adelphi, this ability to truly understand ourselves and connect with who we really are continues to pose significant problems for people and workplaces. The gap between people can be vast, yet the gap within ourselves is often much greater. Our idea of self informs our perceptions, attitudes, behaviours, emotions and, ultimately, our outcomes. Our lives are experienced in the present moment. It's all we have. Yet, deep within us as humans, we are massively susceptible to an incessant dialogue with ourselves about the past and the future – memories or speculative ideas. Many times, we are wrong. Our memories of times past become distorted and our projections of the future can create stress in our present. Navigating life is a constant journey of self-discovery and self-reliance. It is a wholly unique experience to each person.

Everything we'll ever need is within us, but if you don't have the experiences, there are no opportunities for us to find out who we really are. This matters more than you think. One of the first areas of work I do within my coaching is centred around self-discovery. It is staggering the amount of people that do not know why they are here on Earth. On the other hand, it is not so surprising at all given the functions and focus of our education systems around the world. We simply don't ask enough high-quality questions about the things that really matter in life. It is still a rare event for a person to truly connect to their purpose and live it consistently.

We come into this world on our own and we will go out of this world in the same manner. The focus for all of us is to make the period between these two milestones as enjoyable, impactful and fulfilling as is humanly possible, despite each of us experiencing our own suffering and unique challenges. Organizations by their very nature and by the time we associate with them play a major role in our lives. They can help create remarkable moments of joy and astonishing moments of anger and disbelief. In many ways, they are mirrors of the human spirit. It's fragility, weakness and insecurity. It's strength, resilience and compassion.

Stifling human freedom is not good for business

In business circles there is a tendency to want to define and categorize things and people quickly. It provides the illusion of order and the safety of human-made structures. It is the antidote to the perception of chaos. Within this, as humans like to do, there are actions and behaviours that generate policies and practices that increase bureaucracy and diminish human freedoms. This need for control and to assert a form of control is the biggest temptation in business, especially when control is in scarce supply. One example of this is the boom in employee tracking software. One such vendor reported a 600 per cent increase in demand during the COVID-19 pandemic as the global workforce began to work remotely. Rather than build *trust* into their organizations, some companies are opting to *track* their people instead. It's a shortcut many have already regretted, including Barclays, which was forced to stop its programme to monitor and track employees after a very short pilot following a backlash from employees (BBC, 2020). Is this really surprising given the importance of freedom within the human experience? If you want to know just how important a factor freedom is, try taking it away. Other companies have experimented with tracking software to assert some form of corporate control. Imagine if everything you did in work was tracked, every movement, every keystroke, every break. It is a modern nightmare and many knowledge workers have had their first taste of it. Invariably, they didn't like it at all; yet visit fulfilment centres, delivery vans, manufacturing plants and warehouses and you'll find this type of practice comes as standard – humans tracked like resources in the name of profit and productivity. Without a strong voice, dubious business practices like this can do untold harm. It would be excellent to say that this is not the human way to do business, but that would be a lie, for it is humans who are making these decisions within the corporate world. The question is, why? We'll take a closer look at this in the next chapter.

A global reset: work and life reimagined

Did you feel it? COVID-19 brought about a global review of our roles and how we play them in society. It has created a stronger or weaker connection to our jobs, our companies and the people around us. We've had more time to reflect and changes have followed. On the work side, we may not have been working for that perfect company after all. Indeed, what was a positive employee experience (EX) could have very quickly turned sour as lay-offs began to take hold within the economy. How people were treated through that period of time will live long in the memory. On the other hand, employees may well have seen that their companies actually meant what they said – their values counted when it mattered most. In that case, connections were strengthened and celebrated. The gap between these extremes can be vast, with many companies falling into the indifferent middle ground, which is by far the worst place to be. Mediocre, unmemorable or just good enough is not a pleasant place to spend your days as a company.

My research over the years creates a picture of outcomes that can be achieved when we are truly connected to ourselves and the people around us. It is startling what can occur when we know who we are and what we stand for. It can be even more powerful if this is built on elements of our own creation rather than external influences and forces. A reality not of our own design runs counter to what the human experience is all about. Relating well with others can only really be achieved when we relate well with our self. Companies can often fail on two fronts here: not helping people create the best version of themselves while making it very difficult to work with others. So, why do companies create silos and make it difficult for people to relate to each other? It's almost like the organization was designed from the outset to keep us apart and to keep an enforced distance between people. At the individual level, we can understand ourselves that we like to be in control of our own lives and choices. We want and yearn for that freedom. Companies can be similar in the way they ensure compliance and control across structure through what they choose to reward or punish. Control remains as an ever-present theme in life and work. Who is in control of your experience?

A new world of work was delivered in an instant through the COVID-19 pandemic and we had a compelling answer to this question. People have been enabled and emboldened to take more control over their working lives. The hybrid organization has emerged where flexible and remote work practices feature alongside high-impact usage of a company's physical estate. The workforce had more choice than at any time before to determine how work gets done. COVID-19 came along and suddenly we found ourselves faced with a challenge of unprecedented scale – over half of humanity experiencing lockdown conditions with many working from home. More challenging, too, was the fate of those workers that are deemed to be essential to our societies. A new value and appreciation has been placed on the real backbone of the human experience – our nurses, doctors, supermarket workers, delivery drivers, farmers and food producers, teachers and those engaged in roles and supply chains that really do add value and are vital to all human experiences on the planet if we are to meet our basic needs. Without question, COVID-19 has had a profound impact on every inch of our lives. For those who had to juggle family and work responsibilities, these necessary arrangements as a result of social distancing measures prompted a widespread review of what really matters within our economies and the findings have taken many by surprise. Once again, the crisis demonstrates the best and worst of humanity. It shows us who we really are and what we are really capable of. People will flourish and falter in equal measure. Things will never be the same, but what does that mean for the world of work?

Well, it means the possibility to create something better – an organization fit for the future and one that can withstand any challenge or crisis, and one that recognizes the awe-inspiring potential of the human race. Many didn't know they could adapt to COVID-19, but they did. Many people have become digitally savvy and improved their productivity beyond what they could have ever possibly imagined. Microsoft CEO Satya Nadella, in one of his 2020 earnings calls, said, 'We've seen two years' worth of digital transformation in two months' (Spataro, 2020). He was speaking about the impact of the 2020 pandemic on business. A lot is being made about the digital transformation of the economy, and rightly so. Alongside this, many have created stronger bonds with people and between people and their companies – bonds that will last a lifetime and be ever imprinted in the memory banks.

Dehumanizing work

When we use the words 'company' and 'corporation' it can often dehumanize things greatly. It positions abstract things as the prominent entity, not the people within it. What was highly noticeable throughout COVID-19 were the lengths employers were willing (or not) to go in supporting people within and beyond their immediate responsibility and duty. This was demonstrated through countless examples where leadership prioritize people over profit. They demonstrate their commitment through positive actions, and place themselves in service to society. At the outset of the pandemic, companies from across sectors joined together in getting essential supplies to the professionals and services that needed them. Personal protective equipment, face masks and ventilators were being produced by companies, large and small, in a strong and shared experience across the world. I recall at the height of the situation being contacted by and advising head-hunters about a newly created role for the NHS in the UK: a director of staff experience. It is a potent example that illustrates the growing relevance of the human experience in work and why even long-established and iconic institutions are starting to change and reshape their structures to serve people in a better way. To see the NHS investing in such a role during the global pandemic speaks volumes.

If you really consider how the events of COVID-19 unfolded, it is scarcely believable. Many would not have thought that national governments could lock down billions of people in a matter of days. One message cut through: stay home, save lives. All global communications efforts centred on and intensified around this message using a wide combination of science, data, evidence and emotional story-telling to get the point across in the strongest possible way. The World Health Organization, understanding fully the gravity of the situation, called for an army of creatives and high-profile people to get a unified message out. This is the message. How you deliver that message is up to you. These directives and nudges played vital roles, as did the unprecedented financial incentives, particularly across Western economies, where the rulebook was thrown out of the window. The

Conservative UK Government looked more like a socialist government in a time of national crisis with its chancellor announcing the biggest economic package of support for employers and business in history. The relief was palpable and measures like this were decisive and unprecedented in their scale and coverage.

In other words, human beings were put above the economy, not just in the UK, but in many countries. Having experienced this in the UK, I can only comment personally on the profound impact here, yet it is clear there has been somewhat of an awakening globally. Is this an indication that finally people in power are starting to appreciate that successful economies depend entirely on workers? These approaches have broken new ground. Organizations are competing to serve humanity rather than a narrow focus on shareholders. In the process the old view of capitalism has been blown away. Profit and making money is not bad, but doing so at any cost is no longer acceptable. The COVID-19 pandemic has certainly accelerated this business philosophy and consumers will vote with their money post-crisis if they are wise.

Organizing for humanity

The experience of being human is a complex one. We are all experienced in this. We have immeasurable capacity for doing good, yet there are aspects to our humanity that can be self-centred. Money, power and status have been the calling cards of excess, and are also apt indicators that human ego is imperfect and often flawed. We are set up from birth to compete in a similar win or lose pattern. This survival of the fittest philosophy is heralded for the progress it creates and derided for the apparent inequality it can deliver. This is important because it plays out within our companies every day. Companies are a reflection of humanity. They are used to assert control, implement ideas and organize around a proposition to the marketplace, and in the case of the more ambitious tech-driven enterprise, they can transform entire societies. In many ways, an organization is an outcome of what we are willing to tolerate as consumers and citizens.

Are we happy customers if our products and services simply meet or exceed our expectations, or do our preferences change if we fully understand the human lives being damaged and harmed under the intensity of a stressed supply chain and workforce? Is this tolerable in today's economy?

It is easy to become conflicted around this point. Companies like Tesla, driven by an enigma of a CEO in Elon Musk, whose purpose is to 'accelerate the advent of the electric car', are consistently chasing 'impossible' dreams to push humanity forward. Musk's companies are derided and celebrated daily in equal measure. Musk, for all the criticism surrounding the intense and high-pressure work environments that his leadership creates, has created multiple companies that visibly progress and advance humanity. In 2020, space travel became affordable and a new era of space exploration began with SpaceX at the forefront of it. The stated aim of this is to ensure that, as a species, humans become multi-planetary to avoid extinction given the problems humans have created on Earth. So, is there room to discuss these so-called 'challenging' places to work if they are working to an almighty purpose that serves the greater human experience? The question or concerns for companies in this mould may not be about the why, but is often related to the 'how'. Certainly, when thinking about the human experience at work, it is easy to become idealistic about creating happy and harmonious workplaces, but we know from experience that some of our greatest human achievements were delivered on the back of a traditional human framework: pain and progress. The question is: does it need to be that way to create massive impact? Can we deliver progress in a human-centred way?

For the organization, all of this deserves consideration, rather than speculation – tangible thoughts and actions to fundamentally understand what it is to be human. Only then can we really expect an appropriate response or reaction in the way that the business organizes and moves itself forward. The human experience is consistently associated with suffering and pleasure. It seems we are hard-wired to experience both throughout life. In work, the balance between these things has tended to be strongly tilted towards suffering. Work is something people have to do if they have aspirations to survive. Academics have studied why people work for nearly a century, but a major breakthrough happened in the 1980s when professors Edward Deci and Richard Ryan from the University of Rochester distinguished the six main reasons why people work. A short-hand for the modern workplace reported the reasons as: play, purpose, potential, emotional pressure, economic pressure and inertia (McGregor and Doshi, 2015). The first three being positive, the latter three viewed to be negative. All good reasons nonetheless.

The *Human Role* model

To draw all this together, and utilizing the insights from our research and work, I explored a new model to help us better understand the human experience. To effectively develop thriving organizations, the full spectrum of roles that people play will need to be factored in and considered. Each role presents its own unique and enduring challenges across the physical, mental, spiritual and economic aspects of our existence. Through these roles, we are continually shaping and redefining ourselves through life. The roles we play remain consistent and travel with us whether we like it or not. There are certain aspects to the human experience that are non-negotiable. Through birth, we start working to a role description that is not of our making. It has been evolving since humanity learned to organize itself into tribes, communities and societies. Great rewards await for those playing their part, while greater consequences can be expected if they're not. That's life and our workplaces have only just started to truly understand the human being and how they can properly maximize the potential and performance of their workforces. From my work, the *Human Role* model plays a significant part in how we build companies fit for human beings and all the roles they take up. If we can design our companies and experiences with this knowledge and understanding, we can co-create better companies and outcomes all round.

The *Human Role* model centres on what we know to be true about our roles and responsibilities as part of the human experience. Indeed, rather than saying definitively what the human experience is all about, there is the possibility to learn, from observation, what shapes us as people as we follow our path and journey in life. This becomes massively relevant when thinking about the type of organizations we build in partnership with our people. This model is a reflection of reality: we have different roles to play as human beings and the extent to which we play any one of them will affect the other roles we have in life. It is a delicate balance to maintain. At certain points, we may be directed to spend more time in one of these roles, and the others will take less of a priority. Yet, regardless of circumstances, all must be respected and honoured if we are to make our mark as a human.

THE *HUMAN ROLE* MODEL

- **Explorer:** We explore ourselves throughout life, finding and developing our own Truth, sense of identity and determining what brings us joy, fulfilment and happiness.

- **Contributor:** We contribute in multiple ways and across multiple roles and objectives. Through our strengths, talents and characteristics, we make a unique difference.

- **Citizen:** We are inextricably linked with society and the world. We have a role to play in shaping the places and communities around us.

- **Carer:** We care for others. This is one of our highest responsibilities in life – to think beyond our self to support our families, friends, loved ones and communities.

- **Performer:** We are all required to perform in our duties and obligations in creating valuable outcomes in the world and delivering our collective progress.

- **Architect:** We are the architect and grand designer of our life. Our choices, decisions and actions matter more than anything,

---

Explorer

A big part of the human experience is the search for truth. This starts from within and grows outwards, yet for some reason we are taught more in terms of outside–in. From our early education and interactions, we are taught and conditioned to be responsive to external stimuli. This could be authority, accepted wisdom and norms, or the 'way it is' around us. With this view, the path of life is well defined and accepted as 'normal' or 'respectable', and deviating from this path is viewed by society to be maverick, rebellious or strange. The overwhelming strength of social proof, societal pressure and our environments converge to shape us as human beings. This often dictates our expectations, behaviours and actions in life. In effect, most of the script is already written and people just go through the motions on auto-pilot. As a model, it's been very successful for centuries and has churned out an obedient and subservient workforce.

But here's the thing. Humans are naturally progressive, creative and powerful in disrupting the status quo. Francesca Gino and I discussed this during the COVID-19 pandemic. Francesca, who is a Harvard Business School professor and author of *Rebel Talent* (2019), highlights the benefits of having organizations that embrace people who are naturally rebellious and who don't conform to the circumstances and conditions around them. Life and work are as much about system builders as they are about system disruptors. As each generation comes into the workforce, new ideals and expectations are created based on an evolving mindset that is enabled by the technology of the day. The deeper the learning and sharing, the deeper the commitment to positive change. The more we understand about ourselves, the better we can effect this change and move things on. Are we ever really the finished product as human beings, and isn't it one of our major roles to explore our limits and even our morality and the scope of our potential and talent? Would it be a disservice to ourselves if we didn't truly embrace our full capabilities?

One would be tempted to make a very firm conclusion here and say that the best we can ever be as humans is a 'work in progress'. In many ways, that isn't a bad thing. It's just the reality of exploring our potential, our boundaries or our perceived limits. There are countless examples of people striving to achieve something while forgetting to enjoy the journey, or worse, start to take shortcuts to the success they wish to create, but only arrive at their destination with a feeling of emptiness and regret. Jeff Bezos built his Amazon empire on the back of regret – interestingly, not on any regret he will ever experience. His idea of a *regret minimization framework* was noted as the major factor behind him starting Amazon and is an example of inspired human thinking. Looking out to age 80, he asked himself what would be his major life regret. He concluded that not starting his company would fit that description, and the rest is history. Whether you like, loathe or love what Amazon represents, the level of thinking that created it is very much of human origin. Pushing the limits of what's possible is, up until this point at least, a distinctly human trait.

This is the human lot, regrets to avoid, and everyone has choices to make along the way. This is the unique, exciting and challenging aspect to life and work. We can talk about the human experience through a lens of morals, values and purpose, yet we know from experience that a major first task for us is to establish what these things mean. The clear majority of people never meet their full potential, and even 'potential' is up for some debate in terms of how we measure it. Whether looking at this from a spiritual, philosophical, economic or social point of view, the evidence suggests that life is a perpetual exploration that consists of many trials, errors and experiments in finding out who we truly are. It's focused on answering some of humanity's most profound yet least answered questions:

- Who we are? (identity)
- Why are we here? (purpose)
- What are we supposed to do? (mission)
- How are we meant to act and lead our lives? (values)

The greatest exploration we can ever do is the one we do internally. In one of my development programmes, we ask participants about their Truth (purpose, mission and values). The participants are very successful senior leaders from global organizations, and many of them find this exercise extremely challenging. It has nothing to do with their competence and capability. They are exceptional professionals, but it is often challenging because people do not get the chance to reflect on what really matters in the human experience.

When it comes to human behaviours, traits and character, we see more evidence that life, in its most simplistic sense, is exploratory. One term I speak about often is the hexis. This originates from Greek philosophy and is a way of explaining the way in which people build, maintain and sustain character. We can often condition ourselves and move unconsciously into a hexis – a habitual set of characteristics and traits that follow us in life. They can fuel our success or hold us back. Part of the human experience is to intentionally develop it as we go through life. One of the great achievers of any generation, Benjamin Franklin, took this to extremes during his life. On a Saturday night, he would sit down and reflect on his human performance over the previous week, exploring how he did in areas that he felt were holding him back. He would rate himself based on his own observations and seek to make targeted improvements in the week following. It was a process that was influential in shaping his character and his outcomes in life. Franklin understood what many don't. Life happens fast, and if we are not aware of and in control of our own development, it might pass us by completely and irreversibly. In the workplace, this is about being more intentional rather than accidental. Too often, work life is designed, and indeed, experienced, in a haphazard and passive way. There is a need to be present in each and every moment if we are truly to maximize what companies create.

As David Brooks (2012) points out in his book *The Social Animal*, 'the conscious mind writes the autobiography for our species.' This plays out in our everyday life – the back and forth between our conscious and subconscious – the enduring battle between logic and reason on one hand, and emotions and intuition on the other. We rarely look too deeply at ourselves, and companies often miss opportunities to look deeply at their workers from an emotional, and human, perspective.

The human experience is defined by human exploration. As we move through experiences, we are introduced to new stimuli that either helps us grow or holds us back. Not every experience is positive and not all aspects of humanity are benevolent. Jungian psychology talks about the shadow – the darker side of the human being, the unknown that is not visible to others. It represents that inner world where selfishness reigns supreme. In many cases, it is the opposite of what people project on social media and is hidden from scrutiny. Yet, every human must face it and it often presents itself as a challenge to manage within the workplace. The negative aspects to personalities come out and, left unchecked, can help establish a toxicity that takes hold within a business. At an individual level, this is a tough part of the human experience to deal with. At an organizational level, things can quickly spiral out of control if this is ignored. The worst excesses of corporate culture can prevail, and humans are the driving force behind many painful and toxic corporate failures. For these reasons, it may be uncomfortable to address this in the organizational context, yet it is a challenge that most human-centred companies rise to. We cannot ignore the darker side of the human experience, and we may not be able to control it, but we can give people freedom to explore themselves fully, building awareness, acceptance and a greater level of understanding about why we do what we do.

Contributor

No one gets a free ride. We are all required to work at something. Some of us will run the business. Some of us will work in the business. Some of us will work on the business. We will all make our contribution somewhere within the economy. How we do that has fundamentally changed. The nature of the economy now is resetting around a diverse and broad ecosystem of people who come together to support growth and business outcomes. This could be an employee, contractor, gig worker, portfolio career professional, freelancer and any other number of roles that help get the job done. This is becoming the biggest challenge in business – how to define and treat a complex workforce made up of many valuable contributors. The size of the gig economy in the UK has doubled in the past three years (TUC, 2019), and similar patterns are seen globally. The Bureau for Labor Statistics found that the US economy is now reliant on 16.5 million people who work in the contingent workforce through contractor roles, gig economy and alternative work arrangements (BLS, 2018). Platforms for freelancers have boomed in recent years and the very idea of what work is has changed beyond comprehension for many, especially those operating across the digital economy and those at the forefront of these changes. The younger generation is playing its role in shaping new ideas about how positive value can be created in non-traditional ways. In 2019, it was reported that 56 million American workers were Millennials, and there is a noticeable generational shift occurring as more people expect to work on their own terms and in their own way (Desilver, 2019). The ways we contribute are changing, and this coincides with severe talent shortage in places like the UK and the EU. Research is showing that there is a risk that the EU workforce will decline from 239 million to 217 million workers by 2050. This presents a dramatic statistic in the face of an ageing workforce, and this is without considering the impact of Brexit and ongoing trade disputes across the global economy.

In light of this and other challenges, the contribution people make very much depends on their context, career and circumstances. Contribution is determined by people and companies, and it is interesting to see the new models of work being presented; yet this is also a very personal role within the human experience and is experienced beyond a singular job. People may have years filled with national awards, industry recognition, honours, sterling performance reviews and other accolades. Other years could be transitional. Others could be about consolidation and growth. Others will be part of a longer learning curve and experimentation. The strength of the linear career path as the accepted norm appears to be waning. Whatever part of the journey people are at will determine a lot about the contribution they make to the business.

Establishing realistic expectations of people is helpful to avoid any build-up of stress, burnout and resentment. People can be valuable contributors over the long term, and human-centred organizations recognize this within the experiences they deliver by selecting based on human factors rather than trying to categorize people into boxes that don't fit anymore. There are very few superhumans out there. Not even the best of us can consistently be a top contributor. There will be some off days, and maybe some off years, because of our other roles in life. Managing our roles is no easy task, for anyone.

Work could be thriving, but personal relationships could be a disaster zone. Our contribution to family might be tremendous yet our contribution at work may not be. Many people choose to sacrifice something in order to get something else. Some may not have a choice. Work becomes a proxy for something that is missing in life. There's no doubt that the digital economy has shifted the employment landscape considerably, opening new possibilities for people to start their own businesses, work in radically different ways and, for the first time, subordinate work to fuel lifestyle outcomes. Some of the most creative people on the planet are sponsored rather than employed.

Within this role, we also need to consider the unique strengths and talents of people, and where they can make the biggest contribution. In experience terms, this means more personalization of jobs, human-centred job design and changes to the way people think about career paths. The old way viewed a career through narrow paths such as promotion. The new way is about possibility. In human-centred companies, a great deal of thought will be given to help people contribute in their roles and beyond their roles, and this often spills over into wider society.

Citizen

Organizations are certainly not islands. They are part of the world like the rest of us. Trying to keep the world out of companies is proving trickier than ever before. The gold standard for businesses has been to keep their workforce fully focused on their performance and their objectives, shutting out anything that gets in the way of that. This to an extent continues to drive a lot of workplaces in the way that they design their business models, but it's no longer sustainable. Societal causes and topics of great importance to people as citizens have entered the brand narrative in a big way. Indeed, this is about more than being a good corporate citizen. This is about escalating the urgency and attention that is associated with societal issues within the organization. We have seen much evidence of this in recent years – companies thinking beyond their own profit margins to serve society in important and helpful ways. From the production of life-saving equipment to repurposing parts of their business to provide services and products that serve important human needs, many companies have stood up and stood out because they tilted their business in favour of people and communities. This is a key role that all people play. They are world citizens, community members and part of a wider and connected story. Movements and social issues are not in short supply. There are many challenges and problems to solve around the world and within communities. An established pattern in the more enlightened organization is the strength of the connection people have between each other and the society that they are part of. Again, aside from corporate social responsibility initiatives, companies are only just beginning to discover the possibilities (and challenges) this role presents in work. Turning a corporate blind eye to social challenges has never looked so bad.

Carer

In 2020, caring is making its way onto many corporate agendas. While it doesn't traditionally associate itself naturally to business objectives and key performance indicators, caring is becoming an ongoing concern within the economy. Why? Because businesses can't afford not to. Caring about the environment, ethics and society are welcome trends. It's the very same for people and their experiences. As humans, caring is part of our DNA, be it about other people, our planet or any other myriad things. It's one of the better aspects of humanity.

Within this role, one of the most important elements of life is family, but how many companies design their work around this? How many take reasonable steps to ensure we can fulfil all our roles, obligations and responsibilities in life? The inflexibility of employers is a common gripe from employees – the inclination to hide behind draconian work policies and practices to the detriment of their brand and outcomes. Often the phrase 'business is business' is delivered, which means that too often the humanity has been taken out of consideration completely. To create workplaces that don't enable and permit people to fulfil one of their primary roles in life makes zero sense in my opinion. This comes to a head when times are tough and people are required to formally care for others. Whether this is caring for partners, children, parents or loved ones, it is a role that should be celebrated and valued, yet in many contexts people are not given the space and freedom to fulfil their potential as caring human beings. Policies, regulations and rigid bureaucracy treat people like heartless machines. From my research, I have found that people are looking for several important things in work: above all, they want to trust their employer, they want (and greatly appreciate) an employer that is fully committed to them, and they want an employer that demonstrates on a regular basis that it cares about people (and, increasingly, planet). For this reason, when considering the full scope of the human experience, we need to closely and carefully consider the holistic nature of being human and the caring responsibilities we have within it. It's about providing care as well as receiving it in times of need. How many companies are well set up and designed for that?

Performer

Value is created and delivered by performances – more specifically, human performances. Across the length and breadth of the business world, performance and value are critical elements of organizational life. We are all performers in some shape or form. Our societies are built on value, perceived or real, which is the outcome of the performances we deliver. Material success is often determined in direct relation to the extent with which we can create value for others. In the process of creating value for others, we become more valuable. Certainly, value-creation is the driving force behind the business world and often dictates the quality of the human experience in and outside of work. Those deemed to be creating the most value by society are, generally, paid more. It's interesting that if society was viewed as a pyramid, at the top would be actors, celebrities, music stars, sportspeople and business leaders.

This idea of high performance is usually represented by figures, statistics and charts that are all directly connected to bottom-line business outcomes. It's a numbers game, traditionally: delivering more customers, clients or consumers, increasing revenue and profit, creating value within the economy. It's all relatively straightforward to determine a good month, a good quarter or a good year. In an economy that's been totally consumed with the 'what' and with results, it's not hard to understand why businesses take shortcuts, doing whatever it takes to survive and beat the competition.

We have to perform, but an important point to consider is the way in which we perform and how 'performance' is being defined in the first place. Human performance is being reclassified, re-evaluated and recalibrated in leading companies. It considers all the roles we've explored and more besides, rather than solely focusing on corporate contribution and impact. It's about people's impact in life as a human being, not just as a worker. This more balanced view of performance changes the nature of management conversations. If a person is exceeding their objectives, but they are highly stressed and anxious in work, is that high performance? If people hit their objectives, but take ethical and moral shortcuts to do that, is that high performance? If business is good, but life is intolerable, is that high performance? Surely, in this day and age, we can feel good, enjoy the life experience AND deliver high impact at work. That is not impossible, yet some heavy lifting will be required on the part of people and companies in designing the experiences that truly meet this end. We'll explore this further throughout the case studies within this book as there is a need to reconsider performance from multiple angles.

Architect

A life of our own design is a noble and realistic goal. Most people would not object to being the architect of their lives, and though it is a role that we all have, it's one that is scarcely embraced fully, especially within our work lives. Every choice, every decision, every action and every experience has directly shaped what we are today. Whether conscious or unconscious, from the moment of birth to the moment right now, we have shaped our own destiny to a large degree. None of the roles outlined here may be more important than intentionally developing, owning and leading our own lives. In the workplace, this means taking responsibility and operating within a company that provides plenty of freedom, autonomy and space for people to define their work, their impact and their vision.

This role of architect has a lot to do with our own self-reliance, self-discipline and personal responsibility. Within the human experience, it alters our view of how companies can best work with people. It is not about 'engaging' them. It is about co-creating experiences that fundamentally move the control to people – control over the work, the experiences and the outcomes. It also challenges companies to remove anything getting in the way of empowered people. In essence, leaders have a responsibility to architect an organization where people are free to architect the best version of themselves. Whatever it takes to do that is in scope and needs to be explored further.

Summary: the human experience

Our moment has arrived. There has never been as much focus on the experience of work as there is right now. At the same time, people are reviewing the human experience as a whole and how everything can better fit together as part of our journey through life. Within this, there is an opportunity to reflect and deepen our thinking about who we are as people and what the organization now represents to us in the economy given its critical role in human life. This offers the chance to revisit the relationship between people and companies, and how they can interact in a way that enhances outcomes and delivers progress within and beyond the organization.

- Take a step back and consider the human experience: what does it mean to you? What is massively important to you as a human being?

- Explore what is driving and shaping the human experience at work. What factors are leading to change and transformation? What is the state of our evolving understanding of the employment relationship?

- Reflect on the roles you play in life and how the roles set out in the *Human Role* model interact at various stages of your human experience. How do these roles affect, influence and impact your work and career?

- Take a moment to think about any regrets that you would wish to avoid when it comes to your own career and role in leading the important work to improve experiences at work for people. What impact do you wish to have within your organization and the people around you?

02

Why humanity demands
a new model for work

Let's face it, the traditional view that work is 9–5 at a fixed location is not an idea that has been built to last. It's a version, an iteration. So many things are wrong with this approach that it often runs contrary to what we know about human life. People like freedom, autonomy and choice. Rigid workplaces do not deliver that. It's almost as though people are set up to fail. Excelling in one aspect of life leads to negligence of another. Companies have reinforced this through practices that limit freedoms and fix humans in the harsh and unyielding reality called routine, known also as 'same old, same old'. Work, and the associated rituals and routines, becomes a trap and humanity has been the prisoner. Work, when designed poorly, does curb our freedoms, dictates how we live our lives and is the source of much of our stress. Even prior to seismic global events such as financial crashes, the health crises and an increasing instability in geopolitics, burnout, anxiety and stress were all increasing, and it is work that remains a dominant force in creating these within people's existence. There is no room to manoeuvre and no way out for many. For those of the more positive disposition, this may seem like nonsense. We all have choices. We choose to work where we do. We are always in control of our destiny. They're right, of course, but this level of thinking is not commonplace when there are bills to pay, mouths to feed and relationships to maintain. Far easier to think along those lines from a comfortable position, but scarcely available to those who are quietly suffering in jobs and companies they are not comfortable with.

The COVID-19 pandemic, and evolving expectations, changed all that. Instead of just focusing our attention on a select number of progressive companies, we can now extend our view to include a large body of research across the entirety of the global economy. No company escaped the pandemic and very few experiences in work didn't experience some form of reconfiguration, and in many parts, it was a new configuration to be welcomed. A study from the *New York Times* reinforced this, with 86 per cent of people confirming that they were satisfied with homeworking, and 47 per cent stating that they were very satisfied (Strzemien *et al*, 2020). An incredible one in three people would move or relocate if homeworking continued beyond the pandemic. People also reported that they were taking more walks and exercise, and that stress, overall, decreased. This new world of work quickly started to seriously impact life in a profound way. Why wouldn't it? People being given more freedom, more choice, more options and more control over their lives – what's not to love about that? This is the first time in history that work has been designed around life, and not the other way around – and at such scale, there is a very good chance that the lessons being learned about the optimum set-up for humans and work will stick.

A world without humans as 'resources'

A massive shift is already in full swing. Organizations are finding through experience that the status quo is often not helpful when leaning in closer to the human experience. The traditional view that humans are 'resources' to be managed has never faced an existential challenge like this, but it's arrived and it must be faced with candour and a degree of objectivity and calmness. We understand that many professionals are wedded to their professions and disciplines. Communities and long-held beliefs have been formed around them. They are deeply integrated into who we are and how we practise our respective crafts. Reading between those lines, there will in my opinion be a strong resistance from the established orthodoxy, many of whom have built their entire companies, - institutions and programmes of work around the concept of people being managed as resources, which to a large extent reflects an old way of looking at the world. For example, study after study shows an appetite and need for change, yet taking the necessary actions is consistently a lagging indicator. In their view, there are other priorities. In this context, HR as an idea continues to be the default, established and automatic approach to bring in once companies start to scale, develop and grow, but is this the right way to build thriving companies?

I highlighted the potential existential threat to HR in my first book, *Employee Experience* (Whitter, 2019). If colleagues didn't shift their mindset to humans, experiences and creating value in radically different ways, HR colleagues should brace themselves for an uncertain future. The evidence continues to pile up and suggest that. The days of people being treated as mere payroll data and resources are numbered. Conversely, if HR teams continue in this mode, they will find themselves to have a short shelf life indeed. A 2020 study by Deloitte (Volini *et al,* 2020) offered further data that seemingly confirms what we already know – HR is not adjusting well to the demands being placed on the function by a refreshed focus on humans and experiences within companies worldwide. Incredibly, in its global study, Deloitte reported a 64-point gap 'between importance and readiness'. Seventy-five per cent of respondents said that the 'evolving role of HR was important or very important for their success over the next 12 to 18 months'. Yet, in the same study, only 11 per cent stated they were very ready to address challenges related to this new focus on the human experience at work. Once again, the big barriers were ones with which we are all too familiar: the structure of HR within the organizational design of the business and a reluctance to extend impact beyond the traditional boundaries of HR. In no way does this double challenge sit well with a human-centred approach as the lens naturally widens in scope to include any interaction or moment that employees encounter. The traditional and somewhat cumbersome hierarchy within companies is not designed well to rise to these challenges. Indeed, what tends to happen is that progress is halted due to self-inflicted tension between portfolios and personalities. With competing agendas in play, there are simply too many obstacles to overcome.

Are these challenges reserved for newcomers into the human-centred and experience-driven space? Well, no. Even the progressive companies I tend to work with that have already moved strongly into the EX space have reported tension, friction and roadblocks coming out of HR rather than the business. A reluctance to view employees and workers as partners is a common challenge alongside mindset, knowledge and skill deficits within teams. A leading question perhaps, but an urgent question to ask ourselves nonetheless, is about the immediate future of HR. Does it even have a future within our organizations? In the future, one major question will be a primary way of quickly finding out whether a company is committed to a genuine organizational effort to run a human-centred company. It will seem like an innocent enough query, but the implications of the answer will be significant. It is simply this: does your company have an HR function?

Retiring the HR concept

Increasingly, HR offers a convenient image and representation of a changing world. It is, in effect, stuck between two eras: the one where employees were merely numbers on a payroll and cogs in a large machine, and another where humans and their experiences are in full focus in how organizations set themselves up for success over the long term. If we talk about innovation as a key part of longevity in business, we also need to seek innovation in the way we support, organize and design our support services. Root and branch is an expression that springs to mind. The substance is certainly different now than it ever was. HR teams have been busily building up skills and capabilities that are naturally more in service to the brand and the business. Across a whole library of skills and capabilities – human-centred design, people analytics, storytelling, psychology, agile, marketing and many more – there has been a serious and notable pivot from the old to the new. The style, though, also needs to be considered.

CEOs have had plenty of time to enjoy the benefits of a customer-focused approach. It was only a matter of time before they would realize the benefits of applying similar tactics and strategies with their workforces. Peter Cheese, the CEO of the CIPD (Chartered Institute of Personnel and Development), and I joined forces to inspire a new vision for the world of work in 2019. Working with hundreds of HR professionals in Cyprus, we offered both a challenge and an opportunity to colleagues. The challenge was to modernize the work of HR to be more focused on purpose, values and evidence-based practice while embracing a human-centred, experience-driven future of work. Many would be forgiven for suspecting we would be speaking from very different perspectives, yet it was immediately clear that that was not the case. There were some nice overlaps with our respective messages. To me, this was another indicator that established thought was shifting and that HR was evolving into something I could really get behind. It also coincided with a change to the CIPD's Profession Map, with employee experience becoming a prominent development theme. In any case, the CIPD has supported colleagues in successfully transitioning from personnel to HR, and I have full confidence the professional body will be there once again to support the transition from HR to human experience. Similarly, I have also worked with the SHRM (Society for Human Resource Management) in the US, where the employee experience concept has quickly risen in prominence and is now a common expression and approach for HR professionals to embrace. In fact, I think the world's HR professionals will need all the support they can get – shifting mindsets across the economy is not easy work at all. A changing business landscape requires a fundamentally changed HR, not just superficial around-the-edge improvements, hacks or pivots.

Finding the humanity in HR

In the research for this book, I noticed a fascinating trend when interviewing and speaking with HR colleagues. Some very senior HR leaders, global directors and chief people officers spent the initial few minutes of our calls by socially distancing themselves from the HR profession. A common language often emerged that connected one narrative with another, and so on. 'I work in HR, but I'm not *that* HR.' When I challenged this, as I do, the justification was the same in each instance. They simply did not want to associate with the traditional HR profession.

This presents a major problem. Beyond what is often described as an inward-looking profession, there is a whole world out there that does not stand with HR, and more importantly, what it represents. Indeed, they are actively hoping that HR in its current form fades away. Before we get carried away with ingrained professional loyalties, let's take an objective view about this. HR professionals are finding it distasteful to be a part of the HR profession. This is the historical elephant in the room, and is a unique challenge for HR. I hold the same conversations with IT, marketing and other colleagues. There is no immediate temptation to take this sort of approach. So, why is this a huge factor in HR's ability to perform and can it really continue to be ignored in the current economic, political and social climate?

The reality is that this not a new issue. It's just that no one has been bothered to challenge the status quo unless it's for exposure as a firebrand within some fancy business magazine. It's a problem that historically no one wants to solve. The market for change has not been ready. CEOs as they deal with 'real' business priorities often replicate what already exists to effectively cover themselves legally, ethically and sometimes morally. If everyone is doing it, why invest the energy and time to create something different that may not work? HR, in this sense, offers stability that processes, procedures and policies are in place for managers and employees to follow, and more importantly, feel safe among what can otherwise be organized chaos if employees are brought together in a haphazard manner.

To deal with this effectively, perhaps it would be a good idea to separate the many talented people working in HR from the elements of HR that hold them back. Their numbers are vast. Often underappreciated, undervalued and most certainly neglected, colleagues in HR roles are some of the best business professionals in the world, astutely balancing the needs of the business with those of the work-force. Great brands attract truly great people to lead and work in their people functions, yet it isn't enough. The glaring evidence is right before us. The number of HR colleagues rising to the top of companies and landing CEO roles represents truly disappointing performance. I could go further, but this is an indicator of impact. For ambitious executives, the C-suite is the target, but for HR, the story usually ends there. This is a travesty for several reasons when we read and learn about the very best CEOs. What makes them the best is a huge commitment to their people, their brand and their communities. This is the mark of the CEO, and coincidentally, these things should play to the strengths of progressive people professionals.

Has the time come for HR to leave the corporate world?

With the advancement of this 'experience mindset' within companies, it has accelerated efforts to repurpose and reposition support services. Why? Well, historically when thinking about the experience of work, HR has been the function that most CEOs immediately point to. This has developed and reinforced the HR organization while creating additional strings to HR's bow. HR is viewed as a natural home for efforts to improve employee experiences, but is this the best way to organize around people and their experiences?

It would take a brave person to suggest that we now need to elim-inate the many millions of HR jobs across the global economy, yet what we all seem to be saying is more in line with a radical evolution of the people profession – not in any way to diminish people working in HR roles, but to strengthen their hand and positions even more. Ideally, we need a new people profession, one that is fully focused on the human experience that gives colleagues a full licence to innovate, create and design those powerful brand experiences. Freed from a lack of trust and respect, they can lead businesses to new heights by guiding leaders and professionals in ways fit for this experience-driven economy. Idealistic? I think not, because in many instances, it's already happening.

This is not about simply changing HR to something else. It's about redefining everything we know to be true about what matters most to the business. There's no better place to start than with how businesses set up their internal functions for long-term success. Yet, how many times are HR colleagues left behind and forgotten about? HR is expected to play a pivotal role in facilitating a positive employee experience, but no one is looking after HR colleagues. They are human too! It's not good enough anymore.

Then there are the models and structures in place that compound these issues. I recall a discussion about the HR business partner (HRBP) model. In my time at a top pharmaceutical company earlier in my career, it was fascinating to observe the way HRBPs interacted with each other, with leaders and within the HR function generally. The HRBPs often had a big chip on their shoulder, trying to prove that they were all about the business. They dissociated too, but often in a less positive way than the colleagues I mentioned earlier. Then one day, a genuinely world-class HRBP was appointed. Her CV was glittering – a superstar in HR. This type of colleague can be a rarity in the market. Everything about her approach was different. This colleague was oozing all the qualities, attributes and capabilities I'd be looking for in a top-notch people professional. There was empathy, holistic-thinking, commercial savviness, incredible stakeholder management skills, and a genuine warmth and kindness infiltrated every interaction. No one was above her, because no one was beneath her. It was amazing to work with her and the lessons have stayed with me throughout my career.

The downside to this was that, outside of world-class companies, it is difficult to find colleagues at her level because they are often not attracted to working in the HR profession. This is another issue that businesses can solve by placing people at the core of their business approach and philosophy. Indeed, when looking for people to lead in roles like this, it would be wise to only appoint the very best business and people leaders. The example certainly clarified my view that there are a ton of wasted opportunities within HR and this is why the dynamic rethinking of what HR is and does is starting to attract top talent from a diverse range of roles in business.

The endless dialogue between professionals about putting the human back into HR overlooks one very important point: maybe it was never there to begin with. Indeed, all you need to do is simply refer yourself to someone neutral outside of the HR profession. They will when called upon give a real-world and often damning update on the performance of HR. One of the major opportunities is to position HR professionals exclusively on the human part of the HR equation. The time for talk on this front is over, but the first few years of employee experience being applied from and within HR offers evidence that HR is not fully taking the opportunity that the experience economy presents. At the root of this is one powerful question: whose side is HR on? Historically, there has been no confusion on this point. HR has stood on the side of management, not people. The outcome has created a kind of mistrust that is toxic, and many people have similar stories to share about HR in this regard. One colleague I spoke to recently shared a moving story about a mental health crisis they had while mid-career. Unfortunately, it's a story I've heard from countless others. They hit the lowest point in their life and it was seriously affecting their work. Did they approach HR for support or help with their mental health? No, because HR was already working on behalf of management and forcing them through the most stressful of capability procedures. This is not a way to build strong people and communities within companies. The best kind of HR works in the interests of people and the organization.

What if HR didn't exist? This line of thought has been constant throughout my work for the last few years. Would companies be better? Would people professionals finally thrive? From my perspective, based on my research and extensive dialogue with colleagues around the world, it becomes a tantalizing idea. A company I admire in the UK refuses to even have an HR function because they believe it is divisive and runs contrary to their collective goals and responsibilities. *A world without HR*: this could, in effect, be a slogan to launch a human-centred movement globally. Admittedly, it's a message I and many others could get behind, but would anyone else outside of progressive circles care for this radical overhaul of business? Even those who are trying to do something positive continue to build on the old paradigm of HR. Therefore, their actions, their conferences and their ideas, however noble, are limited in scope. They reinforce the long-lived idea of HR. The conclusion is inevitable. Nothing much changes apart from the same cliques and people coming together to pat each other on the back for being so progressive within the world of HR.

Humans first: a sound business idea

Hard science, evidence and data is fundamentally important to running a successful business. The advances in this regard have fuelled growth, guided decision-making and enabled companies to double-down on the things that are really working for them. The rich body of evidence over many decades should be enough to convince the most hardened bosses that putting people first makes good business sense. I think within this we can identify the common challenge. Business is not entirely based on data and numbers. It's based on many factors. A mix of conditioning, experiences, personality and acquired characteristics dictate the predominant approach to company-building. Business is not an all-out numbers game. Indeed, many businesses reflect an overarching and deeply ingrained philosophy. This doesn't go far enough as a description in some cases. The approach to business for some is nothing short of an ideology – a lifelong devotion to making an impact based on a set of values, principles and beliefs that drive value-creation and impact.

Those not developing a coherent and people-oriented set of values may well be playing catch-up for a long time to come, as there is some real urgency around this. According to the Royal Society of Arts and the Food Foundation, only 9 per cent of Britons wanted life to return to 'normal' after the COVID-19 pandemic is over (YouGov, 2020). In their report, they found that people noticed significant changes during the lockdown, including cleaner air, more wildlife and stronger relationships with the people around them. In many of these reports, people are reporting that they are getting closer to their families, their communities and their planet. How organizations build around these elements is going to be significant in the years ahead when it comes to the human experience at work. Fifty-four per cent of the 4,343 people who took part in the YouGov poll reported that they wished to make some changes to their lives because of their experiences during lockdown. People are awakening to new possibilities about their role in the world and the impact they have. Companies rushing to go back to the way things were may have to brace themselves for an awakening of sorts for themselves if they're not careful about the ways of working they create.

A powerful business model is one that places emphasis on belonging, looking after each other and care. One of our colleagues, Nicole Bannell, is Head of Employee Care at SSE and we've been working together to advance an EX approach into the business. Job titles like this are coming to the fore and visibly representing a shift in business priorities. It is similar in a way to companies like Salesforce, which have colleagues with job titles such as 'head of employee success'. A human-centred lens is required across all that a company does and it's another indication of why companies are actively working to demonstrate a high level of care across their employee experience. It is these types of roles and visible commitments that help companies switch gears when it comes to delivering high quality-human experiences. However, it's not just about titles and style. What I find most compelling about these roles is the substance that underpins them. Thinking much more about the whole person starts to come very naturally across business operations because there are a large number of flag bearers in what becomes a collective approach. There is no way good things can be delivered if this isn't the case. New teams, new approaches and new professionals are emerging every day to address human needs in business and create something that people really believe in.

Is this not true when talking about our normal lives? We buy into things that we believe in, that match our principles and that echo the very people we are. We attract and are attracted to people and companies that act like a mirror. In them, we see ourselves. Our experiences then may well be predetermined to a certain extent. We gravitate in one direction or another to experience something that helps us connect to who we really are or who we aspire to be. Bring your whole self to work is a concept and idea borne out of this desire to find a place where we not only belong, but thrive. This is part and parcel of the human experience – a never-ending quest to improve or, at a minimum, better ourselves and our life standards.

Rising friction, tension and misalignment

It is seemingly very difficult for businesses to deliver within the experience economy based on dated structures and methodologies. In 2019, I reviewed and summarized a compelling research project led by *The Economist* which involved C-suite executives around the world. The project explored the state of employee experience and some of the challenges being presented, notably between support functions such as IT and HR. The key themes coming through tally with my everyday experience of coaching leaders:

- There are significant challenges in aligning support functions to common objectives. This applies in terms of the differences in mindset that exist across what are often narrow specialisms and in the way that resources and projects are set up for success. Companies may look and seem 'agile', but competing agendas can still reign supreme.

- If colleagues are struggling to align and unify to best serve people within the company, the next obvious flaw is accountability. This may run very well down a chain of command or departmental structure, yet it is often at the expense of holistic thinking and related outcomes that this creates. Collaboration suffers, as does the overall experience of work.

- This leads into the next issue, which is transparency. Companies actively create teams that are not unified or committed to each other and their objectives. This creates a lack of accountability for shared outcomes and this, in turn, creates a culture of distrust, unhelpful internal political manoeuvrings and a big reluctance to share data, information and knowledge.

Who loses out as a direct result? The business and everyone connected to it. Who created this mess of haphazard and uncommitted functions? The business and everyone connected to it.

Creating experiences to a high standard is a collective approach. When things occur that stifle progress or hold things back, it is, in my opinion, a collective failure. Boards have actively created disconnection. Managers have permitted and reinforced it. Workers and employees have accepted it. If there was a guiding light, it would be the customers and consumers, as their tolerance for poor experiences is capped, to a degree, and they will act if things aren't right (from their perspective). In saying that, they are not entirely blameless in the type of companies the economy creates. Letting the market decide is also not an ideal way to approach business-building. Indeed, some of the most scandal-hit companies in the world have a habit of treating their workers and suppliers in appalling ways. Will the public continue to forgive business models that prioritize profit over people? What they permit and what they reject does make a difference on internal practices and how organizations interact with the world and the communities around them.

A good example of this was an astonishing blog post at the height of the COVID-19 pandemic: Tim Bray, Vice-President at Amazon, dramatically, and very publicly, resigned his position over concerns about the company's treatment of workers during and before the COVID-19 outbreak. Specifically, workers at the company actively protested about the company's safety measures during the COVID-19 pandemic. Prior to the outbreak, there had been a reported clampdown on whistleblowers who were fired on the spot. Commenting on the firings of whistleblowers, Bray said that these offered 'evidence of a vein of toxicity running through the company culture. I choose neither to serve nor drink that poison.' The ultra-successful business, acknowledged by many, including Bray, to be an 'exceptionally well-managed' company, once again found itself in the headlines because of its approach to the experience it provides to its gigantic workforce. With over 500,000 workers, Amazon is operating on a scale scarcely seen before. It operates from pretty much everywhere, and increasingly, has expanded into a wide range of business areas, including space, media, groceries and entertainment. This high-profile resignation and blog post was all the more notable given Bray reportedly gave up $1 million in salary and uninvested Amazon stock to speak out and share his thoughts (Bray, 2020).

Though Google has done some excellent work over the years to provide a world-class work environment for employees, with attention-grabbing perks and benefits, it is also far from perfect. It has been rightly applauded for its work and commitment to progressive people practices and has often challenged the very notion of what work is all about, but in 2020 it was rocked into defensive mode and is, according to staff, trying to do everything it can to avoid unionization. Employee activism and too many bad headlines have led to staff firings, campus protests and a series of problems that have originated from the employee experience (Bhuiyan, 2019). If an employee rebellion can happen at Google, it can happen anywhere. Is it really a rebellion, though, or a failure by management to effectively co-create with its workforce? The evidence points to that latter. Rebellions, wherever they appear, tend to be formed following a lack of voice, alignment, involvement or participation in company decisions or development from a stakeholder group. In this case, it was the workforce and action was taken to correct that by the workers themselves.

Real brand power is not a projection; it's an internal reality

What is striking about some of the high-profile companies that have experienced employee-led protests in recent times is their iconic and expensive physical estates, such as headquarters and office buildings. These high-spec office buildings are an incredible display of growth, power and influence. They are designed to be talent and client magnets, and they often are. There is a solid business reason behind them and it is one based on an unflinching commitment to take on and differentiate from the competition. Attracting the best graduates and talent means investment – everywhere. It is understandable that companies place their bets with best-in-class estates. Some of the slickest operations in the world use their brand as a shield and as a showcase. At the same time, if all is not well inside those buildings, not even a fancy office with all the latest gadgets will protect brands from growth-hurting business outcomes.

Social movements have brought a strong focus on inequality, social justice and fairness that organizations need to respond to internally. With all this happening externally, the focus on developing the inside of business is one of the best steps a brand can take. I worked with a global consumer brand with 64,000 employees to bring together the global HR function for the first time in its history. This was a milestone moment and one that proved to be a catalyst for many excellent discussions across the business relating to how the business can move into a human-centred rhythm across its global business operations while strengthening its consumer brand still further. The business reality is created one conversation at a time. What helps to accelerate progress is a strong and united support service that puts people first and directly leads in the co-creation of a robust human experience.

Brands certainly need this. Spikes in anxiety, stress and other forms of mental ill health are indicators that, collectively, our societies, and organizations, need to do more to support people. This is not a one-way story, though. I'm inclined to treat people like grown-ups to make their own choices and deliver results based on their own responsibilities and commitments. This is part of the human experience that challenges us to grow, learn and develop more holistically. Ralph Waldo Emerson taught us about the value of self-reliance and why it is important to walk our own path in life, sometimes as a nonconformist, but always as a conscious being capable of critical thinking. I fear we need this now more than ever as part of our business approach.

Trust and truth become all-important

In the era of 'fake news', it comes to something when being told the truth is a relief. Yet, this is what we face every single day. Navigating news and social media is becoming more challenging as the fight for our attention intensifies. For companies, there is a constant opportunity to project and promote a brand message in the marketplace. Yet, many are finding out to their detriment that it is a lot harder to maintain an image that is inauthentic. People, candidates for jobs in particular, have more evidence and sources of information to determine how good an employer actually is. Telling the truth in this context becomes a superpower for companies.

For this project, I spoke with a colleague based in the US who has, for several years, been plying his trade working at one of corporate America's truly iconic workplaces. The experience from the outside looked incredible: a best-in-class employer in every regard, or so it seemed. The response to some of my questions surprised me to say the least. I said it must be amazing to work there – a company that really looked after its employees and an employee journey that was second to none. I'll never forget his instinctive and immediate response: 'Yes, we have a world-leading marketing function.' By implication, it seems we were getting a very select version of the real story underpinned by a corporate ecosystem that was very well oiled around brand marketing and positive PR – powerful, but not entirely real. While he conceded that they were doing some very good things for the workforce, his position was that they could do a far better job in many areas. He should know – he worked in their workplace culture team.

This is a problem. Not just on the marketing versus reality front, but even more importantly, there are serious gaps between what companies say and what they do. Within this, the cold hard truth is amplified by people keen to call out hypocrisy wherever it presents. Saying one thing and doing another or, more accurately, claiming to be one thing but being something different entirely, is playing out right now in real time at some of the world's most talked about workplaces. The rise of employee activism has been the spark that has reignited debates about what organizations need to be if they are to honour their commitments as societal stakeholders.

It is worth noting that the 2020 Edelman Trust Barometer special report found that brand trust is the 'second most important purchasing factor for brands across most geographies, age groups, gender and income levels, trailing only price'. A survey, which included responses from 22,000+ people across 11 markets, showed that reputation, performance, customer and employee experience, and environmental impact were all less significant than trust. Other findings of note were that:

- Seventy per cent of consumers stated that trust was more important than ever before.
- Seventy-four per cent say a brand's impact on society is a reason why brand trust has become more important.

Trust has become the biggest issue for brands: perhaps it always was, when we think about the impact that customer and employee experience has had. With these approaches in place, it is much easier to effect change and build trust with and between people. Are brands earning trust through aligned words and actions? Companies will need to accelerate and more strongly bring the issue of trust into their business operations when we start to think about driving performance through the human experience.

Opportunities for positive change

Although 'experience' was, once again in 2020, top of the agenda for companies and HR directors worldwide, there is a lot of work to be done, as I've pointed out in this chapter already. The increasing acceleration towards human-centricity is very positive and it has created a lot of optimism. In a sense, it feels like the time for people professionals has finally come. The Global Talent Trends 2020 survey confirmed as much (LinkedIn, 2020). Results, which included responses from 7,000 talent professionals in 35 countries, reported that the number one trend is employee experience. The script had flipped in an impressive way as functions and professionals apply employee-centric thinking to their work in a big, big way.

In that survey, 96 per cent of HR professionals indicated that employee experience was increasing in importance, but there is some lag with improvement efforts, with 68 per cent of respondents reporting that the EX at their companies has improved. Companies are embracing the trend, but still warming up with their actions and efforts to accelerate their progress. HR functions throughout the economy are being rebranded into people, human or experience-driven functions. In many ways, this is a wonderful time to work in the support services, with the IT, HR and estates triangle combining to innovate people-centred outcomes. Add in marketing and communication, and we're starting to see the potential of these functions come to fruition in a holistic sense. The realization that these parts are connected is dawning on CEOs and they are beginning to do something about it. Whether it is an employee experience conference or workshop, new ideas and practices are bubbling to the surface. They are demanding attention and respect and people are taking notice.

How do you know that you're speaking to a colleague that gets it? Well, it's in their tone, their energy, their language and their focus. Eschewing policy and process, these leaders inspire the people around them about the possibilities that can be created when teams, units and functions develop with experiences in mind. It's a different world. These rebels and mavericks are challenging the status quo to do more and become more. They are searching for truth and meaning, and their ability to bridge those tricky experience gaps – or great chasms in some cases – that have opened up between the workforce and the employer. Leading with head and heart is still massively underrated.

Given the challenges we've already highlighted, there are still some serious and fundamental design flaws within the current and traditional organizational structure. Businesses, in an attempt to organize themselves in an ordered way, have inadvertently created layer upon layer of bureaucracy. A strong advocate for change in this area is Gary Hamel, who argues for the elimination of bureaucracy. 'Bureaucracy saps initiative, inhibits risk taking, and crushes creativity. It's a tax on human achievement' (Hamel and Zanini, 2018).

Gary and I first met when we were both keynote speakers at HRM Asia back in 2017. What came through strongly from our conversation was that organizations needed to change if they were to really unleash the potential of human beings. The HR function, as it stands today, is not outside of this discussion, but a formal part of it. Indeed, when looking at HR and other support services more broadly, it is relatively easy to find patterns of pointless work being done that does not add value to the business or to people. This should be intolerable, but as Gary's work over the years has suggested, there is something comforting about order, structure, rules, regulations and process within business. It is tried and tested, after all. It works and is the accepted way of doing things within the economy for companies seeking to scale their offerings. I enjoy and respect Hamel's enduring crusade against bureaucracy, because it's not the easiest fight to take on in a world so accustomed to their rigid and organization-centric practices.

If people have no choice, they have no freedom to choose. The great monopolies and bureaucracies of our age have enshrined this into business strategy. The global economy is dominated by company-eaters – the great acquirers of our time, the dominant forces in business. Peter Thiel (2014), the famed Silicon Valley investor, is under no illusion about the power of creating a monopoly. Indeed, he believes it should be the primary goal for any business. This type of strategy is attractive for many reasons. Companies can set the pace and control entire markets and industries. This is where the focus on the human experience can balance things out in the economy. The idea that companies can be a positive force for good in the world and a positive force for humanity doesn't necessarily need to run in opposition to the established economic practices and principles of our time. The economy can create strongly performing businesses that are also having a positive impact in the world.

Human experience: a department, philosophy or a conscience?

In my opinion, to fully implement a human-centred approach, a holistic strategy is a prerequisite. It can't really be any other way and this represents a serious challenge for central support services. For every company that has been bold, challenged the status quo, reset their structures and organization in a human-friendly way, there are thousands more barely scraping the surface of what's possible. Too often, they fall into some form of schema that sets an automatic course to reinforce the old rather than building something better. Yes, the rigid organizational chart continues to assert its control, function by function, and in service to anything but people. Companies are adept at repeating this cycle. Growth plans? More managers. More processes. More bureaucracy. More silos. All of this has traditionally equalled less human.

The real challenge is about seeing the world more completely. It is about being better than anybody around you in questioning the very foundations of what's possible. This is what the human condition demands to inspire human progress. It is a blunt rejection of limiting thoughts and beliefs that stifle people from delivering incredible things. This is what connecting to the human experience gives us – unlimited potential. I have explored this problem of HR from multiple angles. There is a growing awareness and acknowledgement that HR may not be the best paradigm to focus on enabling human growth and potential within business, yet the HR establishment is so deep, ingrained and solid that the prospect of rapid change is fanciful at best. Millions of professionals are developed, validated and recruited based on their identity as an HR professional. Students are conditioned and educated based on status-quo HR. This is what HR is. This is how HR adds value. Therefore, businesses need HR.

Is this flawed thinking from the outset? Maybe it is. A controversial survey of 1,000 residents conducted in June 2020 by the *Straits Times* in Singapore found that the role of HR manager was rated as number five in a list of non-essential jobs during a crisis. The job as an artist took the top spot, but the implications for HR professionals were stark. It may have been a brief poll, yet there is a message in there to take note of. Similarly, staffing firm Zety (2020) ran another survey that surfaced another alarming statistic about HR: 50 per cent of respondents viewed HR to be untrustworthy. To compound this, 69 per cent of people also indicated that they felt HR wasn't on the side of the employee. That is not a good place to be at all. A study on the impact of HR by Bamboo (2020) found that 'the majority of people outside HR think HR has little effect, if any, on business outcomes.' Again, is this acceptable? If not, things need to change right now and senior leaders will need to start asking themselves some serious questions about whether HR is fit to serve and deliver the best outcomes across the whole human experience. In the next chapter, we'll consider what could replace it as an approach and what that looks like, but one thing is abundantly clear: status-quo HR is being disrupted all over the corporate world.

The human experience: a CEO's challenge

The idea of change needs to be firmly implanted into the next generation of companies. At a certain point come the inevitable questions as businesses scale and bring in more people. In basic terms, the question revolves around having an HR function. The reality of the question comes from the CEO, and it's more like this: is it time to start viewing our people as resources? Because that's what happens every time this idea is replicated within business. People are resources, and resources require management and control measures. It's an astounding yet unquestioned business cycle. Rinse and repeat. Businesses run through the motions, never really asking themselves if it is the right thing to do, and I believe it makes little to no sense knowing what we know about people, trust and relationships. A manager treating their team as mere resources would be unacceptable and incredibly damaging for team morale, performance and productivity. So, if that is the case (and if you doubt it, just try treating your people, family or teams like resources, and watch the reaction), why do we continue to promote the idea of bringing together hugely talented people into a department that symbolizes the past rather than the future?

Unquestionably, doing something that goes against the grain takes a lot of courage and a big commitment to people. Organizations naturally embody the priorities of their founders and most senior executives. If people flourish, it's because they have been allowed to flourish rather than stifled at every turn. CEOs in the future will be judged harshly or favourably based on the quality of the human experience that they enable within their workforces. Poor human experience? Look no further than the C-suite and assign the appropriate levels of accountability there. Likewise, if there is a positive human experience, CEOs deserve much of the credit if conditions are ripe for humans to be at their best, professionally and personally.

I must say that I am completely biased and in favour of human-centred CEOs or even those CEOs who are trying hard, and with good intentions, to do the right thing by their people. Sometimes it may be clumsy, messy or things may not go perfectly, yet I can't find fault with, nor would I want to, the essential human-centred commitment behind decisions. To keep that commitment, CEOs need a solid and highly talented team to advise, guide and help shape experiences within the business. The surge in chief people and chief experience officer-type roles within companies indicates a shift, and colleagues performing in these experience-driven roles are the new go-to people who help accelerate growth and human performance. But does it go far enough? Do we need to lean in even further across all roles, not just the top ones? The evidence is certainly pointing us in that direction – wholesale rather than piecemeal change.

My organization conducted some qualitative research at the start of the COVID-19 pandemic through global forums and interviews. What we found challenged all manner of widespread assumptions that were previously held in business, namely that:

- People will resist working from home. They didn't.
- People need a physical workplace to be productive. They don't.
- Relationships are entirely dependent on daily in-person communication. They're not.
- Communities are formed through co-location. They aren't.
- People can't be trusted to work from home. They can.
- Engagement will decline because of homeworking. It won't.
- People preferred the way things were before the pandemic. Not true either.

Certainly, for knowledge-based workers, these assumptions have been challenged, and one of the biggest assumptions that still requires some major thinking time relates entirely to the assumed or perceived value that is placed on certain jobs and roles within the economy. Throughout 2020, society found a new appreciation for all manner of people carrying out all manner of roles that were deemed to be essential to human life. Those on the front line who continued to go to and report to their workplaces and places of business. These people were essential to our existence, especially those in the health, medical and food production businesses. There was some fanfare about certain workers, yet the people concerned just went about their business in the most dignified of ways, earning new admirers across our countries. If we are to truly learn from the global crisis, we need to consider value in a way that relates directly to the quality of our human experience. That type of exercise is long overdue, but there is hope given the widespread reconnecting with local and independent businesses, and the renewed appreciation of those who serve us in our times of need. The challenge will be around the maintenance of this once business returns to some form of normality.

A universal and human way of doing business

A role organizations play as a force for good in the world and for humanity aligns powerfully with the fundamental and profound aspiration of humanity, which is to elevate our collective and individual consciousness. This side of an organization's impact is often poorly explained and, as a result, is often misunderstood. I'm talking about companies that change the world, and in so doing, change our understanding and perception around what we think is possible in this world. How do we frame this, though?

Having worked in China for three years, I learned about the teachings of Confucius. The concept of Ren is the core part of a universal value system. It says being human/humane is at the centre of all lives. 仁 from its shape, means two people. The Chinese concept of 'human being' and 'being human' are pronounced the same, and the two Chinese characters are interconnected. The beauty of Chinese characters offers much wisdom. In Chinese philosophy, it is said that when heaven and the earth fall in love, they create a human. I like that metaphor for the human condition given our connection to the wider world and universe. We'll see how one organization applies this level of human-centricity in practice later in the book, as it's important to see how different companies can interpret and drive growth through a stronger focus on people.

Within this exploration of the human experience, as I've highlighted, I do think it is worth the time to consider companies that attract huge criticism at times due to their intense work environments: Tesla CEO Elon Musk demanding 80-hour work weeks; Jack Ma of Alibaba supporting the working culture phenomenon in China of 12-hour work days, 6 days a week; consulting firms and tech companies that burn and churn graduates. Whether Silicon Valley, Hangzhou, London or Shenzhen, there does seem to be some unwritten rules about how people can get ahead at certain companies. I get questions that focus on this category a lot. These are often groundbreaking and earth-changing companies. As people become more enlightened and more experienced of human-centred practices, companies in this mould will, increasingly, face greater pressures around the wealth, health and happiness of their workforces. The wise ones within this bunch will move early to create a more balanced and healthier workplace experience.

Grand designs: a journey full of pivots and pitfalls

We have seen wave after wave of companies and consultants pivoting into the EX field over the years. When I first began introducing the concept globally back in 2014, there were very few of us preaching about experiences and human-centricity on the inside of companies. While it's good that vendors and suppliers are offering their services and solutions to target the improvement of experiences, this has led some astray. Rather than developing solutions for real problems, we've seen many examples of solutions that are still trying to find a problem. Is human and employee experience a technology platform? Is it a design thinking workshop? Is it a set of surveys? Is it a leadership programme? Is it an app? Is it an employee journey mapping session? Is it a compelling internal communications campaign? Is it the design of workplace? Is it a volunteering programme for the workforce? Companies start their journey into the experience of work for different reasons and from different places. The pitfalls come when it is considered from a narrow worldview rather than a holistic one. Actions may well take place and investment may be spent, but too often, it can be in the wrong places.

It's simply not good enough to launch a survey and then do some random, generic things with the data it produces. I view that type of approach as disrespectful. Companies ask their employees and workers what they think, and if it is not to their taste, it can be very often swept under the carpet and forgotten about. On the other side of this coin, Adam Weber, chief people officer at Emplify, exemplified why leadership is now much more focused on listening internally and taking the *right* actions in partnership with staff by announcing to staff that they wouldn't be working Fridays in May 2020. As a co-founder of his business he demonstrated that he took the data seriously, but then also made intelligent improvements to the experience at his company. Weber (2020), who shared via LinkedIn, found that simply encouraging employees to take a break when they needed it wasn't working. There was far too much going on with meetings, emails and workloads for employees to be able to switch off. What did the company do instead? Well, they chose to align all their days off across the month of May to make sure staff were getting the rest they needed without worrying about what was going on at work. They would work and rest as a team at the same times. This also allowed the company to express its support for its workforce through an action that really made a difference to people as they navigated their way through COVID-19 and all its consequences.

With an increasing focus on the configuration of work, whether it remains a five-day week remains to be seen, yet there are opportunities in every circumstance to reinforce and strengthen the employment relationship. The hybrid workforce model is one such innovation I've been discussing with clients. It is a combination of time spent at home or other places, and the workplace. The overwhelming majority of workers have reported positive outcomes so it seems there is now natural alignment between companies and workers on this matter. Not only does the hybrid work model recognize and retain the benefits that materialized through the homeworking experiment that took place during the COVID-19 outbreak, but it also reinforces the way the world of work was going anyway, as companies come to understand that work doesn't need to be viewed as a fixed-location activity.

Not all agree with the hybrid model, though. The obvious pitfall is that teams are divided. There is still much to be said for in-person team sessions and teamwork. Netflix is one company that is leading the charge to keep its workforce together on-site. The critique is that they will lose creativity and collaboration outcomes if their teams are not together sharing and shaping ideas. It's a valid point that needs consideration in any iteration of an organization's design. The question remains clear, though: where and how can people deliver their best work? For companies, in general, the answer to these questions may well take them on a very different path.

Humanizing strong businesses

An indication that employee experience and this human way of building businesses was starting to break out into the wider economy presented when *The Times* published my holistic employee experience model in full over half a page in December 2019 (Raconteur, 2019). What I shared in the article was the notion of strong and stressed organizations. In my own way, I want to move thinking on from simply being fixated on engagement scores, given engagement is a management-centric idea. It is a good indicator of impact, but nothing more. In many companies, it is still viewed as the only score that matters when it comes to critical elements of HR and people work, which is disappointing given the large body of data we can now access across the organization to justify and honour great experience design and execution.

What outcomes are we creating anyway? Well, if we follow the experience path, we are unifying around the need to develop strong organizations – strong in the sense that they know what they are and what they stand for, and this is installed with the experience of work holistically. This matures trusted, human-centred and experience-driven brands. That's really strength in depth and you can feel it every day within these types of companies. This is by no means a new point, but one that needs to be intentionally built into companies. Indeed, John Mackey, the founder of Whole Foods, pointed out that operating an approach based on conscious capitalism can directly shape and deliver high performing-businesses. In his book with Rak Sisodia (Mackey and Sisodia, 2014), they explored companies that were operating more for social good and found that those public companies performed significantly better than the S&P 500 Index between 1996 and 2011. These are companies that back their purpose with positive human and community experience while having a positive impact on the environment. Do we really want to do business with companies that sit outside of this category? In practice, it turns out that companies that do good attract our attention, support and, indeed, loyalty.

Companies like BrewDog, a craft brewery based out of Scotland and the US, intelligently extend their impact in the world by building a community around the company. During COVID-19, the company pivoted part of its manufacturing operation to create hand sanitizer for front-line and essential workers. As a commodity, this was in high demand and society relied on businesses to set up. Doing so proactively and on a voluntary basis only amplifies all the good things that companies create and lead within our economies. This is organizational soft power of the highest order, and the 21st-century company equivalent of winning friends (read fans) and influencing people. They are also going carbon-neutral and have already invested in a new fleet of electric delivery vehicles. This is a brand at the forefront of a mission it is totally committed to – namely, sustainability of our environment. Interestingly, their product may not be the best for humanity, but they are constantly offsetting this through positive actions that reinforce their idea of what an organization is – a community-builder and societal shaper. This is not to everyone's taste, but to many they are a strong representation of the future organization. A choice has been made here. Become a progressive people, planet-supporting and purpose-led company that inspires the human race, or just be another craft beer company? Almost daily and viral content suggests they have made the right choice for their brand.

Similarly, massive pallets of nutritional bars were packed and distributed all over the UK for free to the NHS by one of the country's most exciting and fastest growing brands, Grenade. We'll be meeting the CEO in Chapter 5, but this is a brief indication of the roles companies are playing in this interconnected and interdependent economy. What contrasts these responses to others is the length of thinking time involved in decisions to serve society. There was none. There is an endless list of companies going above and beyond to make a positive impact on the human experience. In this sense, the real challenge is about how we can create and encourage more of these companies to emerge within our economies – companies that care about people, place and purpose; companies that are as a good as their word, do what their values guide them to do and lead in a way that clearly resonates in a special way throughout society at large.

Meritocracy: where human performance counts

Human progress is determined by human performance. This is a simple equation. To do great things, we turn to the best human performers who possess high-quality talents, skills and knowledge. They have, by deed and effort applied over time, differentiated themselves as someone that has reached levels that immediately attract our attention. In short, we want them on our team. Simplistic maybe, but as humans, we get where we get to because of our own drive, determination and persistence. This is sometimes with great support, yet how many top performers have emerged as a sheer force of will? The enduring human spirit that demands progress and movement? Are our companies built on a system of meritocracy? The people who flourish within are the ones with talent, who put in the effort and who can evidence achievement.

Sociologist Michael Dunlop Young made this case in his 1958 satirical essay, which was written to condemn a fixation on testing and scoring students to determine the educational pathway. Their secondary school, and indeed their initial life path, was determined by the controversial 11-plus examination. In practice, it meant that those who performed well would go to a sought-after grammar school, and those who didn't would go to a secondary modern. Straightforward selection, based on exam performance, to effectively write a life script given that grammar schools were considered to be the springboard to better life chances, including university places and the best jobs. This system was abolished, but perhaps the central message of *The Rise of the Meritocracy* was outshone by the introduction of this word meritocracy, which resonated strongly with political and societal agendas, and is an idea deeply held within business. Look no further than the experience of performance management approaches over the last few decades. Like the workplace, these approaches are evolving, albeit at gentle, rather than urgent, pace in some cases.

To consider meritocracy is to exclude our starting positions in life and the experiences that help create us, but one thing is clear: talent doesn't discriminate. Research on FTSE 350 companies, conducted by The Pipeline (2020), found that companies where a third of the bosses are women have a profit margin more than 10 times greater than those without. Yet, in 2020, we have only amassed a paltry 13 female CEOs of these firms – just 5 per cent of the total – and 15 per cent of these companies do not have any females represented on their executive committee. Analysis of the Fortune 100 found similar results, where only 25 per cent of the entire leadership population (level below the board) was female and only 9 per cent held commercial business roles. Indeed, females only accounted for 9.5 per cent of the commercial leadership roles across the entire Fortune/FTSE 100 companies. While the commercial path is viewed to be critical to the CEO role, the female domination of HR roles (close to 60 per cent of chief HR officers in the Fortune 100 are female) doesn't appear to be helping female leaders get to the top of the business. In this human-centred economy, it's statistics and stories relating to these that need to surface more often.

We may not all have equal access to opportunities to cultivate our full range of talents, but it is evident that talent rises unless it is abruptly brought to a halt by the organizations or economies we have built. With 15 per cent of FTSE 350 companies having no female senior executives, it is more than human intuition that suggests the game is rigged and the odds are sometimes not in the favour of certain groups and backgrounds. This statistic seems absurd and out of place in the modern world. We certainly have an embarrassment of riches when it comes to female talent, yet why is the system that we have created, maintained and reinforced creating these kinds of outcomes?

Summary: why humanity demands a new model for work

What I'm interested in here is exploring the full range of human and organizational performance, and how the human experience at work can help enable that. If anything is getting in the way of performance, it needs to be addressed swiftly. This includes the make-up of the board, the management team and every other role within a company. We want the best people doing their best work. If there are factors or biases preventing this from occurring, it is a positive step forward to start questioning the prevailing system and the wisdom of it, together. In my opinion, the best way to build an organization now is by building one that is co-created by and led by everyone within the company. This means that we really do need to question some of the outcomes that are being delivered by the companies across the economy. This requires leaders that can operate with the highest levels of empathy and integrity to unite people from diverse backgrounds while placing a strong emphasis on healthy relationships. When it comes down to it, the success of an organization is determined by how effectively people can work together towards a shared goal. Anything that helps that should be encouraged. Anything that hinders that should be reconsidered.

- Organizations are reacting to a new set of expectations from people and the workforce. Now is the time to challenge existing business models and structures that are getting in the way of high-quality performance.

- Delivering a world-class human experience at work will help companies deliver their best results. A healthy, happy and harmonious workforce is a notable goal; anything getting in the way of this should be challenged, frequently.

- Is it time for *a world without HR*? Discuss this question with your colleagues, teams and the leaders in your business, but most importantly, your workforces – the people who serve your customers and deliver critical value to them every day.

- Building a trusted and human-centred organization will present some tough questions about what functions and roles are now the most valuable to the business and the workforce. This is not just about roles and titles. It's about creating greater impact, alignment and accountability. The system is ripe for change. Let's change it.

03

Accelerating holistic, human-centred and experience-driven business

If we are to create and sustain a purposeful, human-centred and experience-driven economy, we need a different type of organization filled with professionals and leaders focused on the things that truly matter to people. Not simply 'moments that matter', but humans that matter more than anything – more than profit, more than the share price, more than the numbers. Imagine an economy made up of companies acting in the interests of all their human stakeholders, the planet and our collective future. Is this really wishy-washy stuff? You'd be forgiven for thinking it was. The case is still hard to make, for sure. Yet, those CEOs and leaders who 'get it' never look back, and they would never go back. Why? Because of their creations. Their organizations are energetic, inspiring and addictive places. People gladly go there, want to be there and want to experience the environments they create. It's about defining history, being part of it, belonging to it. It's an easy sell once you've experienced it. It's harder if you haven't and you don't even know there is a much better way to advance your business goals through people, purpose and community.

Developing business holistically and through human-centred methods affects all support services and professionals that have historically been set up to enable people to perform at their best. If we are truly and genuinely focused on this, I would see HR, increasingly, being phased out within progressive organizations. Looking through my work, case studies and research, no one has been quite brave enough to say what everyone else is already thinking – HR professionals need to create a bold new future for themselves within our companies, and the HR brand may not survive that change. In my opinion, anyone who says otherwise is simply part of the established order, making money off HR remaining the same, or are strongly invested in maintaining this idea that people are merely 'resources'. Indeed, a 2020 IBM study found that two-thirds of HR executives said that 'the global HR function is ripe for disruption' (IBM, 2020). This disruption has already started, with companies quietly removing HR from their structures for a number of years now. It's been a little under the surface, but a shift has been taking place. Movements relating to the social order, unfairness and inequalities have been picking off bigger targets to address profound and deep-rooted inequalities, but when we look across the organization, HR has been in the firing line for a long time.

Indeed, as I carry out my role as a coach, consultant and researcher, I have found that a differentiated people-centred leader has emerged within the HR profession. What creates their differentiation is a willingness to challenge the status quo, lead with empathy and humility, and enable their organizations to proactively shift to a more humane agenda. It's something we need to embrace fully. This overt attempt by professionals to generate distance between themselves and the HR function, which I highlighted in the last chapter, is indicative of a huge problem within HR. People are very aware of the problem, but it is often unacknowledged. To survive, people quite sensibly continue to build careers (and pension pots) through plying their trade within the concept of HR while simultaneously trying to appear less connected to it. Everywhere you look – from qualifications, entry-level jobs, to senior C-suite roles – there is near-constant reinforcement of this idea of HR. Bottom line: I think we've integrated a company-centred mindset that is no longer suitable for the current and future economy, and it's a big mistake.

A defining moment for HR and organizations

'HR is a joke. They are soulless paper-pushers. It's funny that they're called human resources. They are often the least human people within a business,' says Elizabeth Shaw, a former senior analyst at Gartner and Forrester. 'They have never felt like a partner in my career. What do they do? No one knows what they do. If they don't have the skill sets, creativity and the imagination to deliver better human experiences, they can easily be replaced.' Shaw is not alone in her strong feelings towards HR. Views like this are not hard to find, and when thinking about the less progressive HR functions I've come across, it is entirely justified. HR functions that are constantly in a defensive and reactive posture when it comes to working with key stakeholders create more problems than they solve. Shaw offers a glimmer of hope in that several of her senior colleagues working within people functions are innovating a new and progressive vision for HR, yet it can often feel like they are 'pushing a boulder up a hill'. Shaw spoke with me about a career filled with broken promises, processes and practices across recruitment and on-boarding, often at major corporations, even those that are in the business of helping clients overcome such issues.

Salesforce, however, was a different experience for Shaw. She discussed with me a potent recruitment experience she had at the firm, and although she ultimately didn't secure the role, her advocacy for the 'amazing' hiring team that handled her recruitment process is noteworthy. 'I'm still looking at their job board every day. It hasn't changed my opinion,' said Shaw. The depth of the process, the high-touch personalized experiences, and the support from the hiring team stood out. From Shaw's perspective, it felt like they were on her side and it was a human-centred process. Shaw's critique of HR is strong, yet her praise for Salesforce, a company perceived by many to be getting employee experience right, demonstrates the impact that companies can have on people. Essentially, companies are in the memory and feeling business now, and both last a very long time. It's critical that they start getting their experiences right.

Salesforce is a company that has embraced the holistic employee experience, making it a consideration within every decision. An example of this was recalled by a global director at a launch event for my previous book, who went through 17 interviews to secure her role. It was not solely about assessing competency, but more skewed to find someone for the role who shared the human-centred values of Salesforce. Alongside this values-based experience, it was also about community-building. By the time she arrived on site on her first day as the successful candidate, and new employee, there was already a solid network of colleagues to support her into the business. This is the differentiated approach I mention. It is thoughtful, considered and expertly delivered. It makes a huge impact on the person who experiences it. World-class experiences are powerful beyond measure. Once a worker or candidate has experienced it, going back to anything less is a very difficult process and it only increases the respect for businesses and brands that hit such high notes with the experiences they provide.

This connection between processes, in this case recruitment to on-boarding, is the new standard being set by human-centred organizations. It's an example that helps us understand why people turnover at Salesforce is so low (single-digit), and why, even during COVID-19, Salesforce grew its revenue. With 54,000 employees worldwide, it is often rated as one of the world's leading employers, and they do it by applying a human lens to their business and operations. The company, through its CEO Marc Benioff, has been a leading voice in making the case for stakeholder capitalism. Rather than focusing on maximizing shareholder profit, Benioff believes that all stakeholders should be considered and positively impacted. This was tested during the COVID-19 global pandemic as Salesforce protected jobs with a no lay-off policy, continued to pay its hourly workforce, enabled employees to work from home until 2021 and continued its giving-back work with large grants to support schools. It's a policy and approach that worked, with Salesforce growing revenue by 29 per cent and net income by 152 per cent in 2020 (Clifford, 2020). Humans, organizations and communities growing together is a powerful concept. Internally, this shifts the focus of the professionals and teams working on strengthening these connections.

Workplace revolts: the disconnect between organizations and workforces

Despite how important such considerations are, many large businesses continue to get things wrong at a great scale in how they set up their organizations. It is easy to see that everything is tilted in favour of management and shareholders when it should be that organizations exist to serve all stakeholders. We can map this idea across to HR too. This is a profession that has always been geared up to serve the interests of management as its primary stakeholder. Indeed, there have been some excellent examples of things going wrong on this front, with companies having to roll back their plans or ideas due to workplace revolts:

- A simple dress code policy at Whole Foods prompted a fierce backlash from people at all levels of society, including workers, politicians, community leaders and even a public rebuke from Canada's prime minister (Bochove et al, 2020). The mistake? A policy, in practice, that effectively prohibited workers from wearing poppies to recognize the sacrifice of previous generations. Their intent was to have a consistent dress code, yet it was a change that clearly wasn't thought through with the human experience in mind. A reversal of this policy happened within days due to a large and loud public outcry, and it was a large-scale PR disaster for the brand.

- During COVID-19, Bird, a Scooter rental company in the US, found itself caught in a media storm because of the way it announced and fired 400 employees *en masse* via a 'minutes-long' Zoom call (Sapra, 2020). What caught the public's attention in this, and many other cases, was the inhumane treatment of people.

- United Airlines removed a quarterly performance bonus scheme in favour of a lottery-styled bonus system where employees could win prizes like cars, cash and holidays. On the day of the announcement, the company faced an immediate and chastening rebellion by the workforce (Lazare, 2018). Given the intensity of internal opposition to this change, within days an immediate 'pause' was announced by the CEO with a commitment to work more closely with colleagues in the future.

- BNY Mellon was forced to cancel a proposed removal of their work-from-home policy following 'severe' criticism from employees, with the CEO lamenting the firm's inconsistent implementation and a lack of clarity in the principles underpinning the policy change (Reuters, 2019). Ironically, during and post COVID-19, homeworking was positioned as a key part of its business operations, with 96 per cent of the workforce working from home (Davis, 2020). This is now part of the firm's long-term business plan.

- Google had to pull out of a tender process for a multi-billion-dollar Pentagon contract with the US Government due, in large part, to concerns from workers about how the firm's AI capabilities would be used. There appeared to be a clear lack of internal alignment to projects that are designed to facilitate harm and injury. Following protests, Google withdrew from the tender process (Waters, 2018).

- In 2020, compensation at Blizzard, the video game maker, became a hot topic as employees publicly challenged the company to be more transparent and fair in its pay and reward practices. Employees have railed against perceived inequalities between high and low earners, and the value of their respective contributions to the brand's growth (Schreier, 2020).

- McDonald's, an admired brand when it comes to operational excellence, invests strongly in training and development yet continues to attract scrutiny around its pay practices and conditions. The global 'McStrike' organized by workers once again created negative headlines around the world as its lowest paid workers across the chain of restaurants demanded better pay (Chapman, 2019).

From dress code policies to compensation practices, there is something systematically ineffective in the way that some brands work with their key stakeholders, namely, the workforce. There was a time when there was very little that people could do about their mistreatment at the hands of their employers. Even in unionized environments, it can be challenging as an individual to defend rights and shine a spotlight on poor practices. As the cases mentioned highlight, there is nowhere left to hide. Companies simply cannot afford to get the human experience wrong anymore given how fast bad news travels, not to mention the ethical and moral concerns that can often derail progress and growth.

As I've highlighted many times before, companies are always a 'work in progress' and no company is perfect. To demonstrate this point, I bring us back to Salesforce. The firm experienced its own employee-led revolt in 2018 when faced with intense internal criticism about its work with the US Border Patrol, which at the time was under fire for separating families at the borders. Employees at the firm wanted to have no part of that. How to solve this problem? What the CEO did was look at the problem as a whole and engaged with internal activists in a positive way by setting up 'Silicon Valley's first-ever Office of Ethical and Humane Use of Technology'. He made a decision that encouraged constructive behaviour and positive dialogue. 'I made it in concert with all of those activist groups, with our employees, and we're not going to all agree. But we can have that discussion and we can figure out how to move forward together' (Zetlin, 2018). Rather than condemning activist employees or complaining, the firm continued its human-centred tradition and found a way to co-create and work on this issue at a deeper level. It is a wise approach given the complexities of modern life. The workforce will never be 100 per cent happy with everything a company does, but their views can be respected, valued and used to overcome any obstacles that present for employees and, increasingly, society at large. This is stakeholder capitalism of the highest order and, as Salesforce's remarkable performance confirms, it's very good for business.

Accelerating human and business outcomes

In my view, these negative outcomes are the result of flawed and limited thinking within the corporate hierarchy. The time of human-centred leaders and professionals has only just begun. HR is definitely a key function in the middle of many of these issues and walks a consistently precarious position as expectations around fairness, equality, transparency and human-centricity increase. Trying to hack, disrupt or change its identity and the way the profession approaches things is a good start, but these are only fit for the economy right now. It's part of the transition experience as more colleagues awaken to their potential and possibilities of developing businesses in stronger, people-centred ways. HR's evolution, in this regard, needs to be accelerated.

One company pushing the boundaries about HR's role within companies is JLL, a global real estate firm. It has been taking direct action around this point and is an example of a company awakening to the possibilities of the human experience. With 43,000 employees across Asia and the Pacific, Helen Snowball, head of HR APAC, believes that 'working in a company is no longer just about the people process; we have transitioned into offering an all-rounded people experience.' In practice, this means that there is a firm and focused commitment to transforming the human resource function into a human experience function (Kang, 2020).

This new focus on the human experience respects the increasing awareness that focusing on the experience of work becomes something more holistic and less HR-centred. It is, in a way, stakeholder capitalism on the inside of the business. Every worker has a number of key stakeholders around them. They are all there to enable and, ultimately, help them to be successful in work and life. HR, IT, catering, facilities, estates, marketing and any other professional support service, as well as leaders across management lines, have a direct interest in people being able to perform at their best. Being human-centred, holistic and experience-driven gives all these support services a shared language and a shared mission that is beneficial in unifying and aligning a collective approach. Given the challenges I presented in the last chapter, a radical new approach like this is often the best way to deliver successful outcomes, yet, as usual, fortune favours the bold.

Becoming a rebellious human organization

Resistance to the new world of work is futile, but resisters will be in high supply – yet I challenge you to transform your company into a place that actively seeks out the dissenters, resisters and agitators – the rebels. As Gino, author of *Rebel Talent* (2019), pointed out during a conversation we had during the COVD-19 pandemic, the opportunity for organizations is to welcome all the rebels into our team to positively disrupt the status quo and create better outcomes for all. Cultivating the energy of people by intentionally creating organizations filled with colleagues who are curious about the future and intent on making a difference is something that should be actively undertaken. This aligns very well with our mission to create workplaces where people can flourish by being themselves. This is a very human experience, but how many companies are of that mould? Companies often seek feedback, but any outcomes generated from it may not be clear. The dedication and energy that people commit to employee activism could be harnessed to make improvements to fuel business success, yet support functions, and leadership teams, are often not set up in a way that enables this to occur.

Change the name, change the approach and change the outcomes

If your role exists solely to help people have a positive experience in work and deliver the best possible outcomes they can, there is very little to complain about and there is nothing more powerful as a message to take to the business and workforce. My guess is that you will never go back to what was and you will start to quickly establish a strong partnership and relationship with your people. Sounds easy? It is. The hardest part for established companies is convincing the top team that this is the right approach versus sticking to what everyone else has been doing for years. It's clear from our daily work with leaders that boldness and courage are the hallmarks of human-centred practitioners. HR has never been involved in so many life issues before. There was a distinct line and it was surrounded by policies. For many recent events, there have been no policies available, so for many HR professionals, the guiding light was to do the right thing by people, the business and customers. Included in this is a shift by many companies to the human experience: helping and supporting people in whatever way possible. So, why not now ramp this approach up even further? The timing is perfect.

The human experience platform and team

I've been advancing the idea and fixation on humans and experience for many years, and the human experience is very much locked into and part of this broader work to create an 'experience economy'. Experiences are becoming the currency of human progress and success. The experiences you have had, good and bad, contributed to who you are as a person, much more than possession could. In working on employee experience, it became very clear that human beings were a central part of the idea. The brands that do well in this area see humans more than they see employees, and that view has been at the forefront of major business decisions and epic changes. It is this exciting period of transformation that is really capturing the imagination of chief HR officers (CHROs) around the world. HR used to be the 'everything' service, given responsibility over many things simply because it was people related, even though many of them were outside of its control.

The HR debate should now come to an end in my view. The idea of HR has taken us this far. To its proponents, it has brought fairness, equality and a way of effectively governing workforces. To its detractors, it has created division, mistrust and enabled the continuation of management-centric practices. In many contexts, it no longer fits the brand narrative and is completely out of sync with the times, especially given the massive surge of attention on employee experience, purpose and trust within the economy.

Having met with thousands of HR professionals in recent years, the move to human experience or employee experience functions is viewed to be very good news and is an indication that the widespread restlessness within HR continues to be a catalyst to redefine, re-engineer and reimagine what an organization is. Centring the profession on the human experience is a wise first step, but what does it look like in practice?

Very simply, as in Figure 3.1, the organization is in service to human beings. It's a human lens that infiltrates every area of the business operation. All members of the organization treat each other like human beings and design their products and services with this in mind. This advances the focus for all operational services, employee- and customer-facing functions.

- All services are set up to best serve people.
- All colleagues are co-creators and in service to each other.
- All experiences, interactions and communications are designed and delivered to deepen the connection between people, brand and community.

It is, in effect, a circular organization design that centres itself around the whole human being. It is a 360-degree operating system delivering life-enriching experiences on time and at the right time as people need and want them, making the most important things that really matter to people in life, not just work, a key part of the business model.

A more holistic approach to business, with a different set of roles, skills and capabilities, would be better suited to an experience

FIGURE 3.1   The human lens

© Ben Whitter, HEX Organization Ltd

economy – services filled with people who move forward their work with a human-centred and experience-driven mindset. Colleagues who are inclined to walk this path are in high demand as they can accelerate changes in the right places at a strategic level across organizations, building a philosophy or internal movement, and co-creating the right type of leadership behaviours across management lines. Yes, the workforce, and individuals, have a heavier role to play in the co-creation process, yet there are high-impact roles for highly skilled and high-quality leaders who can help guide projects through to successful implementation and delivery. The onus here is to combine subject matter and contextual expertise with a bias for action and outcomes. This is not busy or activity-based work, nor is it simply fragmented events or experiences that are short term in their nature. This is much more about holistic impact, fixing things that need to be fixed, and making sure, above all else, that relationships are healthy within and beyond the business. It is a wider view than simply seeing people as 'customers of HR', which I tend to think is limiting and defeats the purpose of leading in a more human-friendly way to deliver those much richer connections and more beneficial brand outcomes. This view also plays out in external behaviour. Human or employee experience leaders present themselves first and foremost as human and brand leaders. This is evident in what they share and what they choose to get involved with to further the interests of their businesses. Indeed, they are involved in many more aspects of the human experience than just HR matters.

As I mentioned previously, at the height of COVID-19, I was asked to advise head-hunters about how to fill a very important new role within the people team at the National Health Service – the role was pointedly focused on the employee experience at director level. Employee experience roles of this nature are now popular additions within corporate structures across all sectors, and they do help this shift to experience thinking. We know that the biggest obstacle to change within HR and other support services is mindset, and it leads to all manner of challenges, including transparency, alignment, accountability, balance between people and technology, and others (The Economist, 2019), so we need to strategically and tactically reinforce the most important ideas within the business. An everyday symbol and shaper of this is the structure and philosophy that is visible and experienced daily by people. If you're still set up to reinforce the idea of treating people like resources, this will affect the way colleagues interact, collaborate and work with each other. Therefore, a simple strategic vision anchored around the human experience can be a persuasive one and a consistent theme that ties various units, agendas and teams together, as I pointed out earlier in this chapter.

Breaking down this human experience approach further, we can see that multiple professionals and departments now step up to join at the heart of the human experience, as I indicate in Figure 3.2, alongside the ultimate co-creation partners – the workers and employees themselves. This is a new model to organize internal services, and it's unlike any traditional model we've seen or experienced before – flatter, dynamic, energetic, digital, responsive, proactive and autonomous teams with a mandate to go after anything that gets in the way of strong, sustainable human performance. It always looks different because companies are unique, yet a model is shaping up in

FIGURE 3.2   Human experience platform

Humans

↑

Human Experience Team

- **Wellbeing** (mindfulness, personal development, health, wealth and happiness)
- **Community** (including D&I, recruitment, selection, recognition, promotion, alumni)
- **Marketing** (EVP, employer brand, reputation and PR, internal communications)
- **Workplace** (facilities, estates, assets, catering, homeworking)
- **Relationships** (legal, employment relations, compliance)
- **Performance** (people analytics, L&D platforms, contribution and outcome development, coaching, mentoring, talent, mobility, capability academies)
- **Digital** (runs across, underpins and is integrated into all services)

↑

HEX Accelerators (internal human experience experts, coaches, designers and facilitators)

↑

CEO/Senior Sponsors/Leaders

© Ben Whitter, HEX Organization Ltd

a very similar way to the one detailed in this section, and not a mention of HR in sight.

This human experience platform and philosophy fully commits to the human experience, not just parts of it. Its real strength lies in its shape – the organization in service to people, not the other way around. This may well be an ambitious agenda, yet the opportunities are immense. Scaling a human-centred philosophy into the business requires some fundamental reshaping of all support services into a seamless, integrated and dynamic whole that is accountable for shared outcomes across every journey within the organization. In design, this puts leaders in the role of facilitator and steward. The leader in this context, and especially from a support service background, becomes the shaper and co-creator of experiences that optimize human performance. Narrow thinking and a lack of holistic focus and accountability can be overcome by unifying a service fit for the 21st-century organization.

Progressing through the HEX accelerator

Getting seriously organized and tilted in favour of human experience (HEX) is a good start for companies, but we need some pace, urgency and momentum behind every project to uplift or redesign an experience. Big things can come from smaller actions, yet we need to match the intent with speed, clarity and focus to deliver those all-important gains and outcomes. How can a team or company get started on this journey? In Figure 3.3 I present our process for rapid transformation. My organization usually partners with the accelerators, as referenced in Figure 3.2 – those deemed to be the internal leaders, subject matter experts or designers alongside the strategic senior sponsors. You can see as teams run through these steps that we take a lot of time to *define* the challenge or the experience, with real empathy, evidence and data being used as major parts of the process. From there, the *design* and iteration process begins, as we start to shape up improved outcomes and experiences within targeted parts of the employee journey. An absolutely essential part of this is divergence. We guide companies and colleagues to make specific choices

FIGURE 3.3   HEX accelerator process

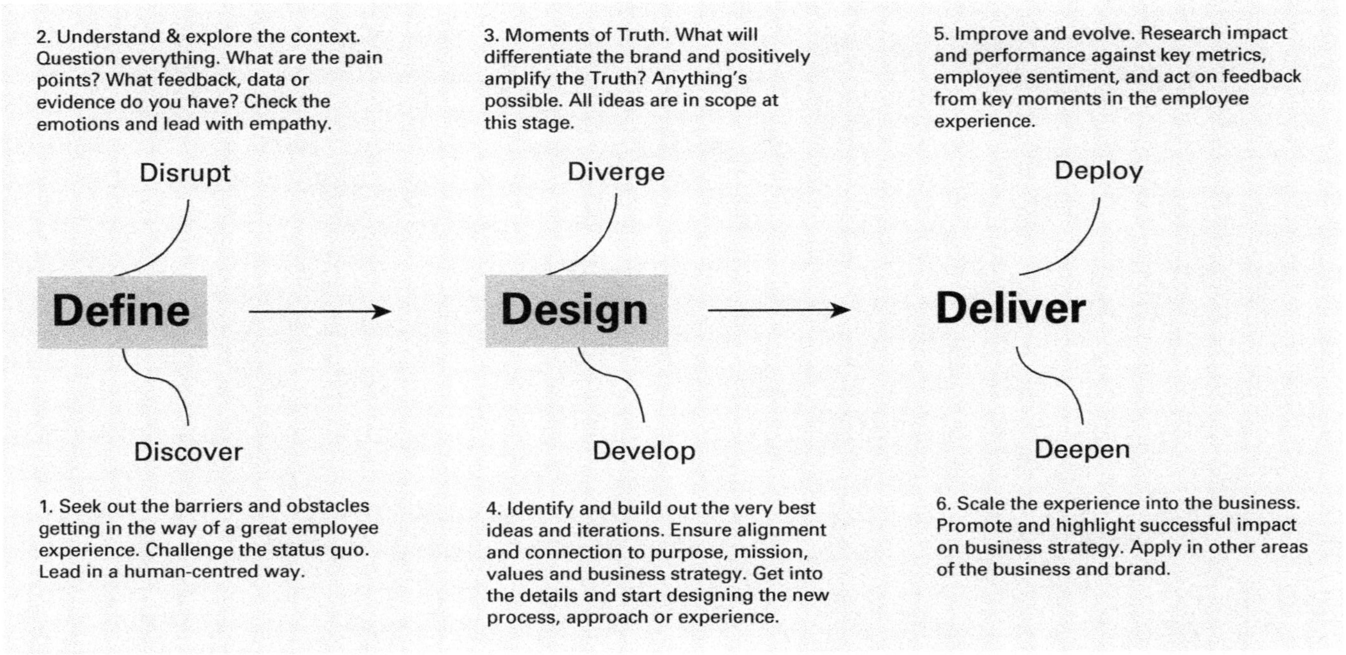

Define

Disrupt

2. Understand & explore the context. Question everything. What are the pain points? What feedback, data or evidence do you have? Check the emotions and lead with empathy.

Discover

1. Seek out the barriers and obstacles getting in the way of a great employee experience. Challenge the status quo. Lead in a human-centred way.

Design

Diverge

3. Moments of Truth. What will differentiate the brand and positively amplify the Truth? Anything's possible. All ideas are in scope at this stage.

Develop

4. Identify and build out the very best ideas and iterations. Ensure alignment and connection to purpose, mission, values and business strategy. Get into the details and start designing the new process, approach or experience.

Deliver

Deploy

5. Improve and evolve. Research impact and performance against key metrics, employee sentiment, and act on feedback from key moments in the employee experience.

Deepen

6. Scale the experience into the business. Promote and highlight successful impact on business strategy. Apply in other areas of the business and brand.

© Ben Whitter, HEX Organization Ltd

around how they can differentiate themselves from others to deliver signature experiences that become real moments of impact and connection within the workforce. Of course, we want to co-create talked-about, celebrated and valued experiences internally, so contextualizing this work locally is fundamental. Finally, the *deliver* stage is all about solid implementation and execution to bring forth successful new prototypes and ideas that resonate within the company and can scale up further.

The strength of the HEX accelerator is the intensity and focus it brings to internal projects and building up internal human-centred capabilities. Any firm can follow a process, but going through this is also about education, knowledge exchange and real-time learning. Therefore, real-time coaching and challenge is built in to the approach with clients to enhance the co-creation process. I have already highlighted that mindset is one of the key challenges, so therefore we take this more integrated approach – off-the-shelf and standard consulting approaches are limited in their effectiveness when it comes to the human experience. Deep co-creation within an ecosystem of colleagues and partners is proving to be a far superior method of developing high-quality, experience-driven work rather than outsourcing leadership to an external firm – the real value is when partners and vendors can be embedded into and serve as an extension of an existing project team. This is partly to build trust internally – too often consultants take over projects that really should be led by practitioners and leaders themselves. Trust is important within the co-creation process and nothing should get in the way of that.

Building trust into the business and human experience

Why is trust important for organizations? 'It's everything,' says Nick Ellsmore, global head of strategy, consulting and professional service at Trustwave. Nick has scaled and successfully sold two companies in his time and they both have trust at the core of their business model and service. As founder of Hivint, Nick says that you need two things to attract people to your brand. 'One is that you need to tell a compelling story about your company – what you're doing, what you're building, what the vision is – and why you're doing all these things, and the second is trust.'

In a start-up, for example, people need to trust and believe in the business, as it is often a risk to join a new venture. People attach themselves to a company and sometimes put their entire career on the line. This is a huge ask. Yes, there is the possibility of a fantastic upside as one of the first employees into a new venture, but there is tremendous risk to bear as well. In practice, people need to believe that what you say is real – the things that you say you're going to do are the things you go and do, as Nick explained.

'If there is no trust, then you're merely paying someone to do a thing. It's purely transactional,' says Ellsmore. A reference point within our dialogue is Atlassian's Mike Cannon-Brookes, who is someone that believes in trust being built up through small actions over a long period of time. Trust cannot be created in one hit. It's an emotional thing. It is a relationship. Whether a vision, product or service, we're selling to people, not legal entities. Contracts are often signed based on one-to-one relationships. From an employee perspective, there are two questions:

- Do I believe that my manager is going to do the things they say they will?
- Do I believe that the organization is arranged and structured in a way that will allow that manager to do the things that they say will?

These are two major elements that prevent trust and there is often misalignment between values and leaders. The structure may well be preventing a company from building trust with employees, but make no mistake, people are the ones responsible for creating trust. Managers making promises that the organization doesn't deliver breaks trust. They may have good intentions, but the system may prevent them from honouring their promises. Navigating this can be a challenge. Trust through transparency is easy when things are going well. It's very difficult when times are tough. People tend to rush to the outcome, but actually taking the time to explain your thinking rationale, and how you've arrived at a decision or position, will be helpful in creating trust. People may never be able to like some outcomes, but in this way they can at least respect the approach. It also opens an avenue for positive challenge, iteration and trust-building dialogue.

In this sense, trust is developed by continuous actions that draw people closer to a brand or a community of colleagues. If trust isn't a major concern, the opposite is true: any actions that lower trust could potentially cause a systemic collapse in trust, and all the fallout consequences that brings. That's why building trust is a holistic and system-wide endeavour, and brands get to do this through every moment and interaction they have with the workforce. This is very exciting, because all of those moments offer a first chance to get things right or a second chance to recover when mistakes are made. In many ways, expanding and leaning in to human experience puts internal services on notice that trust and relationships are now central to business strategy. This, in turn, affects how leaders lead and how things get done within the daily grind of a business operation. Trust becomes valued, and values that deliver trust become a cherished part of everyday business decision-making, data-sharing and strategy development.

Indeed, in human experience terms, values-based decisions are fundamental throughout every conversation, and the questions we ask become even more powerful because of it:

- Is this decision consistent with our values?
- Is this the right thing to do for our customers, employees and stakeholders?
- Is this ethical and good for humanity and the planet?

FOTILE Group (FOTILE is a major consumer brand in China) chooses not to have a CHRO in its business to ensure that this focus on values and people is led directly from the top. Indeed, the CEO takes personal responsibility for the human experience. It is his job to lead the culture and it cannot be delegated to any other senior executive. This is a fascinating approach, and we'll delve deeper into a fuller case study on FOTILE in the next chapter. The role of HR within trust-building does require some scrutiny and HR, given its role in policy enforcement, compliance and sensitive employee decisions, is a poorly positioned function that can often get between leaders and people. Leaders outsource their pain to HR rather than addressing issues or challenges with their people directly. Managers can often secure an easy win by blaming HR for their troubles or failures in organizational leadership, policy or strategy. We need to have a functioning and happy team in the company. If HR is getting in the way of that, then that is a major problem and the ideas contained within this book may well offer a better way to organize around the whole human being while maintaining collective responsibility for outcomes. We understand that business is ripe for disruption, but can the unorthodox and less traditional management ideas really work in practice?

Radical ideas and experiments in the world of work

One such business demonstrating that a radical idea can work is Judo Bank, which was founded in 2018. As a company making some serious waves in the Australian banking industry, it has continued its unique path from day one. This is a brand that offers compelling evidence that even the most radical of business ideas can work if the right level of thought, consideration and care has been dedicated to their ultimate success. Not only is the bank focused on creating fairer outcomes for customers, which is a radical idea itself within the banking sector, it also started life with a co-CEO leadership model. The role is shared between two colleagues who are part of a wider co-founder team.

Joseph Healy joined me for an interview where we discussed the bank's philosophy and how it has achieved so much in its short life. From zero to a $1 billion unicorn in just 18 months is no mean feat. The bank is taking great care to differentiate itself from the status quo and, in uncertain economic times, its fixation with trust and relationships is refreshing in how they build the brand from the inside out. Alignment between the co-CEOs, another unique aspect of the business model, has been critical, but so too the relationships they have formed with a highly talented workforce. Some of the colleagues have come across from big corporate banking and need to learn and deeply understand the bank's business philosophy, which deviates massively from its peers. The emphasis on relationships is what stands out – strong relationships that create strong trust levels with customers and employees. This is what matters to the brand in its growth journey and this is what has helped accelerate its progress. The senior team has great credibility. They come from the system they are trying to reform and have held senior roles in some of Australia's biggest banks. What is incredibly refreshing is that Joseph doesn't try to hide from the fact that he was part of a banking establishment that has been dragged through the mud in recent years for its treatment of customers, the shortcuts and the negative behaviours that have greatly profited from the misfortune of others.

This is what makes his story so compelling. Healy challenged this directly in his book, *Breaking the Banks* (2019), where he forensically picked apart the shortcomings of capitalism and how Australian banks have lost their way. The feelings run deep, but evidence is compelling, in that an industry 'built on trust, professionalism and value' is now more likely to be talked about in more scandalous terms because of greed, complacency and an insatiable appetite for wealth and power. In Healy's view, nothing short of a revolution was required, and with the incredible success of Judo Bank, he has well and truly put his money where his mouth is. Beyond the banking crisis of 2008, a return to purpose, trust and real values was urgently needed. The lessons here apply as much to any other part of the establishment as they do to banking.

Growing trusted, human-centred and experience-driven brands

We have seen the promise of what could be and a glimpse of what is possible when companies become a beacon for humanity – a guiding light to inspire people. As consumers, the choice is ours. Fill our economies with ruthless, cut-throat, profit-seeking machines, or incubate a new generation of organizations that we trust, admire and respect.

My research over the last few years led me to define a new lens and operating model for employee experience, which helped business and HR professionals lead impactful and targeted EX work. Alongside this work to develop professionals practising this new and very powerful holistic craft, we have been helping to create a very different breed of company too. Rightly considered to be among the strongest companies on the planet, those focused on the human experience have major advantages over their rivals. They are the most energetic places to work in any market, and as you'll see from some of the examples in this book, human-centred and experience-driven brands do things differently. I wanted to get to the heart of that and figure out exactly what that was. What has emerged through my current round of research for this book is an organizational lens and philosophy that is starting to emerge in the business world. It's a way of enabling the human being to flourish while building high degrees of trust. In effect, what they do is lead themselves in a way that we have begun to define as a human experience (HEX) organization.

The most defining and prominent aspect of these organizations can be described in one word: progress. This is an over-arching business focus, which I highlight in Figure 3.4, and breaks down what progress is actually made up of. They are visibly leading progress within their sectors – new ideas, innovations or work that simply moves humanity to the next step in its development. They embrace new ways of working and structure their companies so that they are in service to people, planet and performance.

- **People:** They are truly in the people business. There is a deep and unyielding commitment to serve all stakeholders in the best possible way. They want every person that is associated with their company to grow and prosper – to succeed in life.

- **Planet:** They are genuinely committed to the long-term sustainability of the planet and human life. They direct resources to tangibly serve and add value to causes that improve their communities, their countries and the places where they operate. They are active contributors in making the world a better, safer and fairer place to experience.

- **Performance:** They are organizations that set and deliver world-class objectives with their people. They are committed to the highest performance standards, yet performance is delivered ethically, sustainably and in a way that doesn't override the commitment they make to their people and the planet.

FIGURE 3.4   Progress

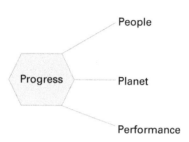

© Ben Whitter, HEX Organization Ltd

Working with some of the top companies in the world, it becomes clear that there are several tangible characteristics that underpin their success in business and in society. HEX organizations move, develop and lead their business in ways that many can't even imagine, let alone emulate. They are distinctly different in the way that they approach decision-making, business operations and service delivery. These characteristics shape their destiny and impact in the world. There's very little room for compromise, if any, when it comes to the things that really matter. Doing something half-hearted is not something they can relate to nor do they tolerate any disconnects between brand, people and society. This is what makes them so special and why they attract advocates everywhere they go. Yet, they are companies still led by humans. They are not right all the time and nor do they need to be. Right most of the time is enough for their stakeholders. Figure 3.5 shows where they focus.

FIGURE 3.5 Human experience (HEX) organization

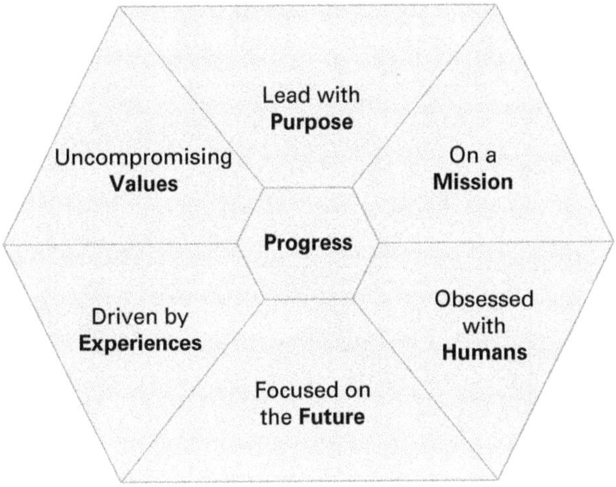

© Ben Whitter, HEX Organization Ltd

Lead with purpose

'Profitability is a shallow goal if it doesn't have a real purpose. We are equally proud of what we are doing in the community, what we are doing with our people and how the company has built itself around a purpose that is not just about making money.' This famous comment from Howard Schultz, founder of Starbucks, sets a lofty goal for everyone at the company, but does it hold up under pressure and when you are forced to shut down all of your outlets? I covered Starbucks as a case study in my last book (Whitter, 2019), and COVID-19 presented an opportunity to revisit the brand to see how it responded in times of crisis. Belinda Wong, CEO of Starbucks China, oversaw the rapid closure of all Starbucks coffee shops in China during the lockdown period, yet ensured that all partners were paid and upgraded insurance benefits to cover family members. In addition, the brand launched a Partner Assistance Programme (PAP) to offer employees and their family members counselling services, which is still a relatively scarce benefit in China. A big part of how Starbucks managed the crisis so effectively was to lean into purpose and make sure that experiences were being lined up to match reality with the stated ideal. It's an approach and philosophy that works and helped the chain recover strongly. Doing the right thing for employees and customers, Starbucks quickly moved into ensuring experiences with the chain were safe and secure. From contactless delivery to reconfigured shop designs, it was careful to put in place the right set-up to protect the wellbeing of its key stakeholders. The biggest standout example from their approach was their enduring focus to put people first and the speed at which they demonstrated their leadership in this regard (Dahlstrom and Duong, 2020).

This is not always the case. There were many companies sat waiting while leadership teams dithered and were holding back to hear what the government would do. The big difference was that human-centred companies reacted faster in a positive way to protect their employees and, ultimately, the sustainability of the business. In calmer times, purpose is often held up by brands as a way of attracting people, investors and admirers, yet on the inside many other factors are in play and can stifle any purpose-based leadership or rhetoric in the long term. WeWork is an example of this and came under intense scrutiny in 2019. 'In one month, the coworking company cut its valuation down to as low as $10 billion from $47 billion, removed Adam Neumann as CEO, and delayed its initial public offering indefinitely' (Aydin, 2019). The brand also made several thousand people redundant and faced a firestorm of negative media attention. WeWork portrayed itself as a tech company with all the usual purpose-based marketing alongside it, yet in the furore generated from its unsuccessful IPO filing, it was shown to be a poorly led real estate company, not a groundbreaking tech firm. This lack of authenticity, greater scrutiny of its management practices and the now well-documented erratic and excessive behaviour of the CEO was a hugely damaging example of why purpose alone is simply not enough for lasting business success. From the outside marketing at least, employees were engaged, on a mission and going after a huge purpose, but this company, at that time, was not a human-centred and purpose-led organization.

'Most people, deep down, are pretty decent' is one of the primary themes of *Humankind* by Rutger Bregman (2020). In his view, it is the institutions that we build and associate with that have allowed corruption to take place. That people themselves are not necessarily corrupt, but rather are corrupted by the entities we create around them, is an intriguing argument. It's one I find favour with. What has replaced profit is now purpose, and we're already seeing some impactful examples of so-called 'purposeful' companies losing their way. It is my belief that the large body of people within these companies continue to want to make a positive difference in the world. It is difficult, and inadvisable, to judge an entire organization based on the actions of a few at the top. That's not right and it's certainly not a balanced view.

Do companies set themselves up to control and mitigate human nature? Is their purpose to help guide people on their life path, keeping them honest and in good graces with society? Are they the positive force for humanity's greatest ideals? The more pragmatic view is that they are there to give us something to do, ensure we are resourced financially so we can enjoy food and shelter, and are able to maintain a quality of life that is acceptable to us. The reality is that many companies are started as a vehicle to make money and sustain livelihoods. Somewhere along the way, and if they allow it, they discover a higher purpose and an organization forms to extend the impact of an idea in the world. They are then ideological entities. They exist to scale ideas into society, and how far their idea goes is the ultimate measure of a successful enterprise. This is where business purpose and philosophy come in, and it is a massive differentiator that separates companies. Organizations as a positive force for good in the world is not a romantic idea anymore. It's becoming a widely respected way for founders, CEOs and C-suites to energize and widen participation in the philosophy and ideas they stand behind. The organization, in my mind, remains one of the most successful ideas in human history, and it's more important than ever that we get this idea right in practice.

On a mission

Gymshark, a gym wear company out of the UK, is a striking example of an organization on a mission. It's been relentless in recent years, and in 2020 earned a $1 billion valuation following an investment round. Not only has it been one of the fastest growing companies in the UK, it has also been quick to ensure its workforce has the best facilities and experience to fuel its remarkable growth and impact. The Gymshark story is very well known as its owner, Ben Francis, has been consistent in documenting the experience throughout the brand's community. From the outside looking in, people can get a sense of the passion, the urgency, the focus, the energy, the challenges and the enjoyment that is related to business growth. They invite their communities to share in the journey and experience the innovation in real time. There is a certain attitude that informs their pace and execution: they're on a mission and it feels like nothing can stop them from becoming the iconic global brand they set out to be. Unifying a company through a solid mission is one of the best organizing strategies in business.

Uncompromising values

There is a ruthless consistency about the way HEX organizations approach their values. Companies are learning that their success in the future depends, to a large extent, on how well they have defined and stood by their values. Plans and strategies can change, but there is something about values that sticks for generations of workers. Values can be strengthened, enhanced and modelled throughout the business or they can be forgotten and destroyed through company actions.

What I've noted about this is that brands leading the way are absolutely ruthless when it comes to the values they espouse – ruthless in the sense that there is no compromise on the things that really matter. Usually ruthless is a term that is deployed to describe a lack of compassion for others. In this case, it means an elevated compassion for people within an organization. Why? Because values mean something to people. They must mean something within the human experience, otherwise what's the point? Gaps open up between the people and the business.

The values, then, within a HEX organization are powerful igniters of sustained high performance. The consistency comes as values roll out, are shared and installed within the business. What companies value is abundantly clear because we see examples every single day – the way decisions are made, the way the community grows together, the way that good business gets done. Organizations at the forefront of the experience economy are ruthlessly consistent went it comes to values. There is no other way it can be for world-class companies. Companies like Airbnb, Patagonia and Costco are notable examples in this regard in how they support, work with people and lead their organizations over the long term. The extent to which companies stand by their values was tested in the most extreme of ways during COVID-19. There was stark differentiation between companies. A major factor in employee experience success has been linked to a renewed focus on values.

Obsessed with humans

Whether it's customers, employees, shareholders or peers, a fascination with people offers a significant path to differentiation and impact. 'Employees who believe that management is concerned about them as a whole person – not just an employee – are more productive, more satisfied, more fulfilled,' which was famously said by Anne M. Mulcahy, the former chairperson and CEO of Xerox who made the jump from HR to the most senior executive at the firm (Derivan, 2003). What Mulcahy found in her long and successful career was that the ability to lead people was paramount and all-important. All key stakeholders are human, so building organizations that reflect this point is critical work, and it takes some real superpowers across management lines to do it.

No one goes to work to enrich shareholders. They go to work to positively impact each other, their customers and themselves. It is perhaps a way of explaining the goodness that exists within the human species and the seemingly unstoppable human spirit. This is what we need to channel and build into the organizational context: our human superpowers. They are all abilities that are respected, revered and valued throughout the entire world. These superpowers need to be translated well into the experience of work. It's about:

- compassion;
- empathy;
- selflessness;
- kindness;
- caring;
- integrity;
- loyalty;
- devotion;
- commitment;
- thoughtfulness;
- creativity.

If there is an employer that represents and encapsulates many of these into their business model, it is Timpson. Based in the UK, it is a company well known for its approach to doing business in a human way. Leading with a philosophy based on 'upside down management', colleagues sit atop the business structure, not the CEO. Sometimes this leads to self-inflicted operational issues in running its chain of shops across the UK, but customers have no real choice but to accept and respect it. A standout example that transcends work life is that Timpson's employees are given the day off to take their kids to school on their first day of the school year. Marking milestones like this within the human experience with an *actual experience* is world-class human-centred leadership.

This is also a company that is famous for its HR approach – it doesn't have one. The CEO finds that having an HR function is often divisive and distracts from the real focus of the business – people.

This being the view, the company is keen to ensure a high degree of autonomy at local level for business and operational practices and decisions. Its chain of shops retain control of decision-making and work with the central office in a style that is more like a partnership rather than a firm. In effect, the company finds ways to work together to make decisions, solve problems and create outcomes at local and national level.

Offering just one anecdotal explanation of why human-centred practices transfer exceptional outcomes to the customer experience, one customer publicly praised the company, writing that, faced with a choice between Timpson and another retailer, they chose Timpson, 'as the service is so good' and because they 'applaud' the employment practices, recommending that 'other companies should take note'. This is a well-established cobbler and locksmith, not a fashionable, fast-paced start-up out of Silicon Valley. Yet colleagues working at Timpson get a range of experiences that connect and interact with the most important parts of the human experience.

Here are just a few:

- **First work day:** all new starters receive a welcome pack (with alarm clock!).
- **Birthday:** every colleague gets the day off (is there a date more important or that we are more conscious of as humans than our birthday?).
- **Financial issues:** there is a hardship fund in place for any colleagues facing personal challenges when it comes to their finances.
- **Marriage:** colleagues get an extra week of leave and a contribution towards wedding costs. Car and chauffeur are provided on the wedding day.
- **New baby:** contribution towards maternity clothes and voucher for new parents.
- **Career growth:** support and access to ongoing learning opportunities.
- **Citizenship:** hires former prisoners to work in all its shops.

- **Holidays:** free access to the company's holiday homes.
- **Services:** a colleague discount of up to 90 per cent off Timpson services and products (Timpson, 2020).

Timpson is a good example of a small organization adapting to the whole human being. With a workforce of 5,400 and nearly 2,000 shops, Timpson stands out in the high street, not just because of its customer experience, but because it serves the interests of all stakeholders, including society. Any company can do this, but they have to want to, and that's sometimes the biggest obstacle to get over.

Driven by experiences

Every experience is a chance to connect with people. Experiences are made up of moments, and so many of them are passed by without a second thought. World-class experience leadership leaves an imprint and a trail of memorable events and interactions. What do you remember in your career to date? What are the positive experiences? What are the negative experiences? What are the most memorable experiences? How do your emotions feel when you check in with these memories? This tells you all you need to know about why brands that are driven by experiences have a strong edge in the attention marketplace and why they fill key leadership positions with colleagues who can lead and deliver industry-leading experiences. Put simply, they make the right choice when it comes to maximizing the potential of key moments within the life journey of their people. They choose to support and strive to help people reach their highest potential as human beings.

Colleagues driving experience can also expertly hover in a holistic sense to get all the fragmented ingredients together and performing well. Just one experience within the employee journey will criss-cross many functions, and being able to pull everything together is a very powerful skill to accelerate progress. Not every company will have the opportunity to build a HEX organization from day one, yet they can apply their well-earned skills, tactics and strategies to bring experiences to life with their teams and for key stakeholders.

Focused on the future

Within experience-driven organizations, there is a relentless focus on being better the next day, the next experience and the next challenge. This is what the human experience is all about: evolution. We evolve or decay. It is a simple choice. As our technology advances, so do we and so should our organizations.

Arrival, a futuristic electric vehicle production firm out of the UK, offers a vision for the future without petrol or diesel cars. Having secured an order of 10,000 electric vehicles from UPS for delivery between 2020 and 2024, Arrival will soon be a household name and will follow in the pioneering footsteps of Tesla. Coincidently, BrewDog has also just placed an order for a fleet of delivery vehicles from the firm. Progressive companies live in the future but enjoy the present. It's the same in relation to the human experience at work. Brands are often fully focused on the next iteration, the next move and the next great innovation that will delight and deliver results for their workforce. Isn't this what our economy should be primed for? To advance the human spirit and create a path for human endeavour and progress? Indeed, throughout history, systems have been built on the shoulders of iconic organizations led by people who have truly embraced their individual truth and have locked it indefinitely into the very fabric of a company construct. Great human progress often follows great examples of inspiring people and organizations that are stretching our imaginations as to what we believe is possible.

Organizations are simply entities that are formed around people. They are designed to spread ideas, philosophies and ideologies further. They are incorporated to attract like-minded people who share similar philosophies about the way the world is, or the way the world could be. Throwing off the shackles of tradition and status quo, organizations are the ultimate expression of human potential. Regardless of what we are told, no company is an island. All that they are and all that they will be is entirely dependent on their ability to build alliances, partnerships and teams to attract investment, resources and commitment from others – whether shareholders, employees, contractors, suppliers or consumers. With this view, companies become platforms, places and spaces to uplift the human experience – to make people and the world better. They are 'out there' in the future preparing the way for all of us to follow – thinking about the next idea, the next opportunity, the next way they can advance the human economy. It is a human economy, after all, though I have never heard it referred to in those terms, it really is. Only humans have the chance to benefit from it, and it's only humans that can decide to make their endeavours deliver benefits beyond humanity in a way that creates a positive impact on the planet and environment. Co-creating organizations that are fixated on human experiences makes everything better – products, services, relationships and outcomes all benefit from us thinking and acting with people in mind. This fixation leads to better questions:

- How can we improve an experience?
- What is the next great idea to take the experience to the next level?
- What are our options?
- How can we innovate or deliver standout experiences?
- In what way can we differentiate ourselves and connect our unique approach within the context of this experience?
- Where is our opportunity to deliver a world-class experience?

This relentless innovation is the modus operandi for the world's elite companies. This is why their organizations are stacked so heavily in favour of the future. There are too many examples to count of companies taking a dive early in their lifecycle due to missed opportunities, erosion of trust or pure arrogance. Innovation must be constant and the experience that surrounds people within their companies is an opportunity to reinforce and focus minds on progress, achievement and success.

Giving people space to *breathe*

Leaders working to develop the human experience move in ways that are different from the norm as they seek to guide their companies in a human-centred direction. It's certainly easy if everyone is on board from the start, yet practitioners can often find themselves as a lone wolf until they have co-created some early momentum to switch up the focus from company or shareholders to a firm commitment to people. From my observations working with practitioners across all sizes of organization, a pattern has emerged in how they go about their business in building human-centred and experience-driven companies. How they do this, and to put it in a form that can be easily remembered, is based on leading in such a manner that quickly helps people in the organization to BREATHE and experience their organizations in a whole new way. Our global research groups reinforced our understanding about where high-quality practitioners focus in their work to improve experiences across the workforce.

For companies, certainly the wise ones, there will be a significant proportion of time dedicated to developing the human experience. Why? Because people need to BREATHE. We need the spaces and places that enable us to do this. For leaders and company-builders, the point is not lost. They serve the fundamental human needs and truths first, not last. Without missing a beat, and we'll delve into case studies on this later in the book, the best company examples we consistently experience within the world are those that have crafted, shaped and delivered experiences in work that connect in the strongest possible way to the human experience – all of it, the whole messy, beautiful, simple and downright absurd elements of human existence.

BREATHE in this context means:

Balance

We know more about balance now than we ever did. Dealing with a sustained global crisis tends to create two directions of travel for most workers around the world. On one side is balance and on the other is excess, and people have been experiencing both as companies experimented with their new operating models for a large period of 2020. A preference has emerged within the global workforce for balance. Having experienced remote working at an unprecedented level, several global polls and research projects are confirming what we already know – that to a large extent, people like working in their own way and in their own home, some of the time.

The emergence of the hybrid organization has already occurred. A good example of this is Siemens, which was one of the first companies to make the hybrid work model a long-term part of its business model. Following internal survey results that indicate a strong preference within the workforce for a more balanced approach to work, the company established a model that empowers people to work from anywhere for two or three days a week. It is worth noting that the approach to arrive at this new global policy was the result of a collaborative effort from colleagues across strategy, HR, IT and real estate in addition to colleagues from general business units. It applied immediately for 140,000 employees working at over 125 locations in 43 countries (Siemens, 2020). This is a glimpse of what can become possible very quickly when you put people at the heart of business transformation. The company is now rolling this out throughout its 300,000+ workforce with a key focus on outcomes rather than how or where the work gets done. I've highlighted before that the workplace is simply the spaces and places that enable our best work, and companies, realizing the potential of this, have seen the possibilities that the huge surge of digitalization in 2020 has unlocked.

React

Is it better to be proactive or reactive? In practice, we are at our best when we adopt a combination of both within our life and work. There are many situations within our control and that we can lead proactively, yet how many curveballs are sent our way in life? The ones we may not have planned for or expected? This is where leaders can start to differentiate their businesses from others – by the way they react to circumstances and challenges. Every action prompts a reaction, and for leaders and professionals, that first reaction is critical. It's the difference between widespread applause or widespread ridicule, and the margins can be tight between the two. When something happens, people expect a reaction. They expect companies to act for them or with them. Airbnb found itself as one firm that was affected in a profound way with COVID-19 and all the disruption it brought to the travel industry. As a result, they made the difficult decision to lay off 25 per cent of their workforce, which was around 1,900 roles. Even in in this scenario it won plaudits and new admirers for the way it reacted and led people through the redundancy experience. In a company blog, the CEO listed all the ways in which the company would be supporting its workforce and departing colleagues, including:

- Equity – to transition people from employees to shareholders, Airbnb announced that qualifying periods for company equity were scrapped, which meant that all departing employees could leave with equity and a stake in the brand's long-term future.

- Severance – a generous leaving package was provided for colleagues leaving the business.

- Healthcare – a significant intervention was made to extend company healthcare to departing employees with extended periods of cover and provision of mental health services.

- Alumni Talent Directory – a public-facing website to help colleagues find new jobs.

- Alumni Placement Team – Airbnb Recruiting became an Alumni Placement Team through 2020 to support people in their career steps.

- Career Support – four months of specialized career services delivered through an external vendor.

- Community Support – all employees formed a community to help people secure new jobs outside of Airbnb and were active on social media.

- Laptops – every leaver was able to keep their laptop (Airbnb, 2020).

Notably, the way this information was delivered directly by the CEO and in a comprehensive and transparent manner was there for all to see. It created a considerable amount of positive PR while ensuring people were supported to the fullest as they moved into Airbnb's alumni community. In my opinion, this was a masterclass in how to react in a human-centred way to be a positive force for good in the world. They didn't make it someone else's responsibility to pick up the pieces of a challenging decision. The brand chose to make itself accountable for the continuing success of its workforce. I can only imagine the incredible emotional impact this must have had on the colleagues who were remaining with the company. To see companies behave in this manner at a time of crisis and treat people right is very inspirational.

It's no accident, though. Human-centred organizations are in a constant state of reaction. I used to view this word negatively and lean in on proactivity, but that may not have been the best way to see things if we are working in line with human experience. There is a delicate, and seemingly incessant, line between absolute chaos and calm within our economies and lives. It is simply not possible to be proactive all of the time. As many employers and practitioners have realized, the mindset and principles that underpin our reactions can be controlled and used in our favour.

Empathize

Very early in the COVID-19 pandemic I gave a webinar to several hundred people about where we should be focused in our response to the crisis. In short, I explained how companies can react in a strong way and what elements of the employee experience would serve them well through those early stages. My obvious early attention was focused almost entirely on safety, security and trust. These were the key themes to start the fightback in the way we developed, pivoted or reshaped employee experiences, especially within the newly created remote-first economy.

Christina Chateauvert, Talent Programmes Manager at Ford, was in the audience. Christina is part of our certified community of holistic employee experience practitioners, and I immediately knew why. While others were still getting their heads around the situation, Christina was already well ahead in shaping the Ford response with her colleagues, putting in place contingency plans and redesigning experiences for the newly configured workforce. Her angle in the question-and-answer session afterwards stood out. Christina was already building the desired welcome-back experience once people could safely return to their workplace. Not only did her reaction consider the here and now, but she was also very quick to empathize with her people, what they were going through and then putting in place a thoughtful response crafted with empathy. At normal times, there are many moments that offer opportunities to empathize with people at a deeper level. They should be welcomed wholeheartedly, especially in times of human suffering.

Accelerate

Every opportunity to accelerate outcomes is taken within exceptional human experience work. A crisis, a change, a difficulty – whatever is thrown our way becomes another step on the way to further reinforce our position as human-centred leaders. As the HEX accelerator demonstrates, rapid iterations and seeking to scale up experiences that deliver results for a business is now essential work. A long-term focus and vision is often in play, but that doesn't mean the pace is slow. Work is considered and is thoughtful, yet it can never be described as slow. With greater use of design thinking and people analytics, companies can get to the crux of any issue quicker and roll out effective and impactful solutions to problems in rapid fashion. As the examples I have shared so far indicate, there is a bias for action and to get things done in a way that is naturally collaborative. This does not mean taking shortcuts. It is much more about focusing energy in areas where serious change can occur that improves outcomes for people.

Whereas previously companies would often introduce programmes and projects that were more aligned to the needs of management, we now have a situation where real challenges that are being experienced in the workforce are being tackled first, not last. This represents a real sea change in the approach to the human experience. In the next chapter, we'll discuss an example based on how one of the world's leading brands has formalized acceleration within their EX strategy.

Think

I recall being asked after a keynote session I delivered about what my advice would be to professionals and leaders that were just getting started on improving the human and employee experience. What should they take away and implement the following morning? 'Nothing,' I said, except for one thing: think. In experience-design terms, practitioners usually work based on longer-term objectives. They have a vision for an overall transformation programme and that usually looks out beyond short-term annual cycles. What I've noticed from companies that struggle with this longer-term human-centred focus is that they are much more fixated on quarterly results or demonstrating value over the short term. This leads to rushed decisions about what to improve, what to invest in and what external vendors or suppliers to work with. This can often lead to poor outcomes. The 'busy' work begins and is disconnected from tangible brand and human performance outcomes. It becomes activity rather than activation.

Indeed, there is a perception that billions of dollars are wasted on employee engagement and leadership development every year, to name two examples. The latter is an industry that attracts upwards of $300 billion in training investment, yet very little of that is considered to deliver a good return (Beer *et al*, 2016). Training is commissioned or delivered, but nothing changes as a result. With employee experience, outside of short-lived workshops, there is a very different approach to this that always delivers something tangible – something changed. This could be a redesigned part of the employee journey, a different set of benefits, higher quality branding and communications, better technology, growth or giving opportunities, and many more. Bottom line, something always gets better. Any waste that does occur is often because the serious thinking about how everything connects within an organizational context just hasn't taken place. It is a costly misstep. What should we think about? Well, everything. This is where holistic thinking proves its worth in practice to target the high-value, high-impact opportunities to improve processes, practices and outcomes. Targeting the right things to change and improve, in partnership with the workforce, is a critical step to take and is part of the change experience. Indeed, thinking and working with the workforce charts a smooth path as part of any transformation work. Things become easier because people are part of the change rather than the victims of it. Thinking things through in an intentional and long-term way presents many opportunities to target projects and work that really makes a difference, and deliver work that doesn't waste time, money and energy – all of which will need to be spent wisely within any organization.

Honour

It may be old-fashioned these days, and we may even now be in deficit as a human species, but there are indications that we are returning to a place where honour means something again within business. There is an unlimited supply of things to honour in our companies, but do we spend enough effort, time and resource to do that effectively? Defining honour can be a challenge, but for my purposes, it is simply this: demonstrating a high level of respect, esteem, and knowing and doing what is right by people. What do we honour within companies? Well, this list is not exhaustive, but some things companies choose to honour are: customs and practices; commitments; tradition; rituals; workers; suppliers; shareholders; fans; ambassadors; values; agreements; promises; heritage; communities; environment; planet; and progress.

The very act of focusing our efforts to improve the human experience is a hugely visible, and often indirect, way of honouring our workforce. I'm not talking about grand proclamations and virtue-signalling attempts by the corporate world. This is more than making statements that do not resonate or have an impact with employees. What we see through our work are diligent, focused, committed and professional people, discreetly working behind the scenes most of the time, to create stronger relationships and better experiences for people within companies. There may be some strategic and tactical PR work to do to ensure our people are being recognized externally and to also help with internal change momentum, but a lot of the time leaders are totally immersed in the task at hand, leading from the front and in the details. This is inspiring in and of itself, and a welcome alternative to people grandstanding about some superficial work that has barely moved or connected with employees. There is an unlimited supply of things to honour in our companies, but do we spend enough effort, time and resource to do that effectively?

Elevate

There are gaps to bridge within the human experience. It is not at all unpleasant to consider the role of companies in elevating the level of human consciousness. We are conscious, intelligent and thinking beings. It is truly outrageous to ignore this point in how we run our companies. It is fundamentally wrong to build companies that don't harness the potential of every person within the workforce. As companies accept an evolved role, they'll also need to take on the associated responsibilities. What I mean by evolved role becomes evident when we look at the modern company. They are social organizations. They lead social narratives, societal trends and can be an incredibly positive force for humanity, if they want to be, yet elevating humanity is a collective effort. Horace Mann put it in terms we can relate to: 'Be ashamed to die, until you have scored some victory for humanity' (Banks, 1992). There is something of a duty for all of us to do something good and become something good in the world. Our companies help us to do this, but can never do it for us in isolation. There is a great human responsibility within this to create, produce and share in life, and make the most of every moment we have.

Living in the moments

It is not easy to apply this, though, without a deep appreciation of how to lead in the details and moments, yet a process we can follow is set out in Figure 3.6.

This frame for an experience-driven approach is the signature of great professionals and leaders. They can go into the details of a

FIGURE 3.6   Moments and outcomes

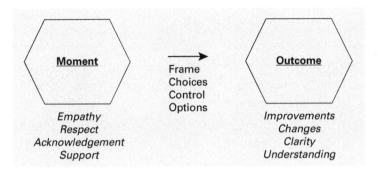

© Ben Whitter, HEX Organization Ltd

specific moment in an empathic way to generate options, choices and solutions. The outcome is progress in actions or progress in understanding without wasting the opportunity to really connect at a human level. The key is to transform moments to outcomes. This is true at the individual, one-to-one level and it is also true at the organizational level – the only difference is scale and scope. The deep skill sets we require, then, should all be focused on harnessing the power of these moments, and then, suddenly, they will all begin to matter across an organization.

Summary: accelerating holistic, human-centred and experience-driven business

Our workforces are made up of human beings. They need air. The failure of robotic and overly bureaucratic companies is that they are often designed in a way that stifles people. It's sometimes the refusal to give people the space and freedom they need that leaves the workforce feeling suffocated. It's sometimes the refusal to give people the equipment and tools they need. It's often the refusal of companies to provide high-quality leadership and a high-quality community. These are all our 'air' in the organizational sense – vital to our success and profoundly missed when they are not present. Indeed, many will leave companies in search of the air they need and find it in abundance elsewhere. This is still a demand and supply issue, though – there are not enough companies set up in a way that effectively leverages the full human experience at work.

What I've presented in this chapter are ideas and tools to help you think more practically about the human experience and what it means to your company. Some of this is operational and some of it will be ripe for further strategic consideration, but it all will serve you well in working out the best way to build your organization's philosophy when it comes to helping people fulfil their potential and deliver results for and beyond your company:

- Consider how well your organization is set up to advance a human-centred and experience-driven approach. What needs to change? What is working in your favour?

- After reviewing the HEX organization concept, how well does your company perform against it? What are your strengths and development areas?

- Explore the human experience platform at your company and how the structure can better serve your work to advance a human-centred approach.

- Challenge yourself and your teams to deeply empathize with people and their needs. Is your company in the best position to meet and exceed those needs?

- Use the HEX accelerator process to target improvements over a specific timeline working with all key stakeholders.

- Take a moment to BREATHE and reflect on the important points we've considered in delivering positive outcomes across the human experience at work.

04

Delivering world-class human experiences at work

World-class experiences in work are delivered by co-creating human-centred organizations. For that to occur, companies need to have their priorities in order. Certainly, the companies I tend to explore are led with purpose, people and planet as key tenets of their business strategy. It is not enough for the modern company to simply develop experiences within the narrow confines of a 9–5 work philosophy. To differentiate themselves, brands are starting to deliver outcomes across the whole human experience in and outside of traditional work time. In effect, we are actively redrawing the lines between life and work – organizations are developing templates for a future economy based on trust, values and mutually beneficial outcomes for both people and the company. In many ways, the organization has become more relevant than ever in the human experience. There is an abundance of choice available to workers in how they develop their careers and contribute to the planet, yet the organization still, in my mind at least, represents a great accomplishment of human endeavour, and an even greater vehicle for future human progress.

Transcendent experiences in work

World-class experiences are naturally transcendent. They can help elevate people to a different level within life. They enable people to feel good and feel joy in their roles and in their lives more generally. This field is so powerful when we consider the possibilities for transcendence – enabling people to go beyond what they thought was possible while enjoying the experience. At an individual level, what is the ultimate goal of our work in this regard? Where do we want to take people and how do all the examples we see and hear about contribute to this? The outcomes I've come across from studying all manner of companies around the world, looking at qualitative and quantities data, highlight several key results of delivering exceptional and high-quality experiences. In Figure 4.1 I attempt to summarize this to help colleagues determine if indeed they have arrived at a situation whereby the employee experience is flowing in the right way. The outcomes associated with this progress are evident every day at an individual level – people flow forward into the future, welcoming challenges and opportunities to grow. This is what we are looking to deliver – human impact. This individual impact, when added up across an organization, becomes the key indicator of company success – organizational impact. To get the latter, it is essential to consciously cultivate the former.

Strong people delivering strong results creates a strong organization. It's that simple. A well-developed organization feels a lot different from an underdeveloped one. What separates the two is often *intention*. One company sets out to be a strong organization across all aspects of the business while others set out to be strong only in certain aspects of the business. In the latter, it is often the workforce that feels left behind, unloved and undervalued. Companies are human creations and vehicles that enable people to create relationships with people at scale. Developing the experience of work with intent enables numerous advantages that come with being human – our creativity, our empathy, our compassion, our resilience, our adaptability and our strength. They can also create a path to unlock the not-so-positive aspects of humanity – our ignorance, intolerance, greed and our tendency to be corrupted by power. There is very little need to spend many hours researching brand failures. They are a high-profile and frequent element of business life. I've highlighted some of these failures already and it's clear that at the heart of all

FIGURE 4.1   Experience impact

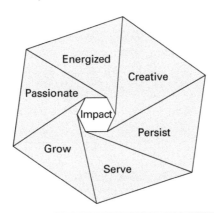

Energized	People are fully focused on the things that really matter. Energy is consistently positive and is used in the best possible way to deliver outcomes at work. Energy is directed towards work that is meaningful and impactful. People feel good about what they do, and where, how and why they do it.
Creative	People express themselves and their unique personalities to enrich their work and the work of others. Their creative powers are unlocked and they are free to explore new possibilities, ideas and opportunities that add value within and beyond the organization.
Persist	Obstacles and setbacks are treated as stepping stones to success. There is a persistence to overcoming challenges to create something better for all stakeholders. This persistence creates an atmosphere that is contagious – people genuinely feel like they can achieve anything.
Serve	People are in service to people. There is a tangible bias in favour of meeting and exceeding the needs of human beings across all parts of the business. They serve their stakeholders to a high standard and are constantly exploring ways to improve experiences. This mentality and approach creates very strong and aligned internal teams and communities.
Grow	People have the space, support and encouragement to grow with, through and beyond their perceived limitations. There is a strong feeling of connection that often dictates career decisions. People are compelled to stay and grow their impact with the organization.
Passionate	A genuine passion is evident in the way that people work and the quality of the results and performance. This passion often transcends a job and becomes part of a wider passion for an organization. They believe in and become very strong advocates of a brand. A notable affection has developed and a relationship is sustained with an employer during and beyond a period of employment.

these examples is a reluctance to lead in a human-centred way with a lack of empathy with the workforce.

The way companies treated people before, during and after the disruption of COVID-19 offers much evidence that a dividing line has emerged between companies and professionals. The examples I relate throughout this book demonstrate the shift that is taking place. There are those on one side entirely focused on profits at all costs, and there are those on the other side putting people first as a core part of their business models and business philosophies. There are a great number of others in the middle confused about the whole thing and looking for inspiration. I evoke the word 'philosophy' very deliberately, because what we've seen at the top of companies from CEOs worldwide is nothing short of business philosophy. This may be dressed up in corporate niceties and language appropriate for businesses and shareholders, but there is no getting away from the point of view that businesses are shaped every day and every way by what their top team and workforce deem to be important priorities. In this sense, businesses are becoming more unique than ever before as companies design their own paths based on what resonates with their key stakeholders. This is to be expected. The more companies can listen to their inner voices, the more distinct they will be as brands. In my view, this is the most exciting element of the change we are going through now – the days of copying and pasting are over. Every organization can build a unique and differentiated brand and human experience. Increasingly, they want to, at least, be seen to be on the right side of history. At best, they are fully committed to business models couched in sustainable, ethical and trust-developing management practices that ensure the workforce feels that their organization cares about them.

In a world that is rife with fake news and misinformation, it is striking when you meet a company that is fully focused on living its truth – the purpose, mission and values that the company has determined for itself. In my experience, the truth about what matters to an organization is discovered, learned and experienced. I pay little attention to noble words, but I do centre my observations on actions. Our workplaces can often stifle progress because, quite frankly, they are not being true to themselves or leading in an authentic way. This stands out and is regularly the reason that good intentions do not translate into organizational success. This is why alignment is a critical issue – alignment between the person and the company, a unification of our individual and organizational truths. With this in place, we start to connect with a positive flow of our energy. I admire people and companies that are comfortable with who they are and what they stand for – it is a compelling and rare proposition. We can start to live more like our true selves with all the accompanying quirks that that may bring. There is no tension between purpose, mission and values. There are no missteps in creating a solid relationship from the outset. Yet, this still seems like the most underrated aspect of great organizational development work, but done well, it can create a world of unlimited possibility. We just need to embrace our truth and install it into every aspect of the organization and the employee experience.

Accelerating its work on the employee experience, Ford integrated my holistic employee experience model into an EX strategy for over 200,000 people. This company, which is one of the biggest and most iconic companies on the planet, has represented so many things to humanity, not least its contribution to the world of work as we experience it today. In 1926, founder of Ford Motor Company, Henry Ford, made a decision that would change the human experience at work forever: the creation of the five-day work week (BBC, 2020). This innovation brought the working week down from six days while maintaining the same level of pay. It remains one of the biggest decisions relating to the workplace in history.

I worked with Ford when the COVID-19 pandemic first hit. Ford was already set on developing an EX approach, and the situation energized this important work and increased the speed and urgency of it in the context of one of the best and most audacious goals I've ever come across: to be the world's most trusted brand.

CASE STUDY

Ford

Kiersten Robinson, Ford's Chief People and Employee Experiences Officer, said:

> Over the past few years, we've seen the pace of change rapidly increase across all areas of our organization and it has required us to change our HR focus. We shifted our processes from 'one size fits all' to 'fit for purpose' in order to enhance the employee experience and instituted new methodologies – particularly human-design thinking – to reinvent our processes keeping the employee top of mind.

Attending to people and culture is critical in how Ford delivers its business strategy today, and for building the company they want for our future. The company's 2030 strategy is enabled by its 2030 people strategy with an integrated aspiration to become the world's most trusted company. With that level of goal-prioritizing, building trust with employees, customers, partners and communities became a core part of its approach to employee experience. 'We know that the experiences that people have shape our culture and our culture enables our business success. This is why we anchor our experience design decisions in the following core rules,' said Christina Chateauvert, Ford's Talent Programmes Manager:

- Design experiences that have integrity, demonstrate competence and are in service to others to build high levels of trust within the organization.

- Ask: how do we put people first, how do they feel? Keeping the questions in mind always.

- Flip perspective and language from the business perspective to the employee perspective (as an employee, I feel…, I need…, I would like…).

- Provide opportunities for sharing, community and connection.

- Collaborate to elevate the holistic employee experience (Whitter, 2019).

- Leverage power of moments to make a meaningful impact (elevation, pride, insight, connection) (Heath and Heath, 2019).

- Use design thinking approaches (seek user input, quick idea generation, rapid prototyping, test and iterate) to co-create experiences.

Co-creating exceptional experiences through truth

Chateauvert said:

> We endeavour to co-create exceptional experiences that reflect a shared set of values, which are known internally as 'Our Truths'. If people aren't experiencing our values, they are just words on paper and that doesn't transform our culture. We also ask ourselves, how might employees experience this at the world's most trusted company? Then we use that inspiration to inform how we solve problems, how we communicate, how we design policies and practices.

While acknowledging that the company is a work in progress when it comes to employee experience, it is a brand intent on co-creating the future with its workforce. They do this not only through core values, but also in how Ford's

Truths are lived in day-to-day experiences. Ford is still early in its employee experience journey. In response to COVID-19, the company transitioned over 100,000 people to work from home very quickly. Chateauvert said:

> Our teams pivoted their ways of working: speed of decision-making increased, collaboration across organizations improved and bureaucracy decreased. Our change management and EX teams are now looking at how might we sustain and accelerate these important behavioural shifts to make us more competitive.

By gaining a deep understanding of the factors that enabled these shifts from an employee experience perspective, the company has learned that policy simplification, clear priorities, transparent communications and extending trust to make decisions all played a role in its successful response. The question now is centred on creating an operating model that helps them to continue this great human-centred work. Chateauvert said:

> One structure that has enabled our ability to better co-create holistic experiences is our Culture Operating System. This important step was led by the Chief People and Employee Experiences Officer, Kiersten Robinson, who aligned support across functions. We formed the cross-functional team with leaders who come together across their disciplines to design and deliver employee experiences, to work on our toughest challenges. They do this by really knowing our people, delivering experiences by engaging teams, and communicating clearly.

COVID-19 presented the ultimate litmus test of this new approach. Using a human-centred approach, Ford has been able to deliver successful outcomes in how it approached the return to work of its large workforce. Within this, a primary task was to return people to work in its manufacturing and test facilities around the world. While the safety and facilities teams had the lead for the protocols and logistics, the EX team was responsible for attending to the fact that real human beings were returning to a changed work environment in a scary or, at the least, an uncertain time while balancing new personal challenges.

Another senior leader at Ford I spoke to summed up the driving force behind this incredible and historic work:

> 60,000 people came back to work on Monday to the manufacturing sites. This is a moment we didn't let slip away. We used the opportunity to demonstrate that we cared and that we recognized their feelings. At the same time, we effectively amplified Our Truths as a brand, and some of the achievements that WE (all of the workforce) have delivered together as one team.

FIGURE 4.2   Ford's Truths

PUT PEOPLE FIRST

DO THE RIGHT THING

BE CURIOUS

OUR
TRUTHS

CREATE TOMORROW

BUILT FORD
TOUGH

PLAY TO WIN

ONE FORD

SOURCE Ford (reproduced with permission)

This is the utopia of exceptional work on the human and employee experience – the feeling and perception that everyone has played their part in delivering a goal, an objective or an experience. This is definitely a feeling we need more of in the world – the feeling that we are human and we are in this together. To deliver it though takes a lot of hard work and actions that lead to increased trust and mutual respect.

Chateauvert said:

> We have successfully resumed these operations and have helped leaders throughout the organization lead with empathy and flexibility, starting from the messages they hear from our most senior leaders. We started with *Put People First*, which meant prioritizing the safety of our workforce.

Using human-centred design, the team got to work on the most significant challenge for the brand, which can be best summarized by the following question: how do people return to work at the world's most trusted company?

Taking this to heart, the team designed and delivered key experiences, which included:

- The Compassion Protocol – a small team of EX and broader HR colleagues worked on how they might best support the workforce as they experienced losing co-workers, friends and family to COVID-19. The compassion protocol consisted of supportive resources, caring communications and personal one-on-one support from a hand-selected HR team, prepared to help in the most serious circumstances.

- Playbooks – cross-functional teams designed and published return-to-work playbooks to be clear and aligned on how Ford would prepare facilities and its workforce to be ready to return to work. It included protocols for entering facilities, cleaning practices, personal protective equipment requirements, safety practices, accountability measures as well as how the company would work together to ensure the collective safety of all teams returning to work. The EX team contributed to this by ensuring the playbooks were easy to understand, aligned across multiple communication platforms and easily updated as needed.

- Return-to-work care kits – a small cross-functional team of safety, purchasing, communications and EX worked on the welcome-back experience to ensure that they felt that Ford was a caring employer. As part of their first-day experience, people received a small care kit including face masks, personal hand sanitizer and personal care items like lip balm and lotion. The packaging contained the same #FordProud artwork that is prominently tagged on the ventilators that Ford teams quickly produced for society. While this was an effective way to distribute an initial supply of PPE as it relaunched the plant operations, it also successfully conveyed the welcome-back message. Each region of the world customized their care kits as needed and each location ensured it was distributed with a caring and welcoming experience.

These successes involved working closely with cross-functional and regional teams in order to scale the designs and localize them to be meaningful in a variety of environments. Regional talent and culture leads met regularly to share best practices and support each other as well as to identify emerging needs. Ford is clear on what was the most impactful aspect of the EX approach: leading with a holistic view in co-creating experiences in service of building trust, both internally and externally. As the company embarked on its work to develop the culture, they quickly realized that there were many elements that impacted the employee experience beyond the traditional HR functions and services. 'It was important to bring all of these elements together in a holistic way,' said Chateauvert. To deepen this, Ford looked at EX as operating in three distinct ways that were critical in adding ongoing value:

Create + Consult = Capability

- **Create:** There are some experiences that HR will continue to own, lead and deliver. Ford engages cross-functional teams for input, testing and implementation.

- **Consult:** There are some experiences that require partnership across the enterprise to co-create. This is where the responsibility for design and delivery is shared across the Culture Operating System and with other teams in the company.

- **Capability:** Through creating and consulting, Ford is building broader capabilities of teams to be human-centred, designed to implement exceptional experiences for our workforce within their own areas of responsibility.

A major factor in successful collaboration is about understanding how teams work together as a unit to elevate the experiences people have. The concept has proven to deliver some great results so far. The brand is not shy about using any methods, tools or technologies that improve the experience of work. Confidence in the team is high, with one senior leader saying: 'If I want something to be looked at in a cross-functional and human-centred way, then the Culture Operating System is the go-to team as they can solve the problems that no other teams or structures can.' This perhaps demonstrates the unique value that leaders and teams in the human and employee experience space can offer to senior executives, employees and businesses. This approach enables Ford to better serve employees and centre their attention on them. What is also noticeable is the bonds and relationships that exist between team members. They are all colleagues sitting in their own teams and specialisms, yet if they have a key impact on EX, they are assigned to the Culture Operating System. This type of human experience collaboration is hard to get right, but creating a shared internal (and straightforward) language, a shared way of measuring the EX and the right set of mechanisms within the operating system enables colleagues to feed ideas in to deepen and enrich the experience of work for all employees.

The clear emphasis placed on employee experience by the executive team, as well as the impact of improved experiences across the brand, has encouraged many colleagues to become key advocates for employee experience in a rapid fashion. Chateauvert said:

> One unique aspect of our employee experience is rooted in our history as a family company and culture. We have many multi-generation Ford employees who work here because they are proud of our company, our products and the role we play in our communities across the world. Employees regularly talk about our culture as a family and are proud of the challenges we've overcome together. Considering the size and global span of our company, this aspect of our culture uniquely contributes to employee experiences. Another aspect that might be unique for us is that the value of caring for each other, treating customers like family and doing the right thing for the world is consistently recognized, supported and messaged by our CEO Jim Farley, former CEO Jim Hackett and our Executive Chairman Bill Ford.

Ford's work on developing positive experiences for its workforce has encouraged the company to be even more human-centred in its approach. When challenges or issues arise that require a human-centred view, the Culture Operating System members and others that are relied on come through immediately, whether that's brainstorming new solutions, collecting research on what other organizations are doing, exploring employee sentiment or testing prototypes, as a central team it is fixated on human beings and their experiences.

'We're in the business of helping people connect the dots to the behaviours that lead to successful individual and business outcomes.' Chateauvert believes this is down to 'the connection points between people and teams that are fuelled by the shared vision of being the most trusted company and living Our Truths. Engaging our teams on this higher-level aspiration is a stronger motivator and enabler than we anticipated.' This work hasn't gone unnoticed, with positive polling, real-time feedback and survey results from employees confirming that the work has been very well received across the workforce and has made a noticeable difference in the business. The business has also reported that people are feeling high levels of pride in working for Ford. A sign that there is real human-centred momentum behind the brand is a recent change to retitle the Chief HR Officer role to Chief People and Employee Experiences Officer, which is another important and symbolic step in creating the world's most trusted brand.

If ever there was a time for human-centred leadership, that time is now. Managers are finding, certainly through our research, that managing with empathy, care and concern for the wellbeing of their teams is of critical importance in maintaining positive outcomes. We know from the success of remote organizations and teams that a remote way of working can be effective in practice. It just takes a little more thought around how best to set up and succeed. What practices are of most value? What communication rhythms work best for people? Are there any gaps in technology or equipment that need to be addressed? Are leaders visible, accessible and present for colleagues when they need them? Are managers truly listening and then following up with immediate actions? These are the important things during a crisis, but they are the key things to consider at any time. Netguru, a Poland-based software development business, is a great example in this regard. I spoke with the company's co-founder and executive chairman, Wiktor Schmidt, about how they grew their business to be one of the fastest growing in Europe – and they did this with a remote workforce, which now stands at around 700 employees. Being a remote-first company has certainly served Netguru well and Schmidt attributes this to the fact that it was in the DNA of its business model since inception. He said:

> The type of work Netguru does lends itself to virtual ways of working. A lot of the trends that COVID-19 accelerated, which include homeworking and digitalization, played to our strengths as a business from our first day so we were naturally able to communicate our unique values and proposition to the market.

From the outset, there was a clear understanding that to deliver a world-class business operation, the human experience, and indeed building trust between people, was going to be key to success. Schmidt said:

> We really tried to build a company where we would enjoy working. We wanted to work remotely from the very beginning. To do this, we, as founders or a leadership team, should trust our team in the way that we trust each other. There was never a tracking system focused on what our people are doing.

Schmidt is keen to point out that the brand has still had to evolve its working practices and communications approaches to better suit the team and workforce over time. 'It's a real privilege to be able to work in this way. Flexibility, trust and teamwork allow people to create an experience adjusted to their expectations. For us, remote working is our default mode.' Although a digital-first company, they do not force people to work from home. Schmidt said:

> Our motivation has been to enable choice in where people choose to work. Colleagues can work from home, or they can spend some of their week in the office. We do need physical spaces to facilitate company connection. Every three months there is something happening to bring the team together, whether a company retreat, team lunches or local get-togethers, and there is a lot of activity based on individual interests that enable colleagues to build their relationships.

All of that was moved online in response to the COVID-19 pandemic.

> There was some anxiety as we grew from 300 to 700 employees. People were saying that it felt like we were becoming a corporation with too much bureaucracy. There were too many people and you can't meet everyone. There's too much corporate bullshit. We're becoming less agile. The easy answer is always more bureaucracy, but that will be annoying to people.

Netguru was officially certified as B-Corp, which is a rigorous standard that certifies ethical and sustainable business practices and is a metric that enables the company to balance the needs of all stakeholders. The company has also accelerated work with its team to be more mindful of the mission, vision and values of the company and has started to articulate this in a stronger way through its internal and external communications. The future focus comes through strongly as the company plans beyond 10 years to create a business that lasts and continues to make an impact into the future.

CASE STUDY
GSK

With revenue of £34 billion and over 99,000 employees across 95 countries, GSK is a world-leading organization. At the peak of the COVID-19 pandemic, GSK announced a groundbreaking partnership with Sanofi to pioneer work around a vaccine for coronavirus. This was a company moving into uncharted territory to serve the urgent needs of humanity. As a client of my company, I have worked with GSK since 2019 and worked with its global EX team before, during and after COVID-19 began to place itself into a firm part of human life. It was a fascinating position to be in as the company responded to a major public health crisis and was working to transition to a hugely different business model.

Consistently regarded as one of the world's top companies and employers, there is a striking commitment to evolution, innovation and improvement at GSK. The commitment of its people to providing excellent experiences is abundantly clear with the scale of the investment in its employee experience work in recent years and its global leadership within the pharmaceutical industry. GSK, believing that a strong employee experience is critical to attract, retain and motivate the best people, launched a period of intense focus on the 'experience' work in 2018. The key themes within this were inclusion and diversity, health and wellbeing, and employee development. The primary aims, as one of the world's biggest employers, was to ensure that people were empowered to be themselves, feel good and keep growing at GSK.

Colleen Schuller, who served as vice-president of employee experience, led the global employee experience team at GSK during a period in which the pharma giant was named one of the top workplaces in the world, according to LinkedIn's Top Companies list. Trust was a unifying theme within the strategic and operational work to develop the experience of work. Schuller said:

> Our CEO, Emma Walmsley, set out a strategy, and priorities, to enable GSK to become the most innovative, best performing and trusted healthcare company. Trust is one of our three long-term priorities and is essential to how we deliver our purpose. One of our priority programmes under Trust is called Modern Employer, which is championed by our CEO and executive team and aims to create a differentiated work experience to engage our people and attract and retain great people for the future.

Creating a unique and differentiated employee experience

GSK is a company that recognizes that progress is delivered through continuous actions and experiences that deeply resonate within the workforce. These things are not just critical to the present environment, but are a major factor in trying to secure the future success of what is one of the world's longest established brands. Its importance to GSK is outlined by Schuller, who now heads up diversity and inclusion in the US: they are keen to connect the past with the future. She said:

> GSK has heritage back to 300 years and it became a critical need to modernize. We want to represent the modern world that we live, work and

compete in; this means creating an environment where people feel included, respected and empowered to do their very best work.

In the years ahead, we will continue to ask a lot of people, so in return we need to focus our efforts in supporting all employees to thrive – it's a two-way deal and must respond to a changing world and different expectations of the current and future workforce.

GSK is a company that needed little persuasion to see that crafting and shaping high-quality experiences in work is the right focus to build a pipeline of solid business results.

A new global EX team was established in early 2018 with a mandate to set the strategic priorities and create the infrastructure to create a great EX and lead the modern employer programme. The ultimate outcomes were centred around:

- increasing employee engagement;
- delivering a clear and differentiated external brand that attracts talent and is congruent to the 'Truth' of what it's like to work at GSK;
- improved organizational performance through a positive EX.

The company's purpose, which is to help people do more, feel better and live longer, has been connected to the updated employer value proposition, with the rallying call: 'Realizing our purpose starts with us, when we feel at our best we perform at our best... Be You, Feel Good and Keep Growing.' A huge part of this work was GSK's Truth. With the right articulation of the value proposition, this took hold across an organization of 100,000 people and was a defining lynchpin of the EX work, making it real, approachable and actionable across the global company. This – combined with GSK's values of transparency, respect for people, integrity and patient focus – created strong alignment throughout the organization and support services.

Getting closer to the human experience

When we think about employee experience in global corporations, a common misconception is that the EX team is vast and has unlimited resources. While investment is normally at the appropriate scale for companies with a 100,000-plus workforce, a lot of the ground work is done by a small but impactful team. It's important to point out that, certainly in our work, the experience of work is not about one function or another. It's about all functions working in service to the organization and its workforce. A global EX team, therefore, brings together a range of leaders, subject-matter experts and experience architects whose role is to get things done working with all stakeholders.

Structures can change and often. This is entirely normal and natural in the evolution of an organization and its shifting priorities. What underpins effective EX work at GSK is a shared and collective commitment to improving the holistic employee experience at multiple levels. A key example of these new ways of working was to have the global EX team lead on EX as the 'umbrella programme' and serving as the connector across inclusion and diversity, health and wellbeing, reward, WREF (real estate and workspaces), technology, learning and development, communications, corporate reputation, and people data and analytics. As Schuller points out, 'these functions did not report into the EX team,' which is often one of the primary structural approaches to leading an all-encompassing EX approach; from her perspective it was 'quite disruptive from an accountability and funding perspective'.

Setting the global standard in an authentic and contextualized way

There is no one-size-fits-all approach to employee experience. There are so many unique factors in play relating to the context, circumstances and objectives; it is far more effective to build an approach that works from within, though external advice, coaching and expertise can be helpful when dealing with specific challenges. It is work that has won recognition and plaudits the world over, and it is work that has required a great level of knowledge, skill and judgement to deliver. In many ways, it was structured in a way designed to drive accountability for outcomes. It is not the EX team's job to create a positive EX. They play a major role, like other support functions, but ultimately, the key here is that all GSK colleagues are aware of and play an active role in the brand's business and human success. The sheer scope of this work could have been daunting – a new EX strategy, a new global operating model and the related employer brand approach with key measures of success.

Indeed, the measures really indicate the depth and breadth of its commitment to people. Schuller said:

> In 2020, we now have a set of 20 minimum global standards across our D&I, health and wellbeing, and learning and development agenda that are endorsed by the executive team as mandatory across every market in which we operate, backed by a governance system. The goal here is to increase fairness, competitiveness and improve the impact of line managers.

Even at the outset of this focused period of development, GSK was getting ahead of the curve by clearly linking leader performance to the employee experience. In 2018, the company introduced 180-degree reviews for nearly 9,000 managers to help them improve based on feedback from their teams.

When we talk about the human experience, there is a clear opportunity to move beyond the labels and how we categorize our workforce by emphasizing the humanity within our companies. This is what world-class EX teams do very well. They know and understand that when we talk about any experience – brand, employee, customer, supplier or shareholder – it is the human element that is by far the most important common theme across all stakeholder groups. In turn, then, this focus for leaders is inspired and, unfortunately, still relatively progressive within the broader business world. When we think of our workplaces as communities filled with human beings, it changes how we lead, develop and grow.

Delivering a diverse human organization

There is a feeling and a position at GSK that a robust inclusion and diversity approach helps deliver the best outcomes for every human being. Schuller said:

> Not only is it the right thing to do, but it also leads to business success, unleashing the potential of the differing knowledge, experiences and styles of our people, enhancing our ability to respond to the needs of the patients and consumers that we serve.

One of the goals of the company is to be recognized in global LGBT+ indices. In 2019 and 2020, LGBT+ rights group Stonewall recognized GSK in its Top Global Employers list. In the UK, Stonewall also named the employee resource group for LGBT+ employees and allies as the best in the UK. At a country level, GSK has won awards such as Forbes 2020 Best Employers for Diversity, Best Employer for Women, Working Mother Media 100 Best Company, Disability: In Best Place to Work for Disability Inclusion.

It is this firm commitment and the accolades that relate to it that sends a strong signal to prospective and existing staff that GSK takes this seriously and they can trust that GSK is being built for everyone. GSK has four diversity councils (covering gender, ethnicity, LGBT+ and disability). Each council is chaired by members of the corporate executive team and members comprise senior leaders from across the company, as well as representatives from employee resource groups.

GSK doesn't shy away from the emotionally charged moments that often light up the human experience on the outside of the company. In 2020, and for the first time in the US, GSK hosted a pan-US business unit discussion called 'Let's Listen' on the topic of race and ethnicity – hearing personal stories from black employees about their experiences. With over 5,600 employees together on a Webex with the US senior leadership team, this moment in society was an opportunity for GSK to deepen conversations that mattered to people. In addition, the company also surveyed people in advance with four questions to understand how people are feeling, what do they personally want to focus on, and advice for what GSK can do to lead in this area. There were over 1,400 responses and senior leaders shared the themes/quotes from the questions and made commitments about what would happen next. The feedback was phenomenal; as a direct result, this will be continued within the business over the long term.

The percentage of women in management has continued to rise at GSK. In 2019, women represented 47 per cent of all management roles (45 per cent in 2018) and 36 per cent of senior management roles – VP and above – up from 33 per cent in 2018. The latest Hampton-Alexander Review of FTSE 100 companies found that GSK had the third highest proportion of women on the board (an increase from sixth in 2018), with 45.5 per cent female representation. It also found that the company had exceeded the target of 33 per cent women on the board and in the direct reports to the corporate executive team. Gender balance is being improved by encouraging and supporting more women to develop as leaders. In 2019, the company provided 130 high-performing female managers with coaching and support through its Accelerating Difference programme. GSK is also recruiting and supporting women early in their careers, with women representing 38 per cent of its apprentices and 58 per cent of its graduates in 2019. As a result of these efforts to develop female employees during the year, three women from GSK were included in the Women's Engineering Society Top 50 Women in Engineering – current and former apprentices – and GSK India was named by Avtar as among the best companies for women to work.

GSK is a prime example of how EX is delivered as a collective endeavour. There has been a strong investment in EX roles and leadership positions to advance the concept strongly across all parts of the business, and as this has evolved there has been a big push to localize programmes and approaches and build them directly into business divisions to maximize and broaden the impact of this excellent EX work. In all the available internal and external research, what really stands out about GSK is that it is a purpose- and relationship-centric organization that is dialling up a focus on innovation, performance and trust, as Schuller nicely summarizes. In effect, being purpose-led and performance-driven connects people to the right things – personal and company growth.

GSK's employee experience is a major differentiator and represents a global promise to help its people: *Be You, Feel Good and Keep Growing.* This is underpinned by great managers and technology, and the agenda is driven by the corporate executive team. This meets some amazingly active grassroots activity at a local level to bring it to life. GSK's brand externally demonstrated improvement as measured by a collective index. This assesses performance across social platforms including Glassdoor, LinkedIn and Twitter. The company's engagement scores, which was a major measure in 2018, are at 10-year highs. This is telling. To deliver the incredible engagement results, they focused on humans and experiences first.

Building an organization for the whole human experience

It has often been a complete revelation for companies to consider people as humans rather numbers. It is a change or shift that does not happen overnight. It happens through experiences. What's important to consider within our work is the notion of home life and work life. We've already discussed the accelerated convergence of these two major aspects of human life. The question is: how do companies navigate the more sensitive (and perhaps controversial) aspects of our experience? Typically, there have been areas of the human experience that organizations don't want to go anywhere near. Namely, we can highlight politics, religion, spirituality and societal issues as examples that companies would prefer to keep separate. For good reason, this has been the easy choice. Keep that stuff away from a *professional* organization to keep people focused on delivering their business objectives.

Certainly, companies have never wanted to intentionally fan the flames of division within the workplace or directly sow any seeds that could spill over and damage their external reputation and business standing. The cautious and risk-averse approach has won out. The irony here is that those that try to do this – to keep a lid on the human experience – are often the ones that suffer in the end. Their lack of response, support and advocacy for something (one way or another) can, at times, be deafening to people within the workforce. It's a silence that is losing its appeal. Doing nothing used to be the safe bet, but no more. There is a realization dawning in corporate HQs that they need to get out ahead of issues and take every opportunity they can to reinforce their values, principles and, increasingly, the position a company takes on societal issues. It is not a good look to do nothing or represent a neutral view anymore, but how do companies organize themselves around deeper human topics like character, truth, justice and happiness? One leading company is challenging the world to take a different view on what an organization is and what an organization does.

CASE STUDY

Installing the truth at FOTILE to drive innovation and happiness

In my research for this book, I had the opportunity to spend time with Mao Zhongqun, Chairman and President of FOTILE Kitchenware Co. Ltd. (FOTILE), which is one of China's most admired and respected brands. Mao shared his business leadership philosophy with me in some detail. Business to Mao is about a close connection with the truth (what people stand for and what they believe in) and having a positive impact in society. Business is a vehicle to create happiness for customers and their families. If that happens, and innovation remains constant, business will grow and succeed.

Develop a great human-led enterprise

Role-modelling values is always a critical part of how the business is led and how it selects future leaders. It's not just about integrity. FOTILE is a business rooted in the truth. It is an inescapable part of its business model and the method that enables it to build strong relationships within the workforce. Mao believes that the company's expansion into new and international markets will pose no problems for a company based on a deep commitment to unique Chinese and Confucian practices. 'There is only one Truth. We build our culture based on the universal truth. It is not a problem for us to take our culture, which is based on Chinese philosophy, to the West,' said Mao.

The humanity function – combining people and culture to drive growth

This truth is so important when it comes to developing the organization that Mao refuses to have a chief people officer or even an HR function. Mao personally oversees and leads the work on people, culture and employee experience from his position as CEO. FOTILE has opted to have a people and culture team to best represent their focus in this regard. Interestingly, in Chinese, when you combine the characters of 'people' and 'culture', you get the word 'humanity'. This offers perfect alignment with FOTILE's work to grow people and the brand and to live their truth every day.

In FOTILE's case, the truth is clear:

> FOTILE has its own mission, vision and core values and every aspect of the business operation is driven by these. This is what drives all company progress. FOTILE's vision and core values have evolved and changed since its establishment. Now, our mission is 'For the Happiness of Hundreds of Millions of Families.' FOTILE's vision is to be a great enterprise. FOTILE's core value is the Triunity of Quality of Character, Enterprise and Products. We have made corporate strategic planning and implementation based on these mission, vision and core values since day one.

A great organization is truly made from different ingredients and a different understanding of the world. FOTILE's ultimate vision is its long-term goal to become a great enterprise. Every action is lined up to deliver that. 'A great enterprise is not only an economic entity that fulfils the needs of the customers but also a social entity that proactively takes corporate social responsibilities,' said Mao. FOTILE's corporate social responsibilities include continuously guiding people towards having a positive impact in the world, promoting the true, the good and the beauty of human society.

The characteristics of a great enterprise

In Mao's view, a great enterprise has four characteristics: clients achieve harmony, employees achieve growth, society achieves justice and development is sustainable. When all these four things are occurring in a consistent manner, the organization is serving humanity in the most powerful of ways:

- *Clients achieve harmony:* Heart of Kindness directs the company's brand of innovation. Clients achieve harmony by experiencing quality products that enhance life. There is a purity about the design process and what goes into it. Equally, it is about the kind thoughts that shape and sculpt each of their innovations and products. The first thought is kindness towards the customer and helping them feel and experience a sense of harmony when using or buying products. Thinking about products in this way – as life-enhancers – is an insightful notion. Products serve their purpose by helping us serve ours. It is a profound but practical way of building a company focused on high quality.

- *Employees achieve growth:* FOTILE promotes happy growth and advancement. This means employees acquire both physical and spiritual growth as well as career and life development. There are four steps to achieve this. First, influence employees by caring; second, nurture employees through education; third, consolidate the regulations (the structure/system contains education of civil manners and rules, rules of proper behaviours as well as policies and incentives); fourth, strengthen employees' professional skills. The first three steps focus on employees' character development and the fourth step emphasizes professional skill and management development. In other words, a good employee shall have both a good character and good management/professional competences.

- *Society achieves justice:* This refers to corporate social responsibility, which is a broad concept in FOTILE. There are four components of the corporate social responsibilities. First, legal responsibilities: taking legal responsibilities is a company's fundamental responsibility. Second, development responsibilities: an enterprise needs to have healthy development. On one hand, a company shall provide employment positions and solve the societal problem related to unemployment. On the other hand, a company shall be responsible for its customers. Third, moral responsibilities: a company needs to take good care of all stakeholders, such as employees and customers. Fourth, philanthropy responsibilities: at FOTILE examples of philanthropy activities include propagation of culture and corporate support for community development and education.

- *Development is sustainable:* The above three components need to combine with good business development. Business development and management are the basic competences of a company, helping the company to grow sustainably. There are four management components: strategic management, operational management, humanistic management and risk management. For each component, there is a corresponding implementation system.

A human-centred organization with human-centred leadership

Is FOTILE a human-centred company? Mao is certain it is. 'I think it is. What is a human-centred company? Management at FOTILE are grounded in human-centricity, and humans are driven by heart. A human-centred company is built on the spiritual advancement/growth of the humans in the company,' said Mao.

FOTILE is a company with a really strong identity, but how can this type of philosophy effectively scale into different cultures and markets? It's a question that Mao has considered extensively as FOTILE seeks to grow even further beyond its China homeland:

> We do not only look at the Chinese culture but also the world culture. We found two common grounds in the culture of the world. The first common ground is love. Across all countries and cultures, love is a common driving force. Second, people in all countries pursue happiness. We start out based on these two common grounds – love and happiness – and provide our employees with happiness, education and an experience that enables them to fulfil these deep human needs.

This idea is taken very literally as FOTILE often holds mass wedding ceremonies for its employees who want to celebrate their love in that way. Such a thing would be unheard of in the corporate world, yet FOTILE has blended the human and employee experience to the point where it is not out of the ordinary for people to want to celebrate such an important occasion with the people they work with.

Indeed, this represents the convergence of work, life and spirituality. This is evidence of an organization operating with the total human experience in mind while challenging traditional stereotypes of what an organization should and could be. While Confucianism has been the predominant theme for this Chinese company, it has been a very powerful concept to promote understanding, learning and knowledge development about a person's own beliefs. To explore them, nurture them and to honour them in this powerful way within a company is rare and unique. This goes well beyond the corporate 'norm' and extends into the very nature of people's existence. While materialism and consumerism have often risen to fill gaps within people's pursuit of happiness and meaning, this approach seems quite bluntly to be turning things back to focus on basic character development and rounded human growth. In my previous research, I found that employee experience is a holistic and human construct. To deliver strong outcomes, companies need to think and act with the whole company, society and person in mind, and Mao is keen to reinforce this.

Five 'One' practices within the human experience at FOTILE

Through the Five 'One' practices, Mao helps his company deeply embed an approach that has consistently delivered positive business and human outcomes. It is important to make a resolution. A resolution tells us where we go and develop. Following one's resolution, employees make the effort to develop themselves as people. FOTILE adopts two Chinese cultural routes to develop employees. The first route helps employees understand the truth – what is the truth of life, what is truth in essence and what is the meaning and value of life? One learns about the truth by reading classic books. The second route focuses on character development, that is, be inclined to the goodness and keep away from the evil. While one learns about the truth by reading a classic book, the other three 'One' practices help employees to be inclined to the goodness and keep away from the evil. Correcting a mistake keeps employees away from the evil. The mistake derives from our selfish desire, which is in nature bad. To be inclined to the goodness, employees are encouraged to practise a filial piety and do one good deed daily.

> We help our employees to focus on developing good thinking and eliminating the bad, we help them to contain their egos. Different people are at different spiritual levels. In the Confucian ideology, there are five types of people: the mediocre human who has no experience of spiritual practices, the scholar who has some spiritual practices, the gentleman, the sage and finally the egoless saint who is at the highest spiritual level. I remember President Xi said: 'I am ready to give up the self to serve the people.'

This is a selfless approach. In 2020, President Xi of China talked about people-centred philosophy and people-centred development. FOTILE appears to be a template for the people-centred company within the Chinese economy. It has deeply integrated the culture of China into its business at all levels.

'We influence employees by caring,' Mao said. Nurturing employees through education, Chinese employees study Chinese culture, societal and company regulations, and deepen their professional skills within their craft. A precondition of employee happiness is to be physically healthy. At FOTILE, employees are encouraged to study Chinese medicine. By studying Chinese medicine, employees become more physically healthy. Additionally, employee care shall emphasize developing a sense of safety, sense of belonging, sense of esteem and sense of self-achievement. 'In FOTILE we provide holistic employee experience through a variety of employee care initiatives,' said Mao. For example, the company offers employees about 50 employee benefits/welfares. All FOTILE employees who have worked in FOTILE for a minimum of two years are automatically entitled to hold stocks in the company. Employees can obtain bonuses without paying for the stocks. In FOTILE each employee needs to have a Five 'One' practices plan. Managers must put the Five 'Ones' on the wall and hold regular sharing and reflection sessions to review their five 'One' practices.

Holistic and transcendental development

We foster employees' holistic development, which goes beyond employee satisfaction rate. Although employee satisfaction with the company is one aspect we look at, we do not simply satisfy employees' low-end needs. We strive to help employees develop high-end needs, that is whether they can gain holistic personal development.

This even goes beyond self-actualization and is more transcendental in its approach:

I mentioned employees' high-end and low-end needs. We all know the five levels of Maslow's hierarchy of needs. I read some learning materials. It was said that Maslow developed the sixth level of his needs model in his late age. This sixth level is 'self-transcendence', which is a concept fitting closely with the Chinese culture. From the Chinese cultural perspective, self-actualization, the fifth and highest level in the original Maslow model, is serving the interests of the self, so it is ego-driven/self-centred. The sixth level, 'transcendence', emphasizes that employees shall contain the ego and pursue a transcendent self. This is what we pursue, and self-transcendence is a very important cultural element in FOTILE.

A company talking about transcendence – not just talking about it, but placing it as a high priority within the employee experience – is not normal and is another reason why FOTILE is a unique company. The way they have done this is also impressive. They went back in time to create the company of the future. They've renewed and refreshed the notion of what a company is and the role it plays in the development of people holistically. Many companies would shy away from holistic development because it takes you into traditionally complex and complicated areas, such as spirituality. In an economy that has by and large created 'leave your spirituality at the door' corporate cultures, it is intriguing to find companies willing to stand by deeply held beliefs.

We've discussed that organizations, in reality, are vehicles for human growth. If people grow in strong ways, companies will experience the benefits directly through increased performance and business outcomes. Is this very complicated to deliver in practice? Mao believes it isn't. Indeed, FOTILE has developed practices that tap into the human spirit:

We use a very simple and effective approach – the Five 'One' practices for both Chinese and international employees. The Five 'One' practices are: make one resolution, read one classic book, correct one mistake, practise one filial piety (which is an important Chinese cultural value and is a virtue of respect for one's parents, elders and ancestors) and do one good deed daily. Chinese employees read Chinese traditional classic books and foreign employees can read classic books from their own countries.

Up to now, this Five 'One' approach has been highly recognized nationally and globally, and I can see why. It taps into the human experience in a way that many organizations can't or won't. It's an approach that is helping FOTILE deliver incredible growth and business performance. It is now the number-one kitchen appliance brand in Asia.

Summary: delivering world-class human experiences at work

What does a world-class experience in work look like? Well, that's the great aspect to this exciting new approach to developing organizations – it's anything we, collectively, as workers and organizations, determine it is. It's the value we place on things internally and externally, and what companies consider to be of most importance to themselves. Every company is unique, and how they go about delivering an organization fit for the human experience is entirely dependent on co-creation with their own workforces rather than best practices from anywhere else. In this sense, the examples and practices I share are merely to demonstrate the depth and breadth of the commitment to leading world-class organizations, and some of the unique practices that form part of that approach. These are, in many ways, signposts for inspiration or simple indicators that companies do not need to accept established thought or the status quo. They can diverge in a way that differentiates and is distinctive in the marketplace as well as the world generally. The organization is one of the most powerful ways to change the world and they are statements of intent. What they do and how they do it is their signature in the world. It underlines their progress and rubber-stamps their progress. Whatever path they choose is up to them, and the best judges as to whether that path is successful or not are their workforces and customers.

- Leading companies are leveraging human-centred thinking, data and dynamic team approaches to reshape their organizations in radical and progressive ways.

- Now is the time to reflect on and review business models and approaches to determine if they are really serving the human experience at work.

- Consider how deeply organizations can go in developing their connection with the workforce and their people. How can you create experiences that transcend the workplace to support growth and performance outcomes?

- Organizations are using their resources wisely to better serve people in work. There is a definite uptick in continuous listening, feedback and action loops. Companies are taking the whole experience much more seriously and demonstrating real empathy in the experience they design with and for their workforces.

- Beyond the organization, companies are extending their influence and impact into areas of human life that they can effectively enhance and add value to.

- Organizations are rightly placing a high value on building trust within their business. This involves greater transparency and authenticity, and a stronger commitment to living their truth on the inside and outside of the organization.

05

Reset, refresh and relaunch work around life

Historically, organizations have formed purely as a vehicle to execute and operationalize an idea at scale to create value and profit for investors and owners. It is a relatively straightforward concept that is applied across the economy every day. The real challenge for any organization though is to optimize and get the strongest performance out of the system, both collectively and individually. This is where it traditionally gets tricky. On paper, it sounds easy. In practice, it is often more complicated than people anticipate. A simple change or communication can generate a wave of emotional responses from employees. A simple act can turn employees against a business. The clash of ideas, values and motivations between employees is a constant tightrope to walk in a delicate internal organizational dance. Mutiny and rebellion are never far away, but similarly, achievement and greatness remain constantly in reach if organizations learn how to harness the potential of every stakeholder. It is at this point where we start to consider the role of organization in our lives. It is more than the 9–5, five-day work week. It has a profound impact on every human being. There is now a widespread acknowledgement that work and life have converged in such a way that hasn't happened in our collective memory: the clear line between these two aspects of life has been blurred, perhaps irreversibly. Certainly, knowledge workers have had no choice but to embrace homeworking and take more responsibility for their own working lives and the design of them.

Building organizations around life and moments

If we are to make genuine and impactful efforts on the human experience, there needs to be an almost carte blanche approach to organizational design. Nothing is off limits. As organizational leaders, we need to answer a few fundamental questions at all times throughout the growth journey:

1 Is the organization set up to serve its people?

2 Do we build our companies in a way that helps deliver exceptional employee and human experiences?

3 Are all aspects of working (and human) life considered in the leadership of the business?

Answering these questions will often surface some uncomfortable truths. It is difficult to look at the structures and hierarchies we see as commonplace today as a human-centred utopia of creativity, intelligence and higher consciousness. The alternative is often true and deliberately led. Companies feel like big, impersonal and disjointed groupings of people. Creating a sense of belief and belonging within that archetypal organization set-up is a serious challenge and ongoing concern to all company stakeholders. What is happening is not only a big reset in the world of work, but also a refresh and relaunch of the modern organization.

As indicated in Figure 5.1, there are certain elements being significantly reset within business. Organizations start this process by examining the key set-up of their companies, such as the types of teams they have, the structures in place, the predominant mindset of colleagues in those teams and structures, the underpinning technology being used to support the workforce, and key elements of organizational and brand design such as mission and values. These elements go through a big reset in terms of getting the organization to a place where leaders and support functions are best positioned and able to serve the needs of the human experience at work. Getting this reset right then enables a company to refresh and upgrade all manner of policies, processes, workforce journeys and moments of truth/moments that matter. What this creates, by design, is a whole

FIGURE 5.1   Reset, refresh and relaunch

Reset	Refresh	Relaunch
Teams, structures, mindsets, capabilities, technology, values, mission	Policies, processes, practices, journeys, moments	Ways of working, experiences, relationships
Ongoing real-time data and analytics		

© Ben Whitter, HEX Organization Ltd

new approach and way of working across an organization with an emphasis on human-centricity, collaboration and creativity to deliver strong and aligned outcomes. Supported by ongoing, continuous and real-time data, organizations are starting to more accurately target and build high-quality experiences that matter most to people rather than hurtling down a corporate and company-centric dead-end that develops products or services that have little or no impact. If our starting position focuses on human beings, everything that follows becomes much more valuable, meaningful and impactful.

The great human shift within organizations

A human-centred brand just doesn't happen overnight. It is a serious bet from executive teams and involves resetting many aspects of the organization. This means that fresh eyes will need to look over the big aspects that will need to change to help facilitate a closer connection to people. Refreshing the business practices and policies that are not delivering on the human experience will be an early priority, as will relaunching newly configured and co-designed experiences in work. In effect, the overarching focus is to reset, refresh and relaunch the relationship that an organization has with its people. It is a serious undertaking, and in large part, is a collective effort to build high-performing human experiences. Because this is what the human experience requires – an unyielding commitment to collaboration and co-creation across functional lines. In practice, this means that colleagues should be prepared to confront any sacred cows or elephants in the room that are contributing to any gaps between the workforce and the brand. In the past, these have been avoided in favour of work that is perhaps easier to operationalize. A constant cycle of going after quick wins will not be healthy in the long term when leading projects internally. Instead of quick wins, we should, in the context of the human experience, be going for big, bold and decisive wins. Every experience has the possibility to become something more – to mean something more – and this is where the work gets seriously interesting. There is nothing more satisfying than taking a dated process or experience and transforming it into something that resonates with people and delivers better results. The feedback is instant, and the difference is immediate. This is not simply focused on business performance, but rather, business is also concerned about performance outcomes holistically given the profound impact life has on human performance at work. It is puzzling that so little attention is directed to serve the whole human experience.

Life issues are business issues

A well-rounded experience in work will cater to the human moments. Whatever the life event, businesses are increasingly considering how they can support them. Moving to a new house, having a baby, family issues, financial milestones, health concerns – these, and many more besides, impact on human performance. If they are important to the person, they should be important to the company. It's that simple. Organizations need to be all-in and supporting the total human being and all their needs.

It can be wonderful to see, witness and experience organizations shifting to the human experience, but at the same time, it can be quite disheartening to see progressive individuals and corporations continue to reinforce the idea of HR, which traditionally has only concerned itself with people in their role as employees and workers. This does not deliver a well-rounded, balanced and holistic service. If a company wishes to bring in a new era of human-centricity, it will need to advance a stronger position even if that risks upsetting the status quo. This is understandable, given the vested interests in maintaining HR as a concept; there is a calculated ignorance of what people tell us every day and this will ultimately lead to the profession's undoing, in my opinion. The voluntary evolution of HR must gather pace and human experience feels like the right idea at the right time. Until some of the major players globally embrace a different approach, the odds will continue to favour the incumbent HR model and all the mistrust it brings.

Holding on to this human spirit even through massively challenging times may sound hard, yet for many leadership teams it is a natural thing to do. Every crisis or challenge is another opportunity to reinforce what is valued, and it can be incredibly powerful and inspiring to witness acts and deeds in this regard. Alongside other members of the C-suite, Doug Thompson, the COO at Texas Roadhouse, gave up his entire base salary and bonuses until 2021 to support his front-line workers during the COVID-19 pandemic. This followed an earlier announcement from CEO Kent Taylor, who took a stand in supporting his people at the outset of the crisis (Cawthon, 2020). Values meeting actions. When the crisis came, this company became even more people-centred. 'I have always said we are a people-first company that just happens to serve steaks. Giving up my salary is the least I could do to show my commitment to that belief. This is my family,' said Taylor. We begin to truly know our companies and organizations in the everyday details and by observing their reactions to inevitable challenges that will present in the human and business growth journey.

Leading the human experience

The leadership versus management argument in business is a futile one. Our organizations need both. There are various parts of the company that can be managed through a consistent and established status quo. They are being managed in a way that works for people and the business. That is a given. In stating that, management without innovation and advancement is a cost too many businesses have to bear. The status quo remains because it does the job and is an effective way of doing things. This doesn't necessarily mean it is the most impactful way of doing things – just that it's effective or there is a need to manage something. To help navigate the human experience, many companies are viewing the human journey in work as something that needs to be managed actively. In this sense, the routine practices surround people and experience analytics, technology and user experience methodologies. In effect, there is a system in place that can be bought or built to help leaders and professionals manage journeys in work and improvements to them through real-time data and insights. In a lot of cases, it's a fancy way of saying surveys and actions. In a smaller number of cases, it means a holistic and sophisticated approach to governing, shaping and using data to make predictions about human behaviour. If you change one experience in work, or one part of the employee journey, what impact does it have? How can this be leveraged fully for the individual and the company? The corporate world loves to have things under control and managed, yet there is a simple reality to keep in mind. It is not the data that counts; it's the actions and outcomes it drives.

Working with global clients, I have seen first-hand what is required to effect real transformation and change within large and complicated businesses. Many of the lessons apply equally to businesses across all sectors. To accelerate positive outcomes, we need to think different and be different in our approach to developing the experience of work. Over many years of work on employee experience, mindset is a consistent theme within successful projects and work. The mindset of the practitioners, leaders and employees within an organization is fundamentally important and it's why we integrate its development throughout programmes and projects. The reality is that mindset evolves through experiences. It fuels the focus, energy and actions from day one. It shapes and determines every outcome. For me, it remains the most important part of any project. Getting this right at the pre-hire stage is critical or correcting it within the employee journey is going to be crucial. What is the optimum mindset and the capabilities that go alongside it? Through observation, there are a number of things that stand out from the practitioners we work with. To start with, there is a high and underlying commitment to creating what we have defined as a HEX organization. This comes with a prerequisite and predominant focus on driving improvements across all aspects of the business through the overarching approach to business development – in short, humans, experiences and their connection to the business. These are some of the capabilities that have been evidenced – it's a very different way of leading and being within the business – they are HEX accelerators, and they come with a unique set of skills, attributes and characteristics.

- **Co-creators** – This is the line of thinking that is pre-eminent within practitioners working on the human experience. They are merely co-creators of the experience. Employees, workers and all stakeholders within a business have equal roles to play. They are not solely responsible for outcomes. The team is. This is a collective endeavour and this shines through in their approach to collaboration across services, functions and organization charts.

- **Holistic leaders** – The ability to take actions across the whole rather than just the parts is one of the biggest advantages to their psychological make-up. This takes practice and dedication. It is more than thinking strategically. It's about connecting things across a business – thinking about the whole organization and the whole person. Being a holistic leader and thinker enables them to go beyond their functions and roles to create wider and sustained impact through the work and projects they deliver.

- **Deep listeners** – Reflection is a huge part of their mindset – reflecting on the good and the bad to help determine the right course of action. Yet, it is the listening stage where they come into their own. They listen (and hear) at a level beyond most professionals. Whether one-to-one or through organizational listening exercises, they find ways to get to the heart of issues and successes so that they can be avoided or replicated at greater scale and with greater impact. They are often the last person to speak, but the first one to really listen to what's being said. A proactive response follows as they seek to promote positive subconscious behaviours.

- **Empathetic enablers** – In the age of the experience economy, empathy is gold and they have it in abundance. It is integrated within all aspects of their work with people. Taking this further, they also build this into design approaches and methodologies that are used by leaders at all levels. If empathy within a business can be improved or levelled up, they will be there finding the ways to make that happen. It's that important.

- **Principled** – They will fight for what they believe in. It may not be popular, but their moral compass is centred on doing the right thing by people. This often comes with career risks. Speaking their truth and going against the corporate tide of opinion is not for everyone, but they cannot perform at their best if their principles have been compromised. Invariably, these principles are associated with an unyielding commitment to helping and supporting the people around them.

- **Adaptable pragmatists** – It's not about resilience. It's about adapting to the conditions and circumstances that surround them. They are confidently practical and realistic in their approach. Idealism is evident, but they can move with and balance competing priorities and stakeholders to make tangible progress. Their pragmatism is often strategic and tactical to keep momentum and energy high in projects.

- **Truth-seekers** – Moments of truth are littered throughout the organization and employee journeys in work. These are the moments where a company's purpose, mission and values come together beautifully to create an emotional impact on people. Alternatively, they can crush efforts to establish a strong relationship with people because these moments have not been given the attention and respect they deserve. Personally and professionally, this is often a capability that is underutilized within support functions – the capability to lead by connecting to and amplifying the truth of a business. People want to believe in themselves. Organizations want their people to believe in them. Seeking out the truth and how it is experienced on an everyday basis is what great leadership looks like. Anything getting in the way of the truth and people is sought out and positively challenged.

- **Critical thinkers** – Fixing things is their prevailing modus operandi. They are independent in thought, question things at a deeper level than most, and do not tolerate complacency. Regardless of success, they continually return to critique the organization on what could be improved and elevated further to improve the human experience at work. Judgement matters here a lot. I spoke with one of the top global data scientists at Uber, Mert Bay, who concluded the same. No matter how sophisticated the approach, data is still all about people, their decisions and their actions. It is the way we interpret and utilize information to deliver better outcomes across an organization that helps us achieve more. This requires people to step back and think deeply about how one thing connects to another, and to critically examine the relationships and experiences that people have within the context of a brand and company.

- **Can-do professional** – To guard against cynicism, they maintain a positive and optimistic frame of reference. Rather than focusing on what they don't have or what they can't do, they consistently come back to a solution-focused approach. There are problems to be solved and they are scanning for options and choices to get the job done. The professional aspect of this is connected to their integrity and the high levels of trust they build within their relationships.

- **Compassionate communicators** – What is evident from working with so many experience-driven leaders is that their entire message is often weaved into one of compassion for the human condition. This can be defined as 'using a caring force to change ourselves and the world', and can be associated with an approach built on protecting, motivating and providing in the way they act in the outside world (Neff and Germer, 2018). Businesses that care are filled with people who care and lead with compassion.

- **Experimenters** – They are usually not psychologists and data scientists by trade, but they do embrace many aspects of these roles in an organizational sense. Certainly, if they are in leadership positions, there will be a strong presence of colleagues whose work revolves around data and human psychology. This supports work to predict human behaviour and address any needs before they arise through experimentation and iterative design. People are not lab rats, though – there is always positive intent behind real-world experiments to improve and develop strong, experience-led programmes, policies and practices. Conversely, this is not nor will it ever be about tracking people or performance management by stealth, which contravenes many of the principles they stand for within their pro-human approach.

- **Renegades!** – The status quo is not for them. They are about human progress and human futures. They think constantly about the next iteration, the next step, the next improvement to the organization and the experiences taking place within it.

What we have just discussed, no doubt, is a proposal for the profile of a human experience leader. This, to me, describes a differentiated business professional and leader. Whether this person comes from a background in HR, IT, estates, marketing or any other business function is beside the point. What matters most is that they exhibit this type of mindset and the characteristics that are associated with it.

Ideally, leaders can build their teams with this in mind from the get-go, yet it may not always be realistic to do so. The fact is that practitioners will be on their own journey to understand and connect more thoughtfully to all that it is to be human and how that relates to the workplace. There will be major challenges and obstacles to overcome in thinking and the more practical aspects of delivering good. This is where coaching can help people stay on track and embrace their experiences of operating in this new and redefined way. We can't just say: think about humans now and expect people to just get on with it. It's not something that comes easily to people. Telling people to lead and act with empathy is easy; actually doing it, and in an effective way, is hard. This is why I encourage real-time coaching within any project or approach to improve the human and employee experience. As people move through their work and challenges, we can offer safe spaces for teams and people to come together to experience them from a whole new angle with fresh feedback on what works well and what doesn't. In effect, everything becomes a learning and growth experience, so coaching can dramatically improve outcomes in this regard. The difference is that the learning is tied indefinitely to real work, real objectives and real outcomes. No more abstract learning is the key. In-context and in-challenge learning is far more effective within experience design work.

Indeed, in leadership terms, we are looking to see how people are shaping up when it comes to this progressive and human-centred mindset. We can only really learn this through real-time data, outcomes and insights. Everything that we are as a practitioner and leader shines through in the actual work that is being done – how well it is led, how people respond and how results get delivered.

Breaking old habits to amplify brand impact

The experience of work is less about the new stuff, but more about the way companies address the old stuff – the old way of viewing and doing things to create a viable and scalable business. The work of HR of the past represented many things, but it never really represented what matters most within the human experience, and it often does more to weaken the connection to the brand. But why is that?

Like companies, we have a tendency to get stuck in our behavioural patterns, habits, routines. When change is required, it is rarely embraced. It is just too difficult at times to break our cycles and do things differently. Our outcomes remain unchanged. We don't learn. This has been the way for companies too. It has been an exceedingly slow march towards digitalization, and it has been a frustratingly slow saunter towards greater human-centricity within companies. Even the more progressive companies have blind spots in this regard. Gymshark, one of the UK's fastest growing companies, recently recruited for an HR people partner. There was such a disconnect between what the brand espouses and the advertised job description that several people who were customers and fans of the brand took it upon themselves to call them out on social media. The stinging, but very valid, feedback criticized Gymshark for writing their job descriptions in a way that didn't reflect the progressive nature of their brand. Indeed, the job description was a very typical and perfunctory HR template that was loaded with corporate jargon and business speak. In short, the very inhuman and impersonal corporate language that Gymshark has been so careful to avoid in its marketing and growth story so far had managed to work its way into the brand via the HR function. The feedback, which was shared publicly online, was taken very seriously and the brand vowed to put it right. This is a very good reminder and example that support functions are there to serve people and the brand. It is also another stark warning that HR functions, though well intentioned, can be the source of many disconnects between people and the brand, and they may not even be aware of how much damage they are doing on the inside and outside of the business. One reason this occurs is that people work from what they know and the routine habits they have, rather than from what they know about a brand and how it communicates in the world. There has also been a fear there somewhere – a deep and long-lasting one that wants to protect companies from the risk of dealing with the full human with all its flaws, which generates a need to stay in safe territory. We are emotional sometimes. We can be unpredictably temperamental. We can be rebels and mavericks. Yet, without all those human characteristics, there is no prospect of progress, no chance for betterment, no hope for the world. This is why there is an inclination to support those doing bold and different things, because at our very best, we are all unique beings and entities, and this should be celebrated across all policies, practices and company narratives.

The previous example may appear to be a critique of Gymshark, but in actual fact, it is lavish praise. They have created a brand so strong that its consumers and workforce want to protect it and will hold it to account when it strays from its central brand messages and identity. This, as an outcome, is performance of the highest order and will go some way to sustaining long-lasting growth plans. Creating something people can believe in is not always pretty. From the outside looking in, it may not always be palatable, yet we need companies that are challenging us to think about what is possible for humanity. These types of companies often require some form of sacrifice and suffering along the way. Yet, isn't that true for us as human beings too? If we want something badly enough, we must prioritize it in our minds and in our hearts. We will not be watching the clock when we are geared up to create something that changes the world, changes our markets and changes our future.

Co-creating at the edges of work

This often creates an intensity and contradiction within business. We celebrate companies that push us forward and we rightly condemn them when they get things wrong. When they push themselves and their workers too far, we hold them to account. I still view this as co-creation. It's the type of co-creation in the public – on social media and in the headlines – that most sensible companies would wish to avoid, but it is co-creation nonetheless: the workforce responding to things that don't 'feel' right and taking actions to respond to it. The level of employee and workforce activism has seen a spike in recent years. Calling in the anti-union consultants is a poor move that reflects badly on many employers, including several deemed to be more progressive in their business approach. It's an indicator that they are losing their way. Why? Because a huge part of the human experience is to attach ourselves to things that we believe in and belong to. If we care, we will fight for those things. We will be activated to stand for them and their ideals in society and the world.

Is activism such a terrible thing in business? Yes, it can deliver irreparable damage to reputations and business performance, and it erodes trust. It can be a disaster. Funnily enough, many of the world's top workplaces and brands have experienced activism and discontent in their workplaces, including Google, Facebook and Amazon, yet all of that discontent is just energy directed in the wrong places. These corporates may be intent on stifling debate to suit their brand image and suppressing their people from criticizing business activity that is distasteful, but this is still co-creation. This is still an opportunity to create a better work life and better companies. It is only an opportunity if it is welcome as one. To many now, the world is a divided mess and organizations have become increasingly political places where certain views remain unacknowledged and certain workers feel repressed and silenced. Herein lies a major point about the human experience. Things change quickly. The great technology companies have been pinned down in recent years – often at the forefront of advancing technology and social media. These same companies are being scrutinized to a high degree due to their impact on the human experience. There are ethical concerns. There are economic concerns. There are very human concerns about people being the product and the never-ending fight for attention and consumer spend.

This plays out in the working life of all of us: the constant competition for our attention and to present a perception of ourselves that is liked and validated within and beyond the company. Stress, anxiety and other issues are heading on an upward curve as the workplace, which was meant to be more connected, has become less human in the process – the filtered version of the person winning the day rather than the real one. So too the effect of notifications and loops of communication that has people slavishly referring to their phones and other devices throughout the working day. This has been compounded as more people work from home – the off button and the blurred boundaries between work and life may have increased productivity, but at what cost? Burnout and stress are an unreasonable price to pay, and it is not in any way sustainable over the long term, with many workers putting in more hours than they've ever done. This sacrifices the things that make the human experience worthwhile in the first place, like family time and our own growth and development. If we're not careful, people will forgo all that is good about their time on this planet in favour of work.

This is not what life is meant to be like, is it? Work is never work if you're doing something that you love. There is a balance to be had here too, but it feels good. We enjoy the experience. How many, though, are in that position? Where people have the job that they were born to do and a company that embraces their talents and strengths? Holistically, there are many parts to this equation, yet companies have a major role in supporting people into the right jobs, roles and places where they can make a big impact. Workers and employees have their role, too, in shaping the organization into something more human-centred. Co-creating a human organization never stops. It is a lifelong commitment to positive improvement that ignites human performance. One company that understands this even had its employees design its unique headquarters from scratch and accepted some of the quirkier design elements, including sheep and treehouses.

CASE STUDY
Working life at Moneypenny

A business built from scratch by a brother and sister team, everything at Moneypenny centres around family. This has been consciously and intentionally shaped into the very fabric of the organization from day one and has played a critical role in its success as an employer and its growth as a business. Recognized as a top five *Sunday Times* employer in 2015 and 2017, Moneypenny has found a way to blend work with play, creating jobs that become a lifestyle, and in the process establishing a deeper bond and relationship with employees. Females are the dominant force behind the company and make up most of the workforce and board positions. One employee who has stayed with this business since day one is Moneypenny's CEO, Joanna Swash.

'With 1,000 people, being authentic and true to yourself is critical. You can't pretend to be something that you're not. Everything I do is because it feels like the right the thing to do,' said Swash. There are two simple questions that guide Swash's approach to company leadership and they should be of note to every business leader:

- If I was a client or a supplier, what kind of service do I want?
- If I worked here, what kind of workplace do I want it to be and how would I like to be treated?

The primary element within all this is not up for any debate:

> For me, straight away, business is all about being human. We all experience the same kind of issues and the same kind of things in our home and work life. If you treat people like humans all the way along, it makes everything much richer. It's not about job titles and the things people do, it's about connecting with the workforce in a human way. I've seen the huge gains from the perspective of CEO that this human approach has brought.

Think big, act small

Swash detailed an anecdote of a staff party to bring people together at a special time of the year. Rather than outsource the party or direct others to organize the details, she personally took it upon herself to manage the organization of the event. It is this type of front-and-centre leadership, or servant leadership, that stands out within companies performing well with the human experience. The details matter, and nothing demonstrates an organization cares more than a CEO actively getting out there to set the tone for leaders and the workforce alike. Swash said:

> This is really key. No hierarchy and not asking people to do things that you wouldn't be prepared to do yourself. An example has to be set at every point. It's hard to distil culture into a set of rules and processes. It's very difficult. Freedom, clarity and autonomy are important when moving culture forward within an organization.

Transforming HR into the Working Life team

To build on the progress and cultural work at Moneypenny, a significant decision was taken that perhaps offers a blueprint for others to follow when considering the human experience. Swash said:

> We reviewed our HR provisions and disbanded HR. HR is everyone's job. It shouldn't just sit in isolation as a department, or be there to sign off holidays. There should be self-service and systems in place, but the responsibility for our working life is shared. This change has made such a difference to the business. We threw out the old HR model and asked people how we could do this differently. It's about creating a caring and sharing environment. As part of this, management needed to be upskilled, because if there is no HR department to send them to, managers will need to play their role.

A human-centred company from inception, Moneypenny's business model evolves with its employees, so instead of a traditional HR department, the business runs a function called 'Working Life' and, as expected, it is designed for very different purposes – to develop positive and high-impact experiences in what is a very flat structure that thrives on open and transparent communication. Ensuring people feel valued, engaged and are positioned as a key part of the organization is a collective approach, and the business model reflects that.

One recent example is the relationship they maintain with employees on maternity leave. While most companies view this as an automated letter-sending process, the business ensures that everyone still feels very much part of the Moneypenny family by facilitating connection on Facebook Workplace – they have a mini Pennies site so people can share photos of their new babies and all new parents receive a gift from the team and are invited back into the office for coffee mornings. Everyone feels connected even when they aren't physically working and the outcomes of a strong relationship are earned.

The company has also ditched the annual appraisal, preferring instead to divert the time commitment into something more meaningful for people. So once every eight weeks, employees meet their team manager for a coffee and discussion about work life. Swash has found that people are happier and more engaged with that process. These 'wow chats' were borne out of frustration with the performance management approach and it didn't sit right with the broader approach to colleague development. Swash said:

> We trust people to do the right thing. There is no monitoring or tracking. You won't see any data on our walls or performance metrics. It's all about trust and responsibility. In small teams, people can self-manage and deliver their outcomes together, or challenge each other if things are not going well.

As an obsessively client-centric company, there is a strong emphasis on accountability – people being accountable to their key stakeholders – and this runs through the experience of work at Moneypenny.

An open and honest approach to business

As Swash highlighted during our dialogue, 'clients join Moneypenny because of our culture as do people within the workforce.' There is an open-book approach to sharing the good and the learning as Moneypenny grows, which marks it out as a company that is very comfortable in its own skin. This organizational self-confidence is evident in how it deals with challenges throughout its growth journey. There is also a no-holds-barred approach to internal social media. The company uses Workplace by Facebook to share and co-create across the company. Swash also highlighted that leaders need to be human and authentic in their communication style. As CEO, Swash shared a story of how she used internal social media at the company to share about her new vegetable garden. It is moments like this that extend that feeling that people are working in a human company, and they become especially impactful if members of the top team are sharing freely, openly and with vulnerability.

Inevitably, with this very human approach to business, there is a different view of perceived failure. 'As a management team, I often tell people that if they haven't cocked up, then they are not trying hard enough. Go and try something, if it fails, learn from it and move on,' said Swash. It is this more realistic and empowering approach that is proving its value within businesses like

Moneypenny. 'I do think part of the CEO role is to get out of the way. As much as I can, I create a vacuum for people to step into while you move onto something else. This is helpful in scaling the business and our culture.'

Embracing co-creation and co-design of the workplace

On arrival, it certainly became clear that this was a different type of company. I only had to look around to find evidence of this – a unique-looking treehouse dominates the entrance and the communal seating area played host to several sculptures of sheep that signified the countryside roots of the company. The treehouse creates a memorable experience for guests. It is a meeting room like no other and was entirely the creation of employees, who were asked to design their ideal HQ. It is this level of co-creation that makes it easy to spot a human-centric company. 'We want a treehouse, a statue of a gorilla outside the building, some sculptures of sheep, and our own pub' would cause some eye-rolls at many management team meetings, but not this one. They embrace people and their ideas – Moneypenny is a company that listens to people and weaves their feedback deeply into the company's growth and development.

Happy organization, happy people

For Moneypenny, there is a consistent theme and lens that is applied through the business. It revolves around creating a happy place to work and somewhere that people can see themselves being a part of over the long term. It works, too. Not only are employees at the company sick less, but they also stay with the business for longer periods of time. The company is rightly proud of its low turnover, with regrettable attrition at just 1.4 per cent, and 99 per cent of maternity-leavers return to work. Undoubtedly, people are Moneypenny's best brand ambassadors. The business received over 4,500 unsolicited CVs last year and has no use for recruitment agencies. This is all the more impressive given the small number of roles available to work at the company and the fact that 83 per cent of promotions came from inside the business.

'It's not fake, it's not a PowerPoint. You can feel it here. It's not just a marketing gimmick. It goes throughout the business every day. You can't pretend. You have to be entrenched in it,' said Swash.

The company report a direct correlation between staff happiness and client happiness, which in turn has led to year-on-year increases in both profitability and growth metrics. By any measure, this is a company getting things right on the human and business sides of the equation for company success. To do this, the company has shifted its thinking on how to build a sustainable and saleable human-centred brand, and this includes the way in which they structure around people to create positive outcomes. For them, it means 'HR' needs to play a completely different role to add value to this story.

Supporting wellbeing at work

Moneypenny has implemented a variety of initiatives to support wellbeing outcomes – focusing on the three areas of the whole person: financial, physical and emotional. Everything from its flexible benefits package (recognizing that their people are all at different stages in life) to the design of its offices (communal spaces to promote a family-style feel, dedicated wellbeing rooms, shunning air-conditioning in favour of fresh air ventilation) has been implemented with people at the heart of it all.

Everyone's day kicks off with a free, healthy breakfast with free fresh fruit available throughout the day and subsidized nutritional lunches. The company also offer free fitness classes, both on- and off-site – everyone has access to the free, on-site, state-of-the-art gym, which is open 24/7. Everyone at the company has access to free 24/7 counselling lines, and they recently introduced mental health awareness training. This, for a company in rural north Wales, is still very unusual, yet it again offers evidence that the company is looking at the human experience holistically, wherever that may take them.

This is a business that needed no convincing that putting people first and creating a family-centric workplace is the right thing to do, and it has experienced the benefit of this for the past 20 years. I'm not shocked to learn that the very first employee of the company is still there. Why wouldn't they be with an approach to business like this? Speaking about the way Moneypenny grows and develops in a human-centred way, Swash was firm in her belief that this may not yet be how the world works, but maybe it should be.

Human experiences, human brand

Branding has always been an important part of human history. Delivering a relentless stream of content, information and knowledge about a defined entity in a way that can be felt and understood is an art form. It communicates what you stand for and what makes you different as a company. Good branding nudges and moves people to make choices and take actions. World-class branding creates movements that redefine the human narrative: what was, what is and what will be. The world of branding is very well established, yet only very recently has branding been leveraged within the workforce, and it is almost always viewed through the lens of employer branding. This is the brand development work specifically for the workforce to tie everything together through an employer value proposition (EVP). The EVP details the value exchange between workers and the employer, and answers the most important of human questions: what's in it for me? People give their time, energy, skills and knowledge to an employer, and the employer gives them things in return, such as salary, benefits, perks, growth and a variety of experiences. While an EVP can crystallize and organize a clear set of benefits, experiences and perks associated with an employer for marketing purposes, there is a real danger that this work becomes dissociated from the human experience at work. In effect, it can become pure marketing with very little substance. Do people really get what they sign up for? A brand can deliver what they say in terms of pay, benefits and other related incentives – many are part of the contract – yet when thinking about the human experience, it is manifestly important to consider how the individual can connect to a brand more holistically. With reference to the HEX organization, progress is an important element of any proposition to prospective workers, as are the other components that differentiate a company in the world. Every company can share a list of benefits, but in human experience terms, we'll need to go deeper in communicating why a company is unique and how it contributes positively beyond making a profit.

Another challenge in this regard is that employer branding is often fully focused on employees with permanent contracts, but as many organizations are creating two-tiered workforces, this is something that is coming under increasing scrutiny. A two-tiered workforce can comprise contractors (who can be paid by project or by hour) and those who have permanent employer contracts. The 'core' group of employees are often viewed to be the real company and contractors are there as the necessary but not loved workforce. In practice, this not only causes tension but also shapes the human experience and the quality of it for all workers. Employees get the greater protections, benefits and experiences, while contractors are treated differently with diluted, and often much weaker, access to experiences that are enjoyed by the core workforce. Connect the dots on this and we don't need a stack of research to understand that this will be the root cause of many labour disputes and rebellions within the workforce. Indeed, many companies, like Uber, for example, have been at all-out war with their contracting workforces and those working within the gig economy because of the way these people are being treated.

It is a problem, and it can be a very serious one if companies mishandle or stoke the flames too far in the wrong direction. The headline-catchers in this regard tend to be companies such as Google that rely on contractors or temporary staff as the majority part of its workforce (Bergen *et al*, 2019), which still surprises a lot of people, and Uber, a company that has been involved in an epic and protracted scrap in the courts with its drivers to determine if an employment relationship exists or not. This is now being played out in the Supreme Court in the UK, and any decision on Uber in this regard is also viewed to be a 'defining moment for the gig economy' as a whole (Sheppard, 2020). The muddying of the waters when it comes to workers' rights and the relationships that people have with businesses has accelerated in recent years. If we are talking about the human experience, we need to radically experiment with our system of work and how it gets done. For someone who has spent so much of his career working with employees, I see the latent advantages of the gig economy because we are all self-employed. Whether deemed permanent, temporary, fixed-term, part-time, contractor or anything else, our self-employment, at least in a philosophical sense, is always guaranteed. Pragmatically, though, there are very real differences in the way we are treated by companies, and this is what needs to be clarified if we deem unity, fairness and transparency to be important elements of organizational life.

Asking someone who has taken a temporary role with a brand about this point is enlightening, as they will immediately know and feel the differences that exist between them and their permanently employed peers. A different relationship has been established and these differences can be the source of friction, tension and conflict within the workforce. Everyone is human, and people may be doing similar jobs, yet one group is treated better than the other simply because they have a permanent contract. It could be better pay, benefits or exclusive perks, or even designated company experiences such as celebrations or team development days – if these are exclusive to one part of the workforce, what message does this send to all the other workers? This matters, too, given the potential strength of the emotional connection people have with their companies. It is especially clear at times of redundancy. It is a relationship break-up and often plays out with a high level of intensity. There is a sadness about what has been lost (unless people are leaving voluntarily, and even then, emotions are running high about what is being left behind or what is to come). For those leaving a company, there is often an opportunity to recover, reinforce or reframe the way they see themselves and their relationship with a business. We don't do what we do for a company or entity. We do it for us, or at least we should do. This offers the greatest career protection you could wish for. Every hour of every day is an investment in our life. When business calls for loyalty yet gives none in return, many of us are rightly not comfortable with that. A loyal workforce demands a loyal company.

CASE STUDY

Re-engineering the organization

Let there be no illusions about what we're talking about here. We're talking about re-engineering the organization as we know it. In my view, there is no other way if companies are to truly make the most of the human experience, and I must say that the manifesto for change is being driven confidently by the young and more vibrant companies around the world. With their no-nonsense and human approach, they have struck a chord with their consumers and employees alike. People want to buy from them and work for them in equal measure. What does this manifesto look like? Well, it doesn't look too dissimilar to the edicts of one of the UK's fastest growing companies:

- We don't do normal.
- We never compromise on brand.
- We do it our way or not at all.

- We embrace humour and humility.

- There are no grey areas. If we don't love it, we don't do it. Ever.

- We don't fear failure.

- We take risks.

- We learn obsessively.

- We disrupt convention.

- We are passionate about perfection.

- We bleed orange.

- We are Grenade. We blow shit up.

Alan Barratt, founder and CEO of Grenade, pulls no punches about why his brand has been so successful, and he has weaved those ingredients into the company's approach. As one of the largest protein bar producers in the UK, for Grenade, it's all about standing out and differentiating from others. From humble beginnings, Grenade is now recognized as a billion-dollar brand and one that is taking on all rivals in the sports nutrition industry. With online sales increasing by 294 per cent in 2020, it's been Grenade's best year for e-commerce to date. It already exports its products to over 100 countries and it has achieved remarkable business growth with a relatively small team of 60 people. I met with Barratt the day after he drove a tank through central London – a stunt that amassed millions of social media impressions and widespread coverage across mainstream media. It is perhaps apt given that innovative campaigns like this are part of the guerilla marketing tactics that have enabled rapid success and expansion. They don't do things in a half-hearted way. The brand is strong, and it dictates how the organization develops and in what direction. Whereas it takes a lot of effort to uncover the DNA of many companies, Grenade spells it out, up front and in full.

Brand is everything

Nothing is more important than brand in the context of Grenade. This chimes strongly with what we know about people – they like their symbols, their badges and their brands. There is something here about status, standing and association, and it is very powerful. People like to be associated with brands that reflect their personality, lifestyle and take on things. Indeed, our choice of brands does, to a large extent, provide an opportunity to amplify personalities and preferences, making sure that people are aware of them. Grenade has tapped into this tribal and historic aspect of humanity by putting brand front and centre of its business strategy.

'It sounds a bit obvious, but we do things that we are passionate about. If no one cares about something, then we don't do it. All of the answers come back to our brand,' said Barratt. 'We have to have processes in place, but remain true to ourselves. It's not about creating a corporate nightmare. It's about growing the brand and the culture in our own way.' Barratt is clear that the brand must be protected at all costs when developing an organization for a growing workforce. 'We want people to be themselves. I don't want to go anywhere and not be myself. It is a real shame that people have to do that.' 'Misfits that fit' is the way that Barratt describes who Grenade tends to attract, and getting people into the right role makes a big difference in bringing out the best in people.

On installing a strong ethos into Grenade, Barratt believes that some of it has been conscious and some of it has been subconscious based on his own experiences in life. 'Treat every customer like royalty' was Barratt's response to a senior colleague who was asking about what they do with complaints at Grenade. 'This is our customer experience policy. We give our customers more than they were expecting. Issues never get to my radar because there isn't the need.' Keeping things as flat as possible in a structural sense is a clear advantage in running the business.

Barratt noted that the brand receives an enormous amount of applications per year for a limited number of roles at Grenade, which offers an indication of a brand on the march. Barratt takes a light-touch approach to running the business, with a focus on brand. Everything flows from brand – great for the workforce, investors, suppliers and partners. 'If the brand comes first, who loses? No one.' Within this, there is a special relationship to be built with the workforce, especially for food-based businesses. As Barratt highlighted, with a product that needs to be ingested, there needs to be high trust from the outset of any relationship. The workforce are brand ambassadors and make that all-important connection to consumers. You don't have to be loved, but you do have to be memorable. 'It is not a good situation to have people who feel nothing or indifferent to a brand. Better they love it or hate it. Make it clear and make an impact either way. This helps grow the business,' said Barratt. Branding for many companies reaches its peak as simply an exercise in marketing, yet for Grenade the brand runs much more deeply into the organization, which in turn helps connect key brand stakeholders.

Integrating people and brand

In Barratt's view, everyone is a custodian of the brand:

> They care so much and are protective of the brand. This is a great indication
> that a strong community has been created. As human beings, we know what

the right thing to do is as well-adjusted adults. I try to think with that head on. Not just the numbers and finance, but what is the right thing to do?

Leading from the front is the business philosophy or, as Barratt puts it, conducting the orchestra is the job for the CEO. 'It's not about playing all the instruments – everyone is great at their respective jobs – but it is about keeping people together and in tune. This is what the emphasis on our brand gives us,' said Barratt.

What came through strongly through our discussion was the importance of integrity to build a brand loved by consumers and the workforce alike. It remains a critical part of the human experience since our tribal days. Liking, knowing and trusting someone is the most fundamental sequence of events in how human relationships form, and it's very similar when we think about the way in which organizations build great relationships with their people:

> Isn't integrity a rare trait? It takes a lot of time to build it and a second to lose it. That's important to the team here and is crucial in getting to the right decision. It's suicide for brands to make the wrong decision based on integrity, but it's easy for them to fall into the integrity trap as decisions need to be taken. Trust has been lost from consumers and that's why we hold onto this in terms of what we do with consumers and our people.

Playing a role in building this organizational integrity is HR, a function that often finds itself playing a critical role in organizational rather than brand development. There is a clear distinction between the two and HR, traditionally, has not been the most effective function building bridges between people and the brand. 'HR is not sexy. I don't see HR as that critical. Build a good brand and look after your people. That's it and everything should fall into that,' said Barratt. Indeed, Barratt pointed out that people can be wasted within the function. On that point, Grenade's very own head of HR is also head of customer experience, which demonstrates a stronger positioning as a gate keeper of the brand and serves to connect HR much more firmly to business outcomes.

CASE STUDY
'Don't be a d*ck!' Living life like a Hueligan

There is nothing worse than being like everyone else. It runs counter to everything we know to be good about the human condition. We are unique. There is not another one of us anywhere. It's the same for companies too. They are all, whether acknowledged or not, unique entities. Even if they closely resemble their competitors in terms of products and services, they are all made up of unique individuals and distinctive brands. The great failure of companies over the years to fully engage their workforces and truly differentiate themselves in their market is part of the reason why businesses are not able to sustain themselves in the long term. There is something so very powerful about standing out, doing things on your terms, making a unique difference.

Huel, which is a name based on a combination of human and fuel, offers nutritionally complete food via powders, drinks and bars. Every Huel product includes 26 essential vitamins and minerals, protein, essential fats, carbs, fibre and phytonutrients. It sells over 50 million meals per year, across 80 countries, and has quickly grown its workforce. In just a few years, this UK-based company has turned heads and captured the imagination of an audience looking for healthy and sustainable food products. It's easy to see why. They have a strong community of people making sure that the Huel brand keeps moving forward in a distinctive way. Co-founder James Collier spoke to me about what has been essential in the company's journey and how they have evolved over the years.

A straight-talking human brand

'People, product and brand have been integral to success,' said Collier. 'If you bullshit, people are not going to buy what you're selling. We're honest and it runs through our operations, running with a high level of transparency.' 'Don't be a d*ck' and 'brand is f*cking important' are not phrases that you often seen standing proud on the walls of office headquarters. Yet, this no-nonsense and straight-talking approach has been a hallmark of Huel's journey so far. This level of honesty is no doubt used in equal measure to keep out the people that they don't want to work with while simultaneously attracting the type of people they do. It saves a lot of time and money when it comes to recruitment, but this is all part of what it means to be a 'Hueligan' – a term that was originally used to describe employees, but now encompasses everyone associated with one of the UK's fastest growing brands.

Collier believes that fundamentally 'people need to be comfortable with the brand and the colleagues around them.' Coming from workplaces where that was not always the case ensured that, from his perspective, these were the details that needed some close attention as the team at Huel began to grow. Collier said:

I work with people I like who are really good at their job. I work from home three days a week. There is a company and brand that people can get behind, and I'm really good at my job. Working with good people is key to that. It wouldn't be a pleasure if you didn't have good people to work with.

Overseeing a mental health allies team within the company, Collier feels that this is indicative of the company's approach with things like brew Wednesdays, which bring people together to support each other's wellbeing. As a brand, they performed well during the COVID-19 pandemic. It's been a lesson in that people can work from home in what could be a more balanced way to approach work. 'In my view, we pay people for outcomes that the job creates, and through the pandemic we have realized that a good balance can be achieved in how people deliver results,' said Collier.

Tough but human language

On the tough language and values associated with the company, in particular the 'don't be a d*ck' statement, unexpectedly Collier mentioned that he was against the idea from the start:

> When they put that up on the wall, I completely disagreed with it. I'm more logical and rational. I didn't think we should be telling people not to be a d*ck because why would we recruit those types in the first place? But when I saw the wider reaction to it, the popularity and the way it landed with our audiences, I totally changed my mind. People received it in a way I didn't anticipate and, reflecting on it now, it did represent our style as a brand. I then got totally behind it.

Ultimately, the goal for any brand is to create an emotional connection with their target audience. We all have different tastes, different feelings and different ideas based on our perspective. This poignant example serves to illustrate why it's much more important to focus on the result of a communication or experience. If we're delivering the intended experience, outcomes and our metrics light up, then great. One of the biggest metrics within any new piece of work across any element of the human experience is the extent to which doubters or sceptics self-transform into believers. It is one of the cleanest pieces of data and feedback available. There is also nothing more satisfying than seeing people transition into supporters.

There is a broader lesson about organizational design and development here. If we are to create more human organizations, they will need to be bolder and more in tune with their human stakeholders. Some of the discussion, dialogue and direction that comes from this will be unfamiliar territory and could often be deemed controversial. Humans are sophisticated and complex, yet they are also straight-talking and no-nonsense. The line between personal and professional is often blurred when dealing with the human experience because, if we are truly embracing the human side of things, things will naturally move to a more relatable and human approach. The other benefit of very clearly defining who you are and what you stand for is that the business, and people associated with it, are memorable and different from others – an incredible business advantage that is useful in attracting the right kind of people, resources and partners, as Collier pointed out.

Indeed, this was the case for Huel, too, when it first began pitching the idea of its new product to potential partners. Not all of them welcomed their idea. The one that did has built two new factories to produce Huel products. This is something that is important to the brand: its partners and suppliers. Very early in the COVID-19 pandemic, when things were looking bleak for its partners, Huel announced that it would pay its suppliers immediately rather than place them in a low-priority position as the full scale of the financial challenge presented. Why? Because it was the right thing to do for business and to honour long-term relationships. Brands like this often stand on the shoulders of their actions, and it's a lesson many others can learn from.

An energized (and remote) human workforce

One area of work that used to be a strong differentiator was remote working. Some brands did it, many didn't, but now pretty much every company around the world has quickly shifted into being a digital organization. High-performing remote teams have existed for years, but there was never really the need to delve into why they have been so successful as business models. Now as we build life into work, it is becoming increasingly urgent to acquire the skills and leadership capabilities to run an effective hybrid workforce given the number of employers mixing up their ways of working between home and physical locations. What are the key elements of success?

I recall meeting my colleague, Oscar Fuchs, in Shanghai. We'd quickly arranged the meeting via WeChat, the popular Chinese social media app. Just minutes later, I received a very pleasant email from his PA confirming the timings and location. What struck me was the speed, efficiency and the overall positive experience of this interaction.

Those who often have a need to meet people will understand that organizing meetings is not always as quick and seamless, yet this was his, and evidently his company's, modus operandi. It was built in to the DNA of their business – they were already a mature remote-first business and it felt that way as an external observer. Now, if that was all I had to report, I suspect this would be a relatively weak example. But during my meeting, my colleague shared a piece of information that locked this anecdote into my memory banks. He'd never even met his PA in person.

Fuchs, who was the co-founder of a successful remote-first recruitment firm that initially expanded rapidly across Asia and now operates globally, highlighted his template for success:

> Our unique remote working environment revolved around instilling the right culture, and underpinning that culture with robust systems. In terms of culture, it was important to hire the right people: those who embraced the idea of remote working rather than fight against it. We then encouraged employees at all levels to take the time to build relationships with colleagues digitally, leading by example in treating co-workers with humanity, politeness and respect. This was critical when working without routine face-to-face interactions, since people can very easily forget their manners in the digital world, lapsing into dehumanizing, task-oriented conversations.

Being human, but digitally. It's interesting to note the emphasis being placed on humans rather than technology. Many companies lead with technology, but forget about the human elements, which brings its own problems. What always impresses me about the remote-first companies I've spoken to is their clear bias for people rather than technology. The technology is the tool and equipment to enhance the human experience, not the other way around. With this lens, I can understand why some companies fare better than others, but how can you feel like you belong in a company where physical face-to-face interactions are limited or not even part of the business model? Fuchs said:

> Since the company was entirely remote, colleagues based in locations around the globe never suffered from the mentality of being 'left out' of

decisions made at the global headquarters. The internet was our global headquarters, creating a level playing field in the game of international influence, career progression and consensus-building. Our systems were all geared towards supporting this culture. They created workflows that forced employees to interact on a regular basis and work together as a cohesive team. They allowed for personalization, building on the strengths of individuals and their relationships within the organization. We had no sacred cows: if a legacy system took us away from our ideals, or otherwise became redundant, they were phased out and replaced. And it was this streamlined cohesion of culture and process which we hoped was always felt by our clients and external stakeholders, no matter with which employee and in which geography.

Summary: reset, refresh and relaunch work around life

As we've explored in this chapter, there is no getting away from the fact that delivering a better and stronger human experience at work will require significant changes in the way we think about the organization and how we lead our brands. Brand and organization are, in many ways, more powerful and prevalent than ever, and they are both much needed elements in taking forward ideas and scaling them into the economy and society. Within each brand and organization, there is a workforce and they are central to all the good things that happen for a company. Therefore, if organizations really do want to deliver great experiences to customers and other key stakeholders, they will first need to serve the workforce in the best possible way. A big first step is to recognize the humanity that exists within the context of the organization and find ways to bring that to the surface. As documented, this could mean radical and progressive structure changes, an all-encompassing focus on human beings, embracing all our roles as leaders and practitioners, building honest and straight-talking human brands, or diverging from the norm to do things differently. In whatever way we approach this, we'll need to get very comfortable with new ideas about how to build work around life, rather than life around work.

- Identify what needs to be reset, refreshed and relaunched at your organization, or in the way that you approach your work, to create positive results and outcomes.

- Consider the design of support services, especially HR, and determine how well they are currently serving the workforce. Is there a better way to position and organize teams around people?

- Determine if you are leading as a HEX accelerator and focus on developing these important capabilities within your work. Differences are being made every day through what you do and how you do it.

- Take a look at your brand, or one you are familiar with, to understand how the brand communicates and talks to its consumers. Now, look at how the brand communicates inside the organization to its workforce. What do you see? Is there a strong brand identity and is it evident across the workforce journey and human experience at work?

- A digital approach to business is now prevalent within the economy, but think about your organization's DNA and how technology can be used to enhance and strengthen relationships and human experiences across the organization.

06

Evolving human experiences at work

Redesign an experience. Make improvements to processes. Revitalize an employee journey. Job done, right? Not quite. The human experience just isn't anything like that. Working on developing the human experience at work is less a project, more a calling. Having been privileged enough to coach and guide this new breed of experience-driven business leaders over the years, I can tell you with a high degree of certainty that they are cut from a different cloth. They carry a deep empathy with the human experience at all times. It shows in decisions, actions and outcomes. Courageous and bold, these human-centred leaders serve their businesses in a whole new way using insight, intelligence and skill to chart new ways to connect people to what matters most. This is not simply about so-called 'moments that matter', but is much more about helping people live lives that matter – meaningful lives with meaningful impact. In this chapter, we will look at how this is shaping up within organizations as we embrace the evolutionary aspect of the experience of work.

Evolving experiences as businesses and people grow

Every brand success story starts from within. Organizations simply create the conditions that allow success to occur. It is not enough to stay still. It would be a very limited experience if things didn't progress, improve or evolve. For people and companies, progress is of strategic importance. It helps to do and become more than what we are and what we were. Growth is a signature element of the human experience, but so is decline. The law of nature dictates the same – growth and decline, a constant cycle of life that is guaranteed. This applies to companies too. A study by McKinsey (2015) found that the average lifespan of companies listed in Standard & Poor's 500 is less than 18 years. In 1958, it was 61 years. McKinsey believes that, in 2027, 75 per cent of the companies currently quoted on the S&P 500 will have disappeared. To avoid this fate, businesses have no choice but to maintain a positive relationship with growth and evolution – the growth and evolution of the enterprise alongside the person. Brands that are ahead of the curve are out there working back from the future to reshape and reinvent their business as a continuous process. This is how they stay ahead of others and maintain a strong connection with growing rather than declining. For practitioners and leaders, this means that an evolutionary focus is imperative. The human and employee experience within our companies should always be in a state of improvement and development. We may outrun projects, but the overarching objective is to keep developing experiences that land strongly, make an imprint and fuel business growth. This is an essential service that practitioners and leaders deliver: always-on development to keep pace with changes in social, environmental and technological landscapes.

Future focus is a defining characteristic of HEX organizations. They respect their past but live in the present and grow into their future. It's an observable way of falling forward that can be understood as more effective than a limiting notion of failure. We don't often hear too much about perceived failure because events are mere stepping-stones into a positive future for humans, business and planet.

Uniting people through organization

To unite people across a company, we need to find ways to help unite each individual with their true self. This, in turn, creates the conditions for people to deliver exceptional human performance. Oftentimes, people surprise themselves with what they can achieve. As humans, we are always moving forward, and this evolutionary nature needs to be acknowledged if we are to fulfil our full potential in and out of work. Organizations also need to evolve and improve to encourage and enable this. In a fragmented and divisive world, the organization, whether it likes it or not, steps into and fills a gaping void in helping people become consciously aware of their actions, habits, behaviours and impact on those and the planet around them. This is a new aspect of organizational life that is relatively unexplored in the corporate world. There is no separation between people and planet. Everything is connected. What often pervades society in modern times is a selfishness defined by an excessive materialism and overdependency on factors outside of ourselves. In contrast, the story of life is not about finding joy. It's about knowing that it exists within. We just need the patience and focus to find and access it. It is energized from within. Is a company responsible for your ability to experience a joyful life? I would argue that they are not, but work continues to be a significant aspect of life, and companies are always making a positive or negative contribution to it.

Building the most trusted, admired and respected brands on Earth

When I hear about companies so skewed in the direction of customers, consumers and shareholders, I immediately see flaws and gaps in their business strategies. It is a modern-day version of a strategic and tactical weakness. Not being balanced in a way that considers all stakeholders that are influential to a company is like setting the stage for future problems and issues that could have been avoided. Businesses that are focused on human-centricity naturally seek to serve the needs and interests of all stakeholders. Practically, this not only feels like a better way of doing business, but it also strengthens a foundation that has the potential to lead organizations into a much more sustainable, rather than short-lived, future.

While it's no longer favourable to focus solely on customers, it has never been healthy to be chasing success with one group of stakeholders over another. If customers are winning because employees are losing, or customers and employees are losing because shareholders are winning, it can lead to many negative consequences in the long run. Notably at a human level, stress, burnout, conflict and anxiety can creep into the workforce. For organizations, this results in lower productivity, profitability, morale and business performance. Ultimately, a lack of connection and cohesion within a brand community opens up many gaps in the business model and drives unhealthy outcomes such as the big one – brand decline. So, in this age, it is less about building customer-centric brands and much more about building human organizations. We cannot continue to accept exceptional service from workforces that are under increasingly pressurized draconian and inhumane performance management practices, can we? These are not role-model organizations for humanity, nor do they inspire confidence with their version of an ideal human future, which is based on squeezing every ounce of revenue and profit from a workforce regardless of very human costs.

The evolution we are experiencing now, greater integration of societal, technological and human goals, will no doubt present some major questions about how all three can combine and connect effectively to serve the whole. Humanity is messy and has multiple, and conflicting, agendas to overcome internally and externally. Yet, within all this, the organization is the bastion of hope. The organization now moves into an area where it directly shapes our collective future as human beings.

Inevitably, this comes back to a question of legacy.

- What type of legacy do you wish to create for your organization?
- What does it stand for in the good and the not-so-good times?
- How do people remember and regard it?
- What are the stories and tales that are going to pass through collective memory?
- How will people be positively impacted because of the existence of your organization?

Companies and people still have a relatively short lifespan, so it's important to understand the impact that can occur within that short time. Are our companies a force for good? The ramifications of this question literally change a business overnight – what it does and how it does it. In many ways, wise and intelligent leaders have realized that any separation between companies, people and planet is a complete illusion. We all rely on and depend on each other, and the health of the planet, to survive. In this case, why would we not serve to protect and nourish that at all costs? The immediate answer is a reality slap in the face – there are a lot of people and companies that simply do not care. They serve themselves above all else. Yet, it is what it is, and it's been that way since we started forming the very first organizations. Herein lies the opportunity. In the days, months and years ahead, public tolerance for unethical, corrupt and greed-driven behaviour will continue to decline. Enough will be enough, and poor experiences of companies, and any negative behaviour they deliver, will no longer be ignored or overlooked. The opportunity is to get out in front of this by aligning with humanity – people and planet – before anyone else does. Not in a superficial way, but in a deep and robust way that locks in a human-centred bias throughout what a company does and wherever it does it. This, regrettably, remains an easy path to differentiation and competitive advantage, and companies stand out and grow through the right reasons. We really do need to start thinking of organization-building as an ART form, as I set out in Figure 6.1.

For internal leaders and practitioners, our work is about co-creating ART, and our craft takes place among the living and breathing human experience every day. The great aspect to this is that there is no possibility that shortcuts can be taken. Yes, we can accelerate progress through actions, decisions and experiences, but there are no quick wins or cheats to build long-lasting and widely held admiration, respect and trust. Borne from real and genuine commitments that are honoured consistently over time, brands act from a sense of duty and responsibility to be of service to and beyond the economies in which they operate. Even if companies fall short of their standards from time to time, as they will surely do, organizations that have earned high levels of admiration, respect and trust have already created a solid foundation in stone, and the key will be to maintain that investment in perpetuity.

FIGURE 6.1   A work of ART

Admired	Respected	Trusted
Organizations win admiration from diverse audiences for their visible leadership on issues affecting humanity.	Organizations are broadly respected by all parties, including peers, due in no small part to the way they treat people within and outside of the company.	Organizations develop a high level of trust with all stakeholders, including the workforce, customers, shareholders and supporters.
Admiration is built over time based on factors including impact across stakeholder groups, citizenship, quality of designed experiences, crisis leadership, integrity, sustainability, operational excellence, and by leading in conscious and intentional human-centred ways.	Respect is built through experiences. They may run similar processes and systems to other companies, but the experience of them will be delivered differently, with very close attention to fairness, transparency and ethics. There is a high level of care and empathy.	Trust is built through upholding values, keeping promises and a consistent delivery of experiences that enhance society, people and planet. We know where we stand with companies in this mould and we believe these businesses are operating with sincere intent.

© Ben Whitter, HEX Organization Ltd

One of my clients in 2020 was one of the world's top 10 most admired companies, one of the world's biggest financial institutions and was a co-signatory of the Statement on the Purpose of a Corporation by the Business Roundtable, which shifted organizations away from a principal focus on maximizing shareholder return. What is notable about its business model is just how integrated the business is with community and societal goals – from employment to sustainability, the brand weaves these valuable connections into its business objectives and invests hundreds of millions of dollars every year into projects that deliver value to the community and the localities it serves, while at the same time investing $300 million in employee training and specialist programmes to support the growth of a diverse and inclusive culture.

Brands become admired, respected and trusted because of a long-term continuous effort across multiple stakeholder groups. No brand is perfect, as we've discussed, but overwhelmingly, the companies moving forward with the right intent and to create value for all stakeholders are the ones that are held in high regard on a consistent basis. Doug McMillon, president and chief executive officer of Walmart, who is chairman of the Business Roundtable, put it in these terms: 'Concurrent health, economic and racial crises have made clear how various systems are connected – and that multi-stakeholder capitalism is the answer to addressing our challenges holistically' (McMillon, 2020). Focusing on the human experience at and beyond work, and all the roles that people play in life, will continue to be a major organizational concern in the years to come. It does feel that we are only at the very beginning of a period of massive change to the way business is experienced across the economy.

Evolve or die

With experimentation being the new 'norm' within companies, there is an increasing expectation that organizations can create safe places to fail and make mistakes. That's a tried and tested part of the learning process, and it is a powerful one that helps establish more successful projects, products and services. Learning in real time with key stakeholders is a compelling part of the co-creation approach, and it comes with the understanding that the greatest mistake organizations can make is not to learn, grow and evolve through their experiences. This can cause problems for companies and people throughout their entire lives, and it can cause absolute carnage for organizations that don't realize their faults or the genuine concerns of their people. Mistakes and failures are part of the human experience, so we should embrace them, encourage them and celebrate them within our companies. They not only offer inspiration to keep on improving, but they are also integral to creating our successes when they eventually arrive. One brand that has been consistently evolving and extending its impact in a sustainable way for a long time is IKEA.

CASE STUDY

Delivering purposeful and sustainable success at IKEA

IKEA is guided by one single yet powerful vision of creating a better everyday life for many people – for customers, but also for co-workers and the people who work at its suppliers. The IKEA vision and purpose, introduced in 1976 by IKEA's founder Ingvar Kamprad, is a forever part of the business and will continue to guide the company in the upcoming decades. For IKEA, purpose and profitability go hand in hand. Being a caring business is good for business and part of the reason why they continue to transform the business. They want to become even more accessible, affordable and truly sustainable for the many. Who can argue against a strategy that places people and profit together? IKEA delivered $45.4 billion in revenue worldwide in 2019.

Being a humanistic and values-driven company with more than 211,000 colleagues across 50+ markets, the brand has attracted 839 million visits to its stores and 2.6 billion visits to its website – a big company has a big responsibility, which is why purpose is so prominent within the company's development, as are the common set of values that are shared by a diverse group of people around the world.

A sustainable future for all

The world is changing, fast, and so are consumers. They won't stand still and neither will IKEA. Urbanization, a growth in digitalization and environmental awareness is changing people's consumption and shopping needs. At the same time, new competition, a wider choice of products at affordable prices and providing customers with convenient shopping is also heavily influencing customers' decision processes. Being aware of those trends, and the digital transformation process, IKEA is adapting by strengthening internal capabilities and infrastructure, as well as preparing co-workers to manage these into the future.

A key focus for the company is sustainability, says Nabeela Ixtabalan, who was previously Head of Digital Transformation at Ingka IKEA Retail (Ingka Group), the largest strategic partner to the IKEA Franchise system. Ixtabalan said:

> With more than 76 years of experience in life at home and the retail industry, IKEA has been determined to transform its business in an even more sustainable direction. The business views sustainability as our generation's biggest responsibility and as a global company with a loved brand, they have a huge opportunity to create a positive impact for both people and the planet.

Good intentions are important, but words give them power. Being a sustainable and purposeful business is critical for profitability and long-term existence. Recently, for example, IKEA and other large companies joined a new alliance of politicians and environmentalists to call on the EU to create a wide green recovery strategy focused on sustainability following the COVID-19 pandemic. This is one of many initiatives that the brand has embarked on, which also includes the following goals:

- Only use renewable and recycled materials in its products by 2030.
- Remove all single-use plastic products from the IKEA range globally and from customer and co-worker restaurants in stores by 2020.
- Achieve zero-emission home deliveries by 2025.
- Reduce the total IKEA climate footprint by an average of 70 per cent per product by 2030.
- Expand the offer of affordable home solar solutions to 29 IKEA markets by 2025 (IKEA, 2020).

Daring to be different and daring to make mistakes is part of the IKEA culture. IKEA's founder, Ingvar Kamprad, said: 'Don't be afraid of making a mistake because you can learn so much from your mistakes. People are afraid of making mistakes (fiascos) and this is the real disaster, because mistakes are our very best teacher.' One of his most famous quotes about mistakes was when he said: 'Only while sleeping, one makes no mistakes – making mistakes is the privilege of the active' (IKEA, 2020).

Words and actions must meet. Speaking about a very successful initiative during her time at IKEA, Ixtabalan detailed Failure Friday:

It's an example of where experiences meet values. It is a space where we encouraged learning, knowledge-sharing, openness and growth opportunities by discussing learnings that arise from failure. The main ambition of Failure Friday was to emphasize the importance of failing as part of the journey, especially in times of increasing change and uncertainty.

Failure Friday has four objectives:

- to focus on failure as an important learning aspect of IKEA culture;
- to reinforce the opportunities that come from making mistakes;
- to increase people's comfort level and understanding that making mistakes is part of the process;
- to allow leaders to strengthen a culture and environment where making mistakes is okay.

Ixtabalan said:

During transformations, it is important that the company increases communication about what is changing, and Failure Fridays is an opportunity to talk about culture and values. Ultimately, IKEA is creating a workplace where it is safe to fail and learn from those failures.

The Failure Friday format is a simple unscripted discussion where leaders and co-workers share real-life stories, their thoughts, their fears and their learnings about failure on a monthly basis. Each session explores one key question that employees in all business units are encouraged to discuss. Examples include:

1 How do you define failure?
2 How do you design for failure?
3 What are the cultural dimensions of failure?
4 Are there gender differences when it comes to failure?
5 How do you create psychological safety to fail?

In addition to each monthly question, they ask participants to share one *epic* failure – why they considered it to be epic and what they learned from it. Seeing leaders and their colleagues openly share their failures on 'stage' for the entire company to see is a brave and bold way of celebrating failure. Failure Friday is also intended to help the company position failure in a more light-hearted manner, where the company directly encourages people to view failure as constructive feedback, rather than mere disappointment.

The immediate impact of this initiative has been overwhelmingly positive. The reaction after the first Failure Friday was highly encouraging. Co-workers appreciate the effort and are learning and sharing more about failures as a result.

Taking responsibility for brand evolution

Failure Friday is a great illustration of how companies can leverage the experience of work to connect with the workforce at multiple human and organization levels. In the process, a practical experience showcases IKEA's company values. It emphasizes values about being different with a meaning, giving and taking responsibility, leading by example, and renewing and improving. It also encourages the idea of creating a culture of bold people who stand for what they believe in, and to do so together. It's very powerful when companies give their workforces the opportunity to experience and co-design the future with them – in the process a togetherness is created with a shared sense of purpose to accelerate efforts to evolve a brand into the future.

Facing the future head on

This focus on creating safe places to share learning coincides with a real drive to test and try new solutions. IKEA considers all aspects of the business as it transforms how it does things. This also includes simplifying organizational processes to secure long-term growth. Experimentation and iteration are core aspects of the human experience. At a business level, IKEA embraces this by testing new business models such as renting/leasing. Due to COVID-19 and people's growing need to work from home, the company has recently acquired a company by the name of Geomagical Labs, which will let customers place and design IKEA furniture from the comfort of their own homes.

This, alongside other aspects of digital technology, is allowing the company to develop, adapt and provide a better service to customers using data and analytics to better serve the business and provide more relevant and personalized offers along with its home furnishing knowledge. This is part of a long-term investment strategy to meet current and future human needs – co-workers, customers, suppliers and other stakeholders.

IKEA's success is based on a humanistic view on diversity, equality and inclusion. Ixtabalan said:

> At Ingka Group, there is a firm belief that equality is a human right and that equality is the right thing to do and good for business. Closing the gender gap has been an important goal for the company and involves a variety of initiatives. One such goal was to have 50 per cent of women at all levels of leadership at Ingka Group. That goal has been realized, with 49.7 per cent of managers being female. By 2022, the company will close the gender board gap as well as reach gender pay equality across all levels of the organization.

The future for the IKEA experience

The company continues to invest more in building a better co-worker and customer experience and is modifying its work to become more efficient and increase competitiveness. At the same time, they're creating opportunities for people to learn various skills, to grow and thrive – all while being true to company values. Recognizing the challenges ahead, the company is already out there working back from the future to fully leverage the human and brand experience to ensure the sustainability of its business globally:

- **Empower co-workers with a digital DNA** – By integrating a range of technological solutions, tools and digital resources, IKEA has a strong focus on finding ways to solve problems at scale with its people. Working in a company that cares about people and the planet gives a lot of energy to dream and build the future. Bringing in those positive aspects from the company's values, and embedding them with a digital DNA, will enable the brand to successfully transform.

- **Equality as a human right** – As a humanistic company, IKEA places equality at the heart of human rights. Its aim is to achieve true inclusivity based on equality. They do this by attracting and retaining top talent, serving a diverse customer base and contributing to positive change in society. There is a firm belief that gender equality promotes innovation of thought, drives stronger teams and challenges the company to act and think differently, which in turn results in increased performance, innovation and creativity.

- **Climate positive and circular by 2030** – This means that IKEA will reduce more greenhouse gases than the total IKEA value chain emits. The goal is very ambitious, but the company uses goals such as this as a way to create and unleash innovation within the organization. This challenges people to work in new ways and will contribute to business renewal.

- **Technological disruption** – Technology generates some of the greatest opportunities and the greatest risks for society. Automation will make companies more productive and efficient and many tasks optimized and deployed with better quality. In combination with social and demographic changes, such as urbanization and greater labour mobility, the future of work will look very different and IKEA's commitment to focus on people is the brand's greatest strength. A good example of this is the Customer Data Promise – a new data capability featured through its app that allows customers to fully control their data at every stage of the shopping journey.

IKEA believes that standing with people will have the greatest impact on their business as it becomes much more like a digital business in the future. The key to this is building a workforce that is truly fit for the future while creating the conditions for all its co-workers to be ready for work – equipped and employable within the IKEA ecosystem or elsewhere.

The world as a workplace and you're the CEO

Now that the world is one big workplace and work gets done in so many ways, the CEO will find adaption and experimentation to be high on the agenda. The evolving organization has recognized a connection that exists with multiple stakeholders and that a more holistic approach is required. Indeed, humanity and businesses have been getting the measure of each other for some time and finding mutually beneficial ways for both parties to win beyond the market-place. The CEO continues to hold sway in this regard and organizations can often reflect their priorities and principles. The background, culture and conditioning of the CEO holds a great deal of weight in influencing, shaping and directing an organizational system. As a CEO, you may have opportunity to shape and mould a senior team into a particular image with specific attributes, which, in turn, shapes the rest of the organization. Yet, as a middle manager trying to reshape a system based on your own beliefs and culture, there is often very strong resistance. In any context, co-creating with people and culture in mind is going to be the wise choice and the path of least resistance.

A CEO role is naturally strategic, holistic and accountable. It is a privileged and demanding position that creates an expectation that value is created for all parties within a brand. Managing this has always been the challenge. There is often a false choice in prioritizing one group of stakeholders over another. For this reason, human-centricity comes into its own as a way of leading a business. All stakeholders are human, and we will need to deliver high-quality experiences to each group or individual at as personalized a level as possible over the long term. I tend to treat my coaching clients as CEOs from the outset of the relationship, even if they don't hold that position. I do this because I want to encourage personal responsibility, accountability and ownership for longer-term outcomes. It is noticeable that the higher people go in their careers, the more time is reserved for thought and for thinking through real-time problems and challenges. Indeed, CEOs often tend to use a circle of people they trust and share openly with, which helps them work through solutions to business challenges and to make sense of the world around them. But ultimately, their actions, decisions and behaviours will dictate and determine how well a company develops or navigates every challenge that presents itself. CEOs are in place because they have the capacity to create and lead a vision. Often, the stimuli for progress are directly around them – the people, environments and communities. Astute observation skills are a big advantage, as is a high level of empathy and emotional intelligence. They have little choice but to take a holistic view of their companies, and it is this perspective that I challenge leaders and professionals to rise to – to see the whole picture, not just that of their functions or departments. This is where we can find and connect cross-functional work to deliver a bigger impact. Practitioners often run quickly down the path of practical action – they need to demonstrate progress and deliver results over the short term, yet a long-term view is healthy when we consider the life of organization. It comes down to evolving what needs to evolve in order to successfully meet the future.

- What problem are we really solving with this work?
- What is at the real core of this issue?
- What absolutely needs to change or evolve to create stronger performance and outcomes, today and tomorrow?

It is phenomenal when you see and experience companies that really take the human experience to the heart of their organizations. Not only does it change everything; it re-energizes people to deliver value in ways that would not have been possible without a human-centred mindset. The realization when it does occur is a transformative one as professionals and leaders begin to understand that all organizational success is entirely dependent on human success. If companies are operating from this perspective, what they focus on evolves and what they deliver is greatly enhanced from that evolution – relationships are stronger, healthier and more vibrant than ever, and this ultimately creates long-lasting outcomes. The example that follows demonstrates the connection between organization and people, and how the human experience can be fully integrated into a successful business model.

CASE STUDY

Human experience at Chang Hong Tian Yuan

Chang Hong Tian Yuan (in short Tian Yuan) is a business unit of pan-Asian life insurance group AIA, which is the largest life insurer in the world by market capitalization in 2020. It is focused entirely on the Asia-Pacific region, with

$1.74 trillion assured. Tian Yuan's core business is to deliver top-quality services and benefits solutions to companies of all sizes and assist corporate clients to meet employees' health, protection and retirement needs. By early 2020, 80 employee partners worked in the business unit, all with extensive industry work experience, and over two-thirds as middle and senior managers or entrepreneurs before joining Tian Yuan.

A connected and aligned purpose

Tian Yuan holds a strong vision to be the most pre-eminent life insurance provider in Asia, offering clients professional service of the highest quality. With a committed purpose to serve societies and people, Tian Yuan focuses its energy on creating long-term value for their clients and employee partners. An exclusive focus on clients and employees comes from Tian Yuan's strong convictions to help people live healthier, longer and better lives in every community in which they live and work. A healthier, longer and better life enables people to get more out of life, do more, experience more and live more. It strengthens individuals' self-confidence and wellbeing and helps build meaningful relationships with family and friends. Along with financial security and intellectual fulfilment, people can live life to the fullest and enjoy ongoing happiness. Holding this promise, Tian Yuan has naturally embedded a holistic and human-centred experience into every business decision they take and every movement they make.

The business of trust

Becoming the most trusted partner for their clients and employees is the core value and ultimate goal of Tian Yuan. To clients, Tian Yuan is their trusted insurance partner. It provides solutions that not only meet clients' needs but also helps clients solve life challenges. To employee partners, Tian Yuan is their trusted employer. The brand focuses on continuous self-growth and actualization through day-to-day value-creation for clients, people in the communities and colleagues.

Guided by its core value, Tian Yuan identifies four business objectives:

1 Be known as an industry leader and role model.

2 Establish and maintain trusted relationships with clients.

3 Build a strong employer brand to attract the best people.

4 Enhance employees' sense of meaning and belonging by working in Tian Yuan.

As can be noted here, at Tian Yuan, business success is never measured by a remarkable financial number, but by the value created for the clients and employees and level of trust clients and employees have for Tian Yuan. When talented people join Tian Yuan, they know their mission is not about selling a product or service but about helping clients fulfil their life vision. Their professional services can make a huge impact on the lives of their clients – they do good for people. As Tian Yuan's business unit leader Sheng said:

> The insurance industry is a future-oriented business. If we build the future for our clients, our focus must be long term and human-centric. We must be honest with our clients and try our best to help them tackle life issues at difficult stages. Building a healthier, longer and better life requires physical, financial and psychological strength. We must possess strong integrity to make sure whatever we do serves the purpose of making people's lives better. We are their trusted partners for a lifetime.

Obsessed with humans – an attractive proposition

Insurance is about promoting the wellbeing of people. Dealing with insurance is dealing with people, so a natural obsession with humans is required if the best service is to be achieved. This 'obsession with human' is a powerful magnet to attract the very best people who share the same values and mission. Employees are humans first. Humans have basic needs. At Tian Yuan, many of the employee partners are already financially comfortable before joining the business unit. They work in Tian Yuan not for more financial security, but rather to pursue a more meaningful life and to develop the best version of themselves. Since the business unit was established in 2017, Tian Yuan has achieved very low employee turnover and rapid team expansion. How does Tian Yuan attract and retain a committed and loyal team of high-potential talent in a fast-moving industry known for high employee turnover? The answer is short: they treat their people well.

Valuing the whole unique person

Tian Yuan regards their employees as partners with unique talent, strengths and resources that are valuable to the business and clients. Tian Yuan values every past experience individual partners can bring in from their previous jobs. In fact, the current partners in Tian Yuan have very diverse education and professional backgrounds. It is believed that each partner is a resourceful treasure who carries value and creates value. Because of the diversity of experience, Tian Yuan partners can collaborate and support each other to create more added value to their clients. A guiding principle of Tian Yuan's work practice is that resources are shared with every partner. Every individual has their own limitations and weaknesses, but through collaboration, co-creation and co-development, an individual grows, the team improves and eventually clients benefit – this is 'win-win-win'.

Focus on brand and identity

Tian Yuan believes a strong brand contains three core components: employer, product/service and employee. When employees feel proud of what they do, they feel good about themselves and their profession, thus they are more willing to take full responsibility for their work and go the extra mile to serve their clients. When employees feel good about what they do, they become more confident, motivated and happy. They show their clients a positive image. Tian Yuan's brand is highly inclusive, embracing all the individual uniqueness. In Tian Yuan, employee partners are encouraged to be authentic: they advocate that only when employees are true to themselves can they be true to clients. Being true to clients requires employees to be empathetic and fully attentive to clients' needs and expectations. They can place themselves in the position of the clients and effectively listen and communicate. On this basis, they provide clients with professional services that meet clients' individual needs.

Ignite passion to serve

In a service industry, employees are required to provide the best service to retain clients and build reputations. A passion to serve can be achieved from one's understanding of the job's calling and a person's reason for existence – their purpose. 'For years, insurance companies in China have been stereotyped as being untrustworthy and full of unprofessional people. To become an industry leader, Tian Yuan strives to reshape the image and reputation of insurance companies as well as insurance professionals,' said Sheng. This broader mandate within the industry generates trust and demonstrates leadership.

Holistic and human-centred experience design

The holistic experience of work is, to a large extent, shaped by organizational leaders. Good leaders pay full attention to people and adjust their leadership style to serve their people. In Tian Yuan, employees are well educated and highly capable. These employees can manage themselves and the work following their own way. What they need is recognition, autonomy and emotional support from both supervisors and co-workers. Leading such a team of highly educated talent, leaders need to be fully attentive and identify what types of support employees are looking for from the leader and the organization.

Sheng described her leadership as:

> ...being an unconditional supporter and cheerleader. You need to give your people full attention and full support, but you do not intervene. When they do well, recognize, praise and reward; when they need encouragement, give them all your energy and show strong belief in your people; when they ask for help, support unconditionally.

This may sound like the easiest style in the world to apply in practice, yet so many leaders across the global economy struggle to move their mindsets in this human-centred direction because of the way they have experienced companies and leaders. One HR director at a global company told me that his organization was numbers driven and the board were intent on delivering productivity at all costs. This dictated a lot of the approach from HR too – it was very transactional, functional and compliance-driven. This led to an overly performance-managed, frail, anxious and stressed workforce that began to buckle amid widespread discontent. So, when I see a commitment to human-centred leadership, I reflect on the senior leadership team, what they did to enable this style to occur and how they also role-modelled within the organization.

Tian Yuan can be summarized in three words: empowering, collaborative and safe. At Tian Yuan, employee partners are fully empowered to do what they think is best for the clients and co-workers as long as they abide by the corporate values and legal principles. They can flexibly arrange their working hours and decide where their working space is. The autonomy employees have at work enables them to be more adjustable to clients' needs, on the one hand, and find their own work–life balance on the other. As mentioned, collaboration encourages co-workers to share their resources with other partners, help team members who face difficulties and co-create innovative solutions for clients. Open sharing platforms are created for employee partners to exchange thoughts, practices, problems and solutions. The company reports that this successful collaboration experience enhances levels of trust, creates stronger emotional bonds and increases employees' psychological safety. They become trusted partners to each other.

Growing together

One basic human need at work, according to Tian Yuan, is to gain self-growth and actualization. To support this, the company has a comprehensive employee development system to help employees grow and develop. Training is provided at different stages of an employee's journey with the company. Early-stage training helps employees to learn the corporate truth (mission, purpose and values) and successfully navigate the way the company operates. Tian Yuan offers a variety of learning platforms so that different growth needs of the employees can be met. It also encourages staff to self-organize training – choosing their own learning activities and courses – and perform as a trainer to develop other co-workers. In Tian Yuan, learning opportunities are accessible to all employees and, in 2020, all the training was moved online into an open learning platform called Ding Ding. Supported by technology, employees are able to track their development and keep a record of learning on a continuous basis.

A rewarding experience

Employees expect to be rewarded fairly. In Tian Yuan, a reward system has been implemented to foster collaboration and reduce internal competition. When a team signs a new client contract, rewards are distributed to everyone based on their individual contributions. While members who win the contract get the largest proportion of the reward, the team leader is also incentivized based on the team's overall performance. Such a reward system motivates leaders to provide full support for their colleagues and reinforces the positive outcomes related to collaboration and mutual support. Rather than promote a 'winning' team or individual, employees are encouraged to see each success as part of one high-performing Tian Yuan Team and one shared true interest – that is, to serve the needs of clients and make their life better.

Tian Yuan's employee partners are also committed to building a vigorous community. On a voluntary basis, employee partners organize health-related workshops, lectures and activities for clients. For example, during COVID-19, employees of Tian Yuan organized free open-access online lectures delivered by renowned medical experts. As Tian Yuan's clients are all corporate clients/ employers, Tian Yuan also provides free wellbeing training and activities for the employees of client companies. Community service under one shared purpose brings meaning to employees' work and life and subsequently helps them to become more valuable and stronger people.

This commitment to the whole human being and how they successfully experience the workplace is something that makes a significant contribution to a brand's stated goals and objectives. If you're serious about business, you're going to need to be serious about people too. This considered, careful and detailed approach speaks volumes about a brand and what it stands for, and regardless of any challenges that arise, there is a foundation in place that encourages and fosters a genuine connection between colleagues, teams and clients. This togetherness becomes invaluable within the human and business growth journey.

Why bother sitting back and letting circumstances dictate the moves we make? We have a finite amount of time on projects and programmes to make a truly profound difference. This is what I have discovered during my research when it comes to the HEX organization. These companies that are fundamentally focused on elevating the human experience do so with an intensity, energy and vigour that cannot be matched in their industries. They take their time and are extremely deliberate in building trust with all stakeholders yet when it comes to taking actions that do just that, there is no hesitation. They are out there making decisions that immediately create an impact and lead with a genuine sense of purpose in all that they do. The joy in work really comes out with the teams and people I get to work with and study. There is compassion, commitment, honesty, empathy and love in what people do. It oozes from these unique practitioners and leaders. It draws people to them and creates long-lasting internal support. This requires a firm commitment to building world-class leadership across a business, and world-class leadership these days is human-centred.

Human-centred leadership

There is an intelligence about leaders focused on improving the human experience because they innately understand that people are at their best when their head and their heart are in harmony. Life should be a positive and joyful experience. We really should be in our element every day. Work becomes hard when people land themselves in the wrong situation, role or company and with the wrong leader. Then people really feel it. Yet, every successful employee I speak to confirms that when reflecting on major wins in their career and the quality of their overall experience, organizational leadership was a critical part of the experience. The work may well have been challenging at the time, but because of the people, the journey, the leadership and the adventure, the experience was enjoyed and filed as a critical memory. How many times has that happened with you? To have the commitment of a leader that you know cares about your success, wellbeing and health in life is a powerful aspect to a successful career and role. This is why the leadership community within a company remains an extraordinary platform to fully utilize every moment across the employee journey to create connection and elevate business and human results, but what does this look like? What leadership experience can we co-create that would best serve the human experience at work?

CASE STUDY
Building a pipeline of human-centred leaders

Kevin Graulus, who is the employee experience manager at Securex, considered this specifically during our work together. Developing the experience of work at any organization is a collective and individual endeavour that requires a major shift in how we develop and grow human-centred leaders. Building this future takes effort, skill and patience, but it is a future worth building, as Graulus suggests as he considers the type of leadership future he would wish to create within his organization:

> We developed our company strategy in co-creation with our people. In that strategy, we've come to realize together that humans are our greatest asset. Whether it is the human customer, employee, shareholder. We reached complete alignment on the human-centred approach in everything we do and develop. Processes, tools, structure, workplace... and also our leadership principles. In order to develop the key behaviours we expect from our leaders, we first went through the data regarding the current leadership experience in our company. We identified the moments that matter, assessed

our strengths and defined which leader behaviours would be most impactful to the future employee experience. The co-creation community was a mix of employees and existing leaders. One of the first events we organized with them had a clear and specific goal to create trust and psychological safety within the group. Without this, we wouldn't have produced the leadership principles.

We've also decided to change our reward system. We noticed that salary increase was at some point only possible if you'd switch to a leader function. But that resulted in a group of leaders where a significant proportion didn't actually feel comfortable in the role of leader. We organized a massive selection day, which was open to all prospective leader candidates, and then we assessed preferences and key behaviours to form the new leadership team. Those who were not selected as leaders became experts in their field again. Everyone recognized and appreciated the role of each other much more than before.

We changed the workplace infrastructure to allow more quality moments between employees and leaders, but also for leaders to meet and exchange their experiences in order to improve the overall leadership experience in the company. With remote work intensifying, we built a digital leadership community too through which we provide interventions and learning sessions on the most effective human-centred practices for impactful remote leadership. We continued to measure progress thanks to our continuous listening approach, capturing the full human experience cycle. This allowed us to tweak specific moments in an efficient way. For example, for certain life events – wedding, birth, divorce, hospitalization... that do not occur every month or year – we developed a specific leadership toolkit where leaders can find the best human-centred practices to make the best out of these employee moments.

It is having this foresight or future vision that is key to understanding and delivering in our role of human experience architects, engineers and leaders – thinking through the vision you wish to create and then working back from it to determine what actions and steps need to happen to make it so. This will surface the big and small obstacles that can be picked off and developed as themes to unleash the potential of all those who are holding a leadership position. The great advantage of leading in moments with people in mind is that this is not only work for the charismatic and extrovert leader archetype that we've been sold over the years as the definition of leadership success. No – it's the quiet, focused and committed leadership that is personalized and tailored to each unique experience and each unique person. The predominant and underlying theme throughout is: how can I help you fulfil your potential as a human being?

Imagine an organization being led from this perspective across all leadership lines. Indeed, I would argue that this type of leadership is as important to the human experience at work as anything else. When we arrive at the conclusion that the whole human experience at work matters, there is a recognition that things will need to change if companies are to drive the right leadership behaviours that enable people to do their best work. The system changes and so too the people within it. If we were to codify what occurred in the previous example of visioning the future of the leadership experience, it would be experienced in a manner set out in Figure 6.2.

FIGURE 6.2 Human leadership

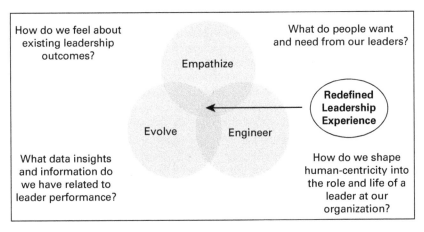

© Ben Whitter, HEX Organization Ltd

- *Empathize*: we step back from looking at corporate needs, and directly step into the real human needs of the people working within the organization. Thinking about how things are experienced and lived from their perspective, we can understand how they see the world, their leaders, their expectations for life and work, and the gaps there are in the existing business model and leadership approach. Thinking holistically, we can start to discover the full potential of each unique person while creating an organizational path to open spaces for candid, trusted and powerful dialogues over the long term.

- *Evolve*: using insights, data and information from the first step, we can then begin to assert some energy in targeted parts of the organization that will deliver stronger outcomes and impact. The often-ignored issues with leadership will have come to the surface and now is the moment to plan and strategize actions that harness the full potential of the leader role.

- *Engineer*: now is the time to engineer and truly enable the leader within the organization as an accountable, responsible and human-centred facilitator. We're not talking about every leader being a coach, though capabilities in that regard are helpful. We are also not talking about adding another layer to the current role of leader. What we are saying, as Graulus perfectly illustrated above, is that being human-centred should now be a primary role of leadership and delivering human outcomes should be the primary objective. The workforce has evolved in a profound way, as we've discussed throughout this book, and such is their impact on the employee experience, leaders will urgently need to evolve with it if organizations are to thrive now and in the future.

A major technique that can help us with this can be borrowed from lean management philosophy. It lends itself to our work to develop better experiences at work for people and offers leaders an opportunity to get closer to the action. Taiichi Ohno, an executive at Toyota, developed the gemba walk as a way to continuously improve business processes at the real place where the work gets done. Prior to any such walk, a specific theme would be chosen by a leader, such as safety, productivity or efficiency, which would then be observed and studied in detail. Originally designed for the shop floors of manufacturing facilities, gemba is a concept that I have adopted and adapted as part of our HEX coaching approach. Our focus is on the connections between human and brand experiences – on the physical, emotional and intellectual growth and success of the people within the organization to ensure that they are using their energy fully and in the right places. Turning the gemba walk into a human experience walk quickly enables improvements to be made that are getting in the way of the workforce. As part of a broader co-creation and listening strategy, it adds a very real lens in how people are feeling and experiencing a business. Leaders have the experience, talk directly to people and work begins on solutions in real time backed by evidence and data, rather than just surveys or other sources that don't really bring things to life in as powerful a way as this. The themes can vary, but I am very focused on whether or not people are experiencing the real truth about a business. This is the purpose, mission and values of the brand. I want to see how effectively they have been installed across different parts of the employee journey and how closely people feel that they are attached or connected to an organization. This helps to identify gaps and challenges, some of which I document in earlier chapters, and then we can immediately fix or resolve them. Nothing should ever come between people and the brand – it's one community and needs to feel that way. As we've seen from multiple case studies, working in partnership with the workforce is now default in world-class companies – any technique or approach that helps us do this more effectively is in scope, because if we are to fully embrace the humanity within companies, we'll need a new operating mode: *bold*.

Bold leadership: flowing forward with people

Transparent, trustworthy and human-centred companies create a platform for success – a togetherness that quickens the step and helps people to think bigger and bolder in how they approach their work. People and leaders seem to flow forward where others falter because of this powerful togetherness they create internally. There is also a greater comfort in risk-taking, trying new things and throwing caution to the wind knowing that there is a supportive community behind them. This is, by far, one of the most impressive outcomes of any work on the human and employee experience – the collective and individual lift a great organization provides to people.

It was this kind of bold leadership that one of my clients demonstrated during COVID-19, and in doing so, set the standard for its sector. Ogilvy, the iconic advertising, marketing and PR firm, arrived at a moment where the company was challenged in a way they hadn't expected. With the workforce being forced into a scenario where they were all working at home in 2020, this proved to be an especially difficult time given the nature of their creative work and the critical importance of rapid, effective and high-quality collaboration within its organization and industry. In this situation, the company started asking: how do we make people feel safe in coming back to the workplace? Yet, the question proved to go far deeper than this and turned out to be more about the kind of workplace they could create that will serve them well into the long-term future of the brand. Helen Matthews, Ogilvy's chief people officer, said:

> When people started to work from home we started to notice themes coming through around three areas: mental health, growth and opportunities for collaboration. We started to analyse this and think about what plans we could put in place for different groups with very different needs. Those with families, those living on their own and those struggling with different priorities. We didn't see the need to rush people back, so that was the underlying principle. This would be very employee-led. We had already proved that we could make it work during the early days of the pandemic.

Matthews put some ideas and business solutions to an internal group called the side-board, which was a group of employees whose purpose was to co-design the workplace and employee experience. The over-riding question for the group was around the right model for work between homeworking and office working.

> It was quite disconcerting to hear that some of the tech giants had all announced that they wouldn't be bringing employees back into the workplace until 2021, and I'm sure we could have gone down that route, but we wanted to do the right thing by our people, and didn't feel

that that approach would do that. What was coming through loud and clear through surveys and data is that they wanted to come back, but in different ways. They missed the human interaction. One of the biggest fears in relation to coming back to work was the commute into central London and a packed transport system around the capital. If this was a worry, it would need to be addressed while avoiding any culture of presenteeism. When we announced it, we were clear that whatever happens with COVID-19, this was about working in a more meaningful way as an organization and team. This set the tone from the outset that this was not a reactive situation. This was a long-term approach to deepen a new way of working and collaborating together.

The company opted for a hybrid 3:2 working model, which meant in practice that there would be three days working remotely combined with two days dedicated to the office for those who are comfortable to do so on a weekly basis. 'It's a big experiment. I'm so thankful to have a boss who is working with me on this and in alignment with the outcomes that we want to deliver for staff,' said Matthews, who continued to work with the side-board and colleagues to maximize the two office days that people were together.

Matthews and I discussed this major organizational change, but within this, there were other powerful moments. In what would be seen to be somewhat of a risky move in traditional HR circles, the company wanted to find new ways to bring people together as it transitioned to full-time remote working, and then subsequently into a hybrid organization – employees asked for something fun – literally, a comedy night. Many organizations in this position would flinch and go another way – a comedy night has the potential to offend and cause a lot of unnecessary hassle for managers and HR. Indeed, many companies wouldn't even risk a comedy night for fear of repercussions within and outside of the workforce, yet this is what colleagues came up with as a way to maintain bonds, connections and relationships at such a challenging time.

I was nervous. I was thinking, will someone sue us and that's my career over, but it went so well. It was brilliant. It was such a good example of our networks collaborating to pull it off. It was also a signal that we are treating people like adults. The company doesn't want to tell people what to do, but rather, work with them to find the right solutions that meet the challenge. We're getting really good at using the side-board to co-create experiences earlier in the process, which enables people to feel closer to the leadership team and encourages stronger peer-to-peer human relationships across an organizational network of colleagues.

For approaches like this to work – at a major and minor scale – whether changing a working model or doing something that hasn't been done before – courage, commitment and boldness are required in abundance, but also a deep-rooted respect for the whole human being, not just the parts deemed suitable for a corporate environment. This respect for people often starts from within, but can also be a major indicator that a brand is on the right path when it comes to connecting what they do with the wider human community.

Respecting humanity

There is a real sense that organizations of today understand the importance of demonstrating a strong connection to human outcomes. Suntory Group, which is one of the world's leading consumer products companies, is a brand that has truly been embracing the human experience challenge, seeking to maintain a relationship between consumers and the workforce while developing the employee experience.

Indeed, one of the five principles of the Suntory Group Way, which helps to define how 'each employee should think and act in their daily work to ensure that Suntory Group is supported by its customers and continues to grow', is: 'We respect humanity.' To back up this pledge, the brand successfully took direct action on the matter. In November and December 2020 they launched the first ever 'Suntory Group's Global Action for Humanity' programme. As part of this initiative, all 40,000 global employees were encouraged to reflect on the importance of respecting humanity through various activities, such as taking part in volunteer work. Indeed, for several years the company has run its annual 'One Suntory Walk', which is an event and campaign that is designed to 'promote healthy workplaces and lifestyles by encouraging our employees to exercise and give back to society'. In 2020, Suntory donated $10 per participant, up to $100,000, to charitable causes that were supporting people affected by the COVID-19 pandemic (Suntory, 2020).

Having worked closely with Suntory over the past year, I learned first-hand about the rich heritage and deep human-centred philosophy behind the brand and what it means to the workforce. Sarah Langley, chief operating officer, global HR, talked with me about what is important to the company when considering the experiences that the brand delivers:

> Suntory is built on strong foundations dating back to 1899. Our vision 'Growing for Good' inspires us to grow our company and strive to live in harmony with people and nature. This means that we are only successful if we contribute to the communities in which we live, and respect the world around us. Inspired by our Japanese heritage, we are guided by our values: Yatte Minahare and Giving Back to Society.

Both values are built into the foundations and philosophy of the business:

> Yatte Minahare is our relentless pursuit of reaching beyond the ordinary and through Giving Back to Society we recognize the importance of the world around us and our commitment to building a sustainable future. Ultimately, we believe our success is underpinned by our gemba mindset and expertise, which is our unique way of understanding the needs of all stakeholders and continuously looking to exceed their expectations.

Earlier I discussed the benefits of a gemba approach to developing the employee experience, and it is one that Suntory has long embraced for consumers. Langley said:

> Our gemba mindset guides us in how we really listen to and learn from others, and while this is critical to understanding our consumers, it is also critical for understanding and listening to our employees. For us, this is the connection to employee experience, and how we think about

creating an organization that people really want to be part of where they can do work they are passionate about, make a difference to others and communities, and build incredible experiences and career journeys.

Leveraging differentiation through employee experience and a gemba mindset

The gemba lens has proved to be highly effective in enabling people to align and work together successfully on key projects. As Langley highlights, this year Suntory started exploring how it could accelerate its ability to tune in to its employees, more overtly talk to and adopt an employee gemba lens and work hard to consider what matters the most for its people:

> Due to our heritage and our shared values, this is not so much new for us, but a way to frame up how we approach this, and shape our people initiatives in a way that ensures we keep our values and founding spirits at the core, ensuring efforts are more overtly aligned with this. The key projects we have taken this approach with this year include a revision of our Suntory Leadership Competencies, developing a global employee value proposition and considering our mobility practices.

Noting that the gemba mindset and this EX way of thinking and working resonated well, Suntory is already exploring other areas to apply and extend it as an approach across the business. Langley said:

> We are looking forward to amplifying it as a way of thinking and leading across our HR and leadership communities in the future so that we can really leverage what differentiates us in our mission, vision and values, strengthen this across all our people, deliver great employee experiences and as a result power our business ambitions through this unbeatable combination.

The redefined organization

If you're a leader or HR professional, you'll know that the path to transformation is challenging. Where do you focus time, investment and resources? Becoming a truly human company was never meant to be easy. It is, after all, the path less trodden. Therefore, it still offers a rich reward for those who dare to go there first. Taking the traditional organization that has been built off long-established theories and norms towards a model that focuses solely on things that matter to people is legacy-defining work. It needs to be backed at the highest levels for a great chance of success, yet pockets of human-centred excellence can emerge across any company.

The conclusion I've drawn from observing several global studies, such as IBM's 2020 study on the future of HR, is that while such studies confirm that the HR function, and companies in general, are 'ripe for disruption', there is always a caveat. It is that HR or companies are not ready to embrace the new paradigm that is being created. As usual, the best performing companies are already on top of thought leadership, given their future focus, and simply work their way through in a constant state of change and improvement. They thrive off it and it helps them outperform their peers across revenue, profitability and invocation metrics, according to IBM.

Don't copy anyone; evolve from within

While the value of the consulting industry is to help companies with specific challenges, it should not be at the expense of the organization's collective growth. There is a constant reaction mode for organizations to deal with. A new trend emerges and there is a tendency to reach for external provision immediately to fill any gaps. This often occurs to the detriment of internal team-building. Consultants come in, present their model and process, and then move on. This is flawed from the outset, because organizations don't often get the chance to build their own unique approach and they simply end up as a copy of another organization. With the human experience, this really shouldn't be the case, and it's certainly not the case with companies I work with. The joy that is found in this work is doing things your own way based on your own terms, but, importantly, in partnership with the workforce. This is real evolution in the partnership between an organization and its people. The traditional change curve that the workforce experiences when anything new comes along is eliminated. There is no need to manage change because employees are deeply emerged in and leading the change themselves. Co-creation continues to be the calling card of exceptional employers, and the extent to which they do co-create with their workforces will be a major factor in sustaining organizational success.

Having led a coaching, consulting and certification business for the past couple of years, I've had to clearly differentiate what we do in a way I didn't expect. The ownership and responsibility for creating great human experiences rests with the business. There is no external saviour in the same way that there is no external scapegoat either. Total responsibility lies with the organization and its people. We help develop, guide and validate, perhaps, but the only thing that matters is the brands and organizations themselves. For example, the way my company works well with clients over the longer term is to embed one of our coaches into a project or experience redesign as an extension of the existing team. They are not there to be the all-knowing expert, but with their expertise they are strongly positioned to accelerate positive outcomes while ensuring companies avoid any costly mistakes. We do not come in with our fancy models, PowerPoints and 'best practices' and impose them on the client in the mould of traditional consulting. As a practitioner, I always, as a first principle, sought to leverage the people and resources within a company as a centrepiece to the overall approach. Co-creating is fundamental. It helps build trust and successful change as part of the process. Too many external influences and the magic is often diluted or weakened, or it turns into a consultancy thing in the minds of employees, much in the same way that any projects allocated to HR functions can often be dismissed as simply an 'HR thing'. This is detrimental to any business. To me, working on the human and employee experience at a company is a deeply personal endeavour. Every thing and every person matters. An over-reliance on traditional consultants or, indeed, any one team can cause weakness and internal division, especially if the people in the business have not used their guidance to grow and develop in a meaningful way.

The alternative is an approach I have built into my business model, which combines consulting and coaching. We are not there to create dependency or upsell. We function as part of a broader coalition that serves only the interests of a business and its people. We are only there to serve colleagues and teams that are working hard to elevate the human experience at work. This offers a marked difference. The company retains all the power, all the control and all the accountability. We are simply there to guide, offer our specialized expertise and challenge our clients to become world class in employee experience. This is also a positive approach internally, as companies bring together colleagues that can seriously develop and design experiences with impact. We can integrate insights, research and thought leadership to give additional perspective or inspiration, but our primary focus is to bridge the gap between people and the brand, and nothing should distract people from that. We want to co-create an incredibly strong connection between the employee and customer experiences. This is the brand experience. Now, within this – and our work backs this up – is a leader that respects all talents and expertise and can bring it together seamlessly. Working with multiple stakeholders across multiple themes of work, there is often a differentiated leader pulling the strings and leading with the whole picture in mind. Making connections, building bridges, nurturing relationships, they expertly get the maximum value from an internal and external ecosystem of colleagues who are all working to transform the way work is experienced across an enterprise. This is a key characteristic of a HEX Practitioner. Naturally strategic and holistic, they lead with the whole company and whole person in mind in a way that many professionals and leaders do not.

Summary: evolving human experiences at work

It is no coincidence that companies at the leading edge of the experience economy put a lot of time and effort into their community outreach and charitable programmes. It is a distinctive quality of coherent and confident brands. When discussing human experience, it is an inevitable question that arises: how does a company serve humanity and the planet we live on? We may be very well aware of the financial performance of a company, but when we get a little deeper into our association, we want to understand more about positive impact in other places, not just in sales, revenue and profit. From an emotional perspective, good companies help human beings to feel good about themselves in life. Therefore, a company's impact is inextricably attached to people through the companies they ally with throughout their careers. What the company does or does not do consistently reflects on those who have had a connection with it. Being open and humble about a company's place in the community can help to foster and grow new connections, while also deepening existing relationships within an organization. This may be considered a defining aspect of the HEX organization, as it does not take long to know which companies are considering the whole human experience rather than just financial or market success. If we evolve our strengths in this regard, what becomes possible? Well, that's an easy outcome to understand – anything. Organizations have an opportunity every day to set higher standards, elevate their standing in the world and evolve the outcomes of everyone connected with their brands – it's an opportunity that's ready for focused development.

- Consider the companies you *admire, respect and trust*. What experiences have they delivered that have led to this outcome? How does your organization compare?

- Failure is not possible if you learn in the right way. Through feedback, experimentation and data, failure becomes a gift to improve experiences. Focus on 'failure' and find the big wins for your company and career.

- If you were the CEO, where would you focus your efforts to improve the human experience at work? What would be your absolute priorities in evolving experiences to a high level?

- Take a gemba walk around your organization to identify the value that can be added to the human experience at work and any barriers preventing *progress*.

- Brands are renewing the role of leader and re-emphasizing a commitment to human-centricity. Start to vision a human-centred leadership community at your organization and how you're going to help deliver it.

- Don't be afraid to lead in a bold way. Co-creation with the workforce will help you to deliver superior experiences in work and will also mitigate any risks. Human-centricity will demand new ways of doing things. Embrace them.

EPILOGUE

Though people have explored it from their own experience and perspective, we are no closer to truly arriving at a moment of profound clarity about the true nature of the human experience. We are operating from some knowledge, but not all knowledge. We can only do the best we can with what we've got, or what we co-create along the way. In this sense, and the way this book has looked at the human experience at work, the greatest opportunity we have as human beings, and indeed as leaders in this world, is to represent progress – not just any kind of progress, but progress that advances humanity and our world. In this context, the examples we have shared and the ideas we have reflected on indicate that something profound is happening within the world of work right now. The evidence suggests that work is becoming more human, and in the process, more impactful in our lives and the communities around us. Is now not the time to truly embrace all the facets of humanity within our organizations and build accordingly?

The human experience has been evolving for thousands of years to get to the point where people can access more of their potential, capabilities and consciousness, and to secure the necessary freedoms to make the most of them. Challenges remain, yet as I hope I have demonstrated in this book, there is reason for optimism that humanity and organizations can thrive together, now and in the future. Rather than small-scale reforms of existing systems and approaches for building companies and brands, the new generation of people professionals and leaders is demanding massive action to repurpose everything that is getting in the way of people and positive outcomes. This calls for bold and courageous leadership across organizations to bring this vision to life, especially in light of the resistance that may occur. Many of the changes we discussed and explored in this book have brought significant changes to the way organizations structure, develop and lead themselves. Leaders may well find themselves in a fascinating situation where they will need to deeply consider the value, standing and results of their roles and services. This is not a bad thing. In fact, it can be reinvigorating to contemplate wholesale changes to our organizations and our own lives in the search for excellence and impact. One function continues to represent the challenge and the opportunity before us: human resources.

Goodbye HR?

Is the jury still out about the future of HR in our organizations? I hope in some small way this book can help accelerate a definitive conclusion to this decades-long debate on HR's long-term future. More movements and groups are popping up daily to preserve status-quo HR. However well-intentioned these campaigns and initiatives are, there is a feeling, shared among many, that HR is about to enjoy a wholesale and positive transformation. I do admire the affinity that many professionals have with their HR profession, yet I can't help wondering if their energies are being spent wisely in constantly defending HR's relevance, impact and contribution to business. The previous sentence defines the challenge: HR requires a defence, given its reputation with employees and lack of progress at the top of organizations. As a management idea, HR remains formidable. It is an idea that broke through and took hold within the economy. Having considered HR from the human experience angle and in reflecting on just a small percentage of the examples that I've been exposed to during the research for this book, my view on the matter has not changed nor has it weakened.

Quite simply, if the human experience is important within companies, I can see a time in the short-term future where the HR function will be completely transformed out of the business. The decline of human resources has begun and will only intensify in the years to come. In my opinion, it will soon become very unfashionable to play host to an HR function and department. Indeed, I expect one of the signature marks of the most progressive brands in the world will be that they do not, and nor would they ever, entertain the idea of an HR function. Their direction will favour community-driven approaches and developing teams with a strong, and visible, bias for people. Within that, these teams and colleagues will carve out one of the most important innovations in business for generations – a strategic and operational commitment to the human experience at work. The possibilities this creates will be a sight to behold. Practitioners and professionals with in-demand human-centred skills, expertise, capabilities and knowledge will find themselves in roles and teams that better serve people and the organization. Without the division that the 'HR' label brings, these people will deliver their best performance. Through working closely with colleagues who have transitioned their services into human and employee experience, I have observed first-hand the difference it makes to them. They are fully focused on what genuinely matters in the business – building positive connections, relationships and outcomes. In its current form, and for all the reasons I have documented, HR simply does not deliver what it could in this regard, and in my view, it's time for a new proposition for HR and all the other support services within an organization. Having spent over 15 years of a wonderful career in the HR profession, I could have made this case within 15 minutes of my first HR job. The problems with HR were as clear then as they are now, and there has been little evidence that suggests positive change in this regard, despite bringing elements like employee experience into the function.

In my previous book, *Employee Experience*, I highlighted that organizations working on EX were in a state of evolution, not revolution. They are always looking to innovate and scale successful ideas that deliver better experiences and business outcomes. In taking this approach, they tend to avoid the need for a more significant revolution. On reflection, this holds true when considering the organization in the context of human experience, but when we focus in on specific functions like HR, I believe there is a strengthening case that evolution just won't do what is needed. In the case of HR, a full-scale revolution may well be required to overhaul how we develop a people profession that is fit for now and the future of work. In my view, colleagues and companies who are determined to 'put the "human" back into human resources' should really ask themselves if it was ever there in the first place – there may be a lot of energy being wasted in propping up an old idea that is no longer relevant to today's economy and expectations. Building relevance and overhauling the concept of HR will need to include business schools, associations, institutes and any other body that educates, certifies and develops professionals and leaders who will soon find themselves in re-energized people and experience functions and roles. The establishment around the HR idea is strong and this will be a significant challenge to overcome, but it is an important one nonetheless, and it will require an incredible level of collaboration to achieve if we are to co-create truly human-centred organizations.

Progressing humanity to new levels of impact

We can help each other along the way and share similar missions, but ultimately, every organization and leader needs to find their own unique path that enables them to contribute to the world in a meaningful way. For us to do this, we'll need a bit more candour about who we are and what we stand for. This matters to human beings and it should matter to us as leaders and human-centred practitioners. Throughout history, we have institutions that have taken on roles to help develop the character of people. From education to employment, as people we are conditioned, grown and developed with values in mind. That's what we are good at understanding – right and wrong. Our behaviour is evolved along the way and through our experiences. Today, there are fewer and fewer role models in this regard, and this is why organizations will need to invest even more in nurturing the talent and character of their workforces through a firm commitment to human values. In my opinion, a material, consumer and social media-driven world has perhaps led to a distortion about what is most important within the human experience as people fly through life looking to get more for themselves rather than give more to the world. This is a challenge that surfaces within organizations too as they prime people to grow and win at all costs. Complacency or a sense of entitlement could also creep into the workforce unless companies have fully considered what they mean by progress. A superficial and shallow workplace that only serves itself is the antithesis of progress. This is not a satisfactory situation, as we've explored, but one that needs to be highlighted when thinking about the human experience. Is it our job to change this picture to create a more values-based, compassionate and selfless business world?

I don't think this challenge rests with any one person or team, but we can contribute to a better version of the world, and our businesses, through the roles and responsibilities we have. We can become human-centred leaders above all else. We can lead with empathy and emotional intelligence to unlock the potential of people. We can build communities and connections where none existed before. We can celebrate difference. We can, in our own way, make our difference. This is often a mindset thing and applies to all areas of our work and life. If you looked across all of your projects right now, can you identify areas that could be more human? Many of us can and that underlines the huge potential of the human experience at work.

Unity is strength

In creating and leading an organization, we'll need to consider how each element serves as a unifying force within the company. Every day we learn about more things that divide us as human beings. This must be acknowledged, yet it shouldn't in any way control the organizational narrative. Is it not wiser to focus all efforts and energies on what unites people? This is where our view of progress can help. Differences are leveraged and guided to serve the greater good of the organization and the people within it. Naturally, human experience organizations create more unity through their policies, processes, procedures and everything else that people encounter at work. If we stand for a progress built on people, planet and performance, a unified workforce is an outcome of this. Indeed, unity is strength, and what binds us all together is our humanity. That illusive togetherness, which is not experienced enough within careers, can be a powerful and profound part of the human experience at work. It takes time and many experiences to build, yet it is incredibly worthwhile to do. Do you feel a togetherness at your organization? If so, I would encourage you to explore exactly why that is. If you don't, I would suggest the same. As you do, you'll understand that the human experience is not so complicated at all. Indeed, the reasons will be self-evident as you recall the memories and moments that made an impact on you.

Co-creation at the heart of the human experience

In my opinion, there is no doubting that one of the primary enablers of the remarkable outcomes within the employee experience field to date is that of co-creation. A hallmark of mature EX approaches, co-creation has been a major factor in the delivery of better experiences in work. The combination of deeper listening, empathy and harnessing powerful insights from data alongside progressive design approaches that encourage greater partnership and collaboration within the workforce has delivered a platform for continued human success. There is an opportunity to go further. With evidence of challenges across functions and disciplines, a genuine human experience platform or collaborative enterprise centred on human-centricity can help to overcome any alignment or accountability issues within an organization. Co-creation, therefore, will continue to be a significant part of our work on human experience. In my view, it is the best part and is a natural approach of a strong and confident organization. Any power-, knowledge- or information-hoarding by leaders will simply fall away if they are all unified around the human experience and are expected (and incentivized) to co-create within and throughout projects. How can you co-create at a deeper level with people? How can people be your partners in driving programmes of work from the outset? Structure is the obvious first place to look, as is the way project teams are formed across different areas of responsibility.

The interesting thing about the human experience at work is that co-creation is always on and always happening. There is no escaping it – for good and bad. Increasingly, as I've shown in this book, the workforce will become active participants in the co-creation process, especially when it is not an established part of the business model and strategy. Ensuring co-creation is a fixture and fitting with any aspect of business life is a wise move. This is not only a visionary approach, but it also a human one – a commitment to make progress with people, not through them.

Human issues = business issues

Business is so dominant in the lives of people that it may be unwise if companies don't more fully embrace their responsibilities within the human experience. Whatever is experienced on the outside has originated from the inside of a business. In this context, our people become critical. Their world becomes our world, and leadership is right to concern itself daily with the health of its workforce. In fact, the human experience naturally becomes something that business is right to obsess about. In my opinion, this notion that business is all about profit is something that belongs to the past, and it is the work that we do inside our organizations that is going to support and stabilize this idea that people and planet matter more, however challenging that may seem from the outset. This could be a bolder people strategy, it could be a management team proposal that reshapes an entire organization or any other way in which we can seriously nudge senior leadership and key stakeholders in the direction of human-centricity. In this era, some companies are comparable in size, scope, influence and even impact to that of nation states. Working on the human experience now in a holistic and in-depth way is preventive and practical action – the company is preventing and minimizing risks around generating any self-inflicted organizational damage relating to human-centric issues in their workforce.

Part of this is to recognize all the different roles people play and be in support of them. It's that straightforward – caring and being there for people, not payroll numbers. It's amazing how good we can feel when we know there are people that care and want us to do well in life – the organization will, increasingly, play a serious role in this regard, especially with mental health issues set to rise in the coming years. In human-centred organizations, there is no real debate or indecision when it comes to mental health. If a company is taking the human experience seriously, mental health will hold the same status and importance as physical health, with related investment and provisions in place. The emotional wellbeing of the workforce is a primary concern. Indeed, this is built into and integrated into the very fabric of a company throughout its employee experience and the values of the business. In any situation, people will have the support they need. Whether through a caring leader, an impactful human-centred policy or a service, experience or forum dedicated to their ongoing success, people should always have options and choices available to grow through any life and work challenges that present themselves. You can tell a lot about a company by the way it supports people through their worst moments as well as their best ones.

A moment of opportunity, a milestone for humanity

One moment has the potential to impact many others, in numerous ways, and from a work perspective, how we are treated by managers and colleagues through both our employee journey and our personal experiences can have significant effects. From my work on employee experience, I have observed up close how practitioners and leaders have set up their services to lean in totally to the people they serve. It makes a profound impact and, in many ways, is a mere evolution on the path to better serve people in work – better *serve* people, a reversal of what may be considered the more 'traditional' view of work. This human-centred mentality overhauls the current nature and structure of work, which has limited the creativity, ideas and potential of many people and therefore impacted the sustainable growth of companies. The opportunity is here for organizations to address this by supporting people to perform to their true potential in life and work. In doing so, they will redefine what it means to be a world-class brand.

If we really question everything about the company, and its relationship with the human experience, in my view there is no choice but to create a different type of organization – one that is good for the *planet*, *humanity* and *business*. Indeed, evidence is suggesting that this triangle of impact could well become a standard for organizational success in the future and what we consider to be real *progress* in this world.

REFERENCES

Chapter 1

BBC (2020) [accessed 27 January 2021] Barclays scraps 'Big Brother' staff tracking system [Online] https://www.bbc.com/news/business-51570401 (archived at https://perma.cc/QP3E-B2TM)

Brooks, D (2012) *The Social Animal*, Short Books Ltd, London

Bryson, B (2004) *A Short History of Nearly Everything*, Black Swan, London

Bureau for Labor Statistics (2018) [accessed 7 January 2021] Contingent and alternative employment arrangements summary [Online] https://www.bls.gov/news.release/conemp.nr0.htm (archived at https://perma.cc/S6ZW-MCXH)

Credit Suisse (2019) [accessed 7 January 2021] Global wealth report [Online] https://www.credit-suisse.com/about-us/en/reports-research/global-wealth-report.html (archived at https://perma.cc/33AU-QCQH)

Desilver, D (2019) [accessed 7 January 2021] 10 facts about American workers [Online] https://www.pewresearch.org/fact-tank/2019/08/29/facts-about-american-workers/ (archived at https://perma.cc/CP5M-KJSL)

Economic Policy Institute (2019) [accessed 7 January 2021] [Online] https://www.epi.org/publication/ceo-compensation-2018/ (archived at https://perma.cc/G3DN-L5LP)

Gartenberg, C and Serafeim, G (2019) [accessed 7 January 2021] 181 top CEOs have realized companies need a purpose beyond profit, *Harvard Business Review* [Online] https://hbr.org/2019/08/181-top-ceos-have-realized-companies-need-a-purpose-beyond-profit (archived at https://perma.cc/9T3K-X8ME)

Gino, F (2019) *Rebel Talent: Why it pays to break the rules at work and in life*, Harper Collins, New York

Health and Safety Executive (2020) [accessed 7 January 2021] Work-related stress, anxiety or depression statistics in Great Britain, 2020 [Online] https://www.hse.gov.uk/statistics/causdis/stress.pdf (archived at https://perma.cc/L4BE-NR9M)

McGregor, L and Doshi, N (2015) [accessed 7 January 2021] How company culture shapes employee motivation, *Harvard Business Review* [Online] https://hbr.org/2015/11/how-company-culture-shapes-employee-motivation (archived at https://perma.cc/C499-PKC8)

Spataro, J (2020) [accessed 7 January 2021] 2 years of digital transformation in 2 months, *Microsoft* [Online] https://www.microsoft.com/en-us/microsoft-365/blog/2020/04/30/2-years-digital-transformation-2-months/ (archived at https://perma.cc/9FYU-XQFX)

Trade Union Congress (2019) [accessed 7 January 2021] UK's gig economy workforce has doubled since 2016, TUC and FEPS-backed research shows [Online] https://www.tuc.org.uk/news/uks-gig-economy-workforce-has-doubled-2016-tuc-and-feps-backed-research-shows (archived at https://perma.cc/Z89Q-YMTS)

Chapter 2

Bamboo (2020) [accessed 7 January 2021] Do people hate HR? [Online] https://www.bamboohr.com/blog/do-people-hate-hr-infographic/ (archived at https://perma.cc/U4PP-AZ64)

Bhuiyan, J (2019) [accessed 7 January 2021] How the Google walkout transformed tech workers into activists, *LA Times* [Online] https://www.latimes.com/business/technology/story/2019-11-06/google-employee-walkout-tech-industry-activism (archived at https://perma.cc/LPH2-WU2L)

Bray, T (2020) [accessed 7 January 2021] Bye, Amazon [Online] https://www.tbray.org/ongoing/When/202x/2020/04/29/Leaving-Amazon (archived at https://perma.cc/KV5R-U65X)

Dunlop Young, M (1958) *The Rise of the Meritocracy*, Thames and Hudson, London

Edelman (2020) [accessed 7 January 2021] Edelman Trust Barometer special report: Brand trust in 2020, *Edelman* [Online] https://www.edelman.com/research/brand-trust-2020 (archived at https://perma.cc/5CBT-QYXR)

Hamel, G and Zanini, M (2018) [accessed 7 January 2021] The end of bureaucracy, *Harvard Business Review* [Online] https://hbr.org/2018/11/the-end-of-bureaucracy (archived at https://perma.cc/2XVE-WTPJ)

LinkedIn (2020) [accessed 7 January 2021] Global talent trends 2020, *LinkedIn* [Online] https://business.linkedin.com/talent-solutions/recruiting-tips/global-talent-trends-2020 (archived at https://perma.cc/8D6A-CWZU)

Mackey, J and Sisodia, R (2014) *Conscious Capitalism: Liberating the heroic spirit of business*, Harvard Business School Publishing, Boston

Raconteur (2019) [accessed 27 January 2021] Future of work, *Raconteur.net* [Online] https://www.raconteur.net/report/future-work-2019/ (archived at https://perma.cc/X3EE-UFMB)

Straits Times (2020) [accessed 7 January 2021] 8 in 10 Singaporeans willing to pay more for essential service [Online] https://www.straitstimes.com/singapore/manpower/8-in-10-singaporeans-willing-to-pay-more-for-essential-services (archived at https://perma.cc/BT8Q-SQZQ)

Strzemien, A, Bennett, J, Ma, T and Lyons, E (2020) [accessed 7 January 2021] Out of office: A survey of our new work lives, *New York Times* [Online] https://www.nytimes.com/2020/08/20/style/working-from-home.html (archived at https://perma.cc/VE3Z-CM7C)

The Economist (2019) [accessed 7 January 2021] The experience of work [Online] https://theexperienceofwork.economist.com/pdf/Citrix_The_Experience_of_Work_BriefingPaper.pdf (archived at https://perma.cc/55BA-LQYS)

The Pipeline (2020) [accessed 7 January 2021] Woman count 2020 [Online] https://www.execpipeline.com/women-count-2020/

Thiel P (2014) [accessed 27 January 2021] Competition is for losers, *Wall Street Journal* [Online] https://www.wsj.com/articles/peter-thiel-competition-is-for-losers-1410535536 (archived at https://perma.cc/E745-5L87)

Volini, E, Denny, B and Schwartz, J (2020) [accessed 7 January 2021] A memo to HR, *Deloitte* [Online] https://www2.deloitte.com/us/en/insights/focus/human-capital-trends/2020/changing-role-of-human-resources-management.html (archived at https://perma.cc/9V6F-JHCU)

Weber, A (2020) [accessed 18 March 2021] We announced to the company today that we won't be working Fridays in May, *LinkedIn* [Online] https://www.linkedin.com/posts/meetadam_employeeengagement-leadership-activity-6663140458190958593-kjwr (archived at https://perma.cc/UY69-Q8BZ)

Whitter, B (2019) *Employee Experience*, Kogan Page, London

YouGov (2020) [accessed 7 January 2021] Food Foundation survey results [Online] https://docs.cdn.yougov.com/otidumbhkq/YouGov%20Survey%20Results%20-%20Food%20Foundation.pdf (archived at https://perma.cc/Q9EN-QSCB)

Zety (2020) [accessed 7 January 2021] Is HR human? [Online] https://zety.com/blog/is-hr-human (archived at https://perma.cc/9YQJ-2UWX)

Chapter 3

Airbnb (2020) [accessed 7 January 2021] A message from co-founder and CEO Brian Chesky [Online] https://news.airbnb.com/a-message-from-co-founder-and-ceo-brian-chesky/ (archived at https://perma.cc/QW9D-3F8K)

Aydin, R (2019) [accessed 7 January 2021] The WeWork fiasco of 2019, explained in 30 seconds, *Business Insider* [Online] https://www.businessinsider.com/wework-ipo-fiasco-adam-neumann-explained-events-timeline-2019-9?r=US&IR=T (archived at https://perma.cc/2HQB-CNYX)

Banks, JA (1992) *Building Learner-Centered Schools: Three perspectives*, Columbia University, New York

Beer, M, Finnström, M and Schrader, D (2016) [accessed 7 January 2021] Why leadership training fails – and what to do about it, *Harvard Business Review* [Online] https://hbr.org/2016/10/why-leadership-training-fails-and-what-to-do-about-it (archived at https://perma.cc/R94N-DEJK)

Bochove, D, Bolongaro, K and Day, M (2020) [accessed 7 January 2021] Amazon's Whole Foods reverses poppy ban after angering Canada [Online] https://www.bloomberg.com/news/articles/2020-11-06/amazon-s-whole-foods-bans-veterans-poppies-incensing-canadians (archived at https://perma.cc/7FPP-5RRN)

Bregman, R (2020) *Humankind: A hopeful history*, Bloomsbury Publishing, London

Chapman, B (2019) [accessed 7 January 2021] McDonald's staff go on strike and march on Downing Street to demand better pay, *Independent* [Online] https://www.independent.co.uk/news/business/news/mcdonalds-strike-today-mcstrike-higher-pay-downing-street-john-mcdonnell-a9199681.html (archived at https://perma.cc/8YY5-FDEF)

Clifford, T (2020) [accessed 7 January 2021] Salesforce's Marc Benioff claims a 'victory for stakeholder capitalism' [Online] https://www.cnbc.com/2020/08/25/salesforces-marc-benioff-claims-a-victory-for-stakeholder-capitalism.html (archived at https://perma.cc/6N4X-XB5M)

Dahlstrom, L and Duong, M (2020) [accessed 7 January 2021] One global company's steps to navigate COVID-19 in China – and the lessons learned, *Starbucks* [Online] https://stories.starbucks.com/stories/2020/one-global-companys-bold-steps-to-navigate-covid-19-in-china-and-the-lessons-learned/ (archived at https://perma.cc/VLY7-NKU5)

Davis, MF (2020) [accessed 27 January 2021] BNY Mellon tells most employees to work remotely until January, *Bloomberg* [Online] https://www.bloomberg.com/news/articles/2020-08-26/bny-mellon-tells-most-employees-to-work-remotely-until-january (archived at https://perma.cc/4KZR-9D6X)

Derivan, J (2003) Employers challenged to motivate and engage workforce, *Business Wire*

Gino, F (2019) *Rebel Talent: Why it pays to break the rules at work and in life*, Harper Collins, New York

Healy, J (2019) *Breaking the Banks*, Impact Press, Australia

IBM (2020) [accessed 7 January 2021] Accelerating the journey to HR 3.0 [Online] https://www.ibm.com/thought-leadership/institute-business-value/report/hr-3 (archived at https://perma.cc/8QJC-N7D5)

Kang, M (2020) [accessed 7 January 2021] We are moving from HR to HX, *People Matters* [Online] https://www.peoplemattersglobal.com/article/employee-engagement/we-are-moving-from-hr-to-hx-jlls-helen-snowball-25415 (archived at https://perma.cc/UWK7-3HT9)

Lazare, L (2018) [accessed 7 January 2021] United Airlines employees shocked: Bonuses replaced with lottery, *Chicago Business Journal* [Online] https://www.bizjournals.com/chicago/news/2018/03/02/united-airlines-replaces-bonuses-with-lottery.html (archived at https://perma.cc/J377-9R8G)

Reuters (2019) [accessed 7 January 2021] BNY Mellon puts brakes on changes in work-from-home rules for staff [Online] https://cn.reuters.com/article/instant-article/idUSKCN1QO22V (archived at https://perma.cc/7MA2-8ES8)

Sapra, B (2020) [accessed 7 January 2021] Bird employees say they were locked out of their email and Slack accounts as they were told their jobs were gone, *Business Insider* [Online] https://www.businessinsider.com/bird-employees-locked-out-of-emails-layoffs-2020-4?r=US&IR=T (archived at https://perma.cc/CJ9W-W3ZR)

Schreier, J (2020) [accessed 7 January 2021] Blizzard workers share
salaries in revolt over pay, *Bloomberg* [Online] https://www.bloomberg.
com/news/articles/2020-08-03/blizzard-workers-share-salaries-in-revolt-
over-wage-disparities (archived at https://perma.cc/H4CP-D78N)

Siemens (2020) [accessed 7 January 2021] Siemens to establish mobile
working as core component of the 'new normal' [Online] https://press.
siemens.com/global/en/pressrelease/siemens-establish-mobile-working-
core-component-new-normal (archived at https://perma.cc/NS8S-EL25)

The Economist (2019) [accessed 7 January 2021] The experience of work
[Online] https://theexperienceofwork.economist.com/pdf/Citrix_The_
Experience_of_Work_BriefingPaper.pdf (archived at https://perma.
cc/55BA-LQYS)

Timpson (2020) [accessed 7 January 2021] https://www.timpson.co.uk/
about/careers-at-timpson (archived at https://perma.cc/5DG7-UL3N)

Waters, R (2018) [accessed 7 January 2021] Google withdraws from
$10bn Pentagon JEDI contract contest, *Financial Times* [Online] https://
www.ft.com/content/5d680566-cb46-11e8-b276-b9069bde0956
(archived at https://perma.cc/Q7WK-ATNH)

Whitter, B (2019) *Employee Experience*, Kogan Page, London

Zetlin, M (2018) [accessed 7 January 2021] Salesforce employees objected
to its immigration work. CEO Marc Benioff's response was brilliant,
Inc [Online] https://www.inc.com/minda-zetlin/salesforce-ethical-
humane-office-marc-benioff-kara-swisher-employee-activism.html
(archived at https://perma.cc/8SPL-DJAZ)

Chapter 4

BBC (2020) [accessed 7 January 2021] Who invented the weekend?
[Online] https://www.bbc.co.uk/bitesize/articles/zf22kmn (archived at
https://perma.cc/59HT-6SDF)

Heath, C and Heath, D (2017) *The Power of Moments*, Bantam Press,
London

Whitter, B (2019) *Employee Experience*, Kogan Page, London

Chapter 5

Bergen, M, Huet, E and Bloomberg (2019) [accessed 7 January 2021] Not a Googler: The secret, frustrating life of a Google contract worker, *Fortune* [Online] https://fortune.com/2019/11/07/google-googler-tvc-contract-worker/ (archived at https://perma.cc/6EGQ-K6BC)

Cawthon, H (2020) [accessed 7 January 2021] Texas Roadhouse CEO on weathering the coronavirus storm – and giving up his salary, *Louisville Business First* [Online] https://www.bizjournals.com/louisville/news/2020/03/26/texas-roadhouse-ceo-on-weathering-the-coronavirus.html (archived at https://perma.cc/BW4Y-TKSV)

Neff, KD and Germer, CK (2018) *The Mindful Self-Compassion Workbook*, Guildford Press, New York

Sheppard, D (2020) [accessed 7 January 2021] Will the Uber case be a defining moment for the gig economy?, *People Management* [Online] https://www.peoplemanagement.co.uk/experts/legal/will-uber-case-defining-moment-gig-economy (archived at https://perma.cc/6VEL-74U5)

Chapter 6

IBM (2020) [accessed 7 January 2021] Accelerating the journey to HR 3.0 [Online] https://www.ibm.com/thought-leadership/institute-business-value/report/hr-3 (archived at https://perma.cc/8QJC-N7D5)

IKEA (2020) [accessed 7 January 2021] The testament of a furniture dealer [Online] https://www.inter.ikea.com/en/-/media/InterIKEA/IGI/Financial%20Reports/English_The_testament_of_a_dealer_2018.pdf (archived at https://perma.cc/Q6PV-X29S)

McKinsey (2015) [accessed 7 January 2021] Six building blocks for creating a high-performing digital enterprise [Online] https://www.mckinsey.com/business-functions/organization/our-insights/six-building-blocks-for-creating-a-high-performing-digital-enterprise (archived at https://perma.cc/SZN7-PZ2N)

McMillon, D (2020) [accessed 7 January 2021] One year later: Purpose of a corporation, *Business Roundtable* [Online] https://purpose.businessroundtable.org/ (archived at https://perma.cc/3FPQ-NTRK)

Suntory (2020) [accessed 7 January 2021] Suntory Group's Global Action for Humanity [Online] https://www.suntory.com/news/article/13788E.html (archived at https://perma.cc/78YF-P9BH)

INDEX

CPSIA information can be obtained
at www.ICGtesting.com
Printed in the USA
JSHW051338040521
14314JS00010B/129